Dr. R. T. Kendall is one of the most articulate leaders in Christendom today. His insightful teachings and writings have had a significant impact on my own thinking. In fact, one of my books, *When God Doesn't Make Sense,* is dedicated to this godly man. I respect Dr. Kendall greatly and am honored to call him my friend.

—DR. JAMES DOBSON, FOUNDER

FOCUS ON THE FAMILY

My friend R. T. Kendall spent twenty-five years of his ministry at Westminster Chapel, and his book will give you the opportunity to read his unique account of those years.

—BILLY GRAHAM

I thank God for Louise and R. T. Kendall, whom God used so mightily in the UK for His glory. R. T. Kendall served as pastor of Westminster for twenty-five years, following in the footsteps of G. Campbell Morgan and Dr. Martyn Lloyd-Jones. Dr. Kendall is a powerful expositor of the Scriptures and a great lover of souls. You'll be blessed by reading this award-winning book.

—LUIS PALAU, PRESIDENT

LUIS PALAU EVANGELISTIC ASSOCIATION

I have known and loved R. T. Kendall for over a quarter of a century now. During the 1980s it was my joy to preach at Westminster Chapel over several summers. RT and I have discussed the Scriptures sitting in flat-bottom fishing boats in Bimini and in the Florida Keys as well as at dining room tables in London. Although there are points at which we disagree, there is one point at which we are in total agreement—that being the need for a visitation of genuine heaven-sent revival. I have known no one through the years who has consistently beseeched the throne of grace for an outpouring of true revival any more than R. T. Kendall. *In Pursuit of His Glory* is not simply the title of this volume tracing his years at the Westminster Chapel; it has been and continues to be the passion of his life.

—DR. O. S. HAWKINS
FORMER SENIOR PASTOR,
FIRST BAPTIST CHURCH, DALLAS, TEXAS
NOW PRESIDENT, ANNUITY BOARD OF THE
SOUTHERN BAPTIST CONVENTION

Reading *In Pursuit of His Glory* has been for me a special delight. When its author was my student at Southern Baptist Theological Seminary during the early 1970s, I knew that God had something special in store for this man. Yet I never imagined it would be in the heart of London. Converted from Arminian to Calvinist beliefs— or, as he would say, "baptized in the Holy Spirit" while driving on a Tennessee highway—he would write a dissertation that, when published, would become a major catalyst in convincing today's scholars that John Calvin did not teach the doctrine of limited atonement (for the elect only).

Of all my students for more than half a century, I would not know of one who has had a more remarkable preaching ministry than R. T. Kendall. A significant contributor to the renascence of expository preaching, he has also invited to his pulpit charismatic leaders who do not share his reformed theology. In ways that should prove to be helpful to other pastors, Dr. Kendall has been able to narrate his difficulties and his triumphs and to give credit to his congregation while always giving glory to the triune God.

—DR. JAMES LEO GARRETT JR.
DISTINGUISHED PROFESSOR OF THEOLOGY, EMERITUS
SOUTHWESTERN BAPTIST THEOLOGICAL SEMINARY
FORT WORTH, TEXAS

RT had high and holy hopes when he came to tackle London. His confidence was in the Word of God, which he always sought to expound with faithfulness. I admired his courage and his perseverance, and I valued the times we spent together. I am glad, therefore, that he has written down his account of these important years.

—JOHN W. STOTT, RECTOR EMERITUS
ALL SOULS, LANGHAM PLACE
LONDON, ENGLAND

IN PURSUIT OF
HIS
GLORY

R. T. KENDALL

Charisma
HOUSE
A STRANG COMPANY

Most STRANG COMMUNICATIONS/CHARISMA HOUSE/SILOAM products are available at special quantity discounts for bulk purchase for sales promotions, premiums, fund-raising, and educational needs. For details, write Strang Communications/Charisma House/Siloam, 600 Rinehart Road, Lake Mary, Florida 32746, or telephone (407) 333-0600.

IN PURSUIT OF HIS GLORY by R. T. Kendall
Published by Charisma House
A Strang Company
600 Rinehart Road
Lake Mary, Florida 32746
www.charismahouse.com

Unless otherwise noted, all Scripture quotations are from the Holy Bible, New International Version. Copyright © 1973, 1978, 1984, International Bible Society. Used by permission.

Scripture quotations marked KJV are from the King James Version of the Bible.

Lyrics from "Up to Me" by Bob Dylan, copyright © 1974 Ram's Horn Music. All rights reserved. International copyright secured. Used by permission. All rights are nontransferable.

Cover design by Karen Grindley

Library of Congress Cataloging-in-Publication Data
Kendall, R. T.
  In pursuit of His glory / R. T. Kendall.
     p. cm.
Includes bibliographical references and index.
  ISBN 1-59185-454-7
  1. Kendall, R. T. 2. Congregational churches—Clergy—Biography. I. Title.
  BX7260.K39A3 2004
  285.8'092—dc22
                                        2003026541

04 05 06 07 08 — 9 8 7 6 5 4 3 2 1
Printed in the United States of America

To the members of Westminster Chapel
1977–2002

*Not to us, O L*ORD*, not to us*
but to your name be the glory,
because of your love and faithfulness.
—Psalm 115:1

Contents

Foreword
by Jack Hayford

YOU ARE ABOUT to have the privilege of stepping into the life and experience of R. T. Kendall, a man who is beautifully qualified to show us the pleasures—and pain—of pursuing the glory of God through spiritual leadership. Dr. Kendall has just finished fifty years of pastoral ministry, twenty-five years of which he spent as pastor of Westminster Chapel in London, England.

This book chronicles those twenty-five years of spiritual leadership. Dr. Kendall makes no attempt to hide the difficulties he faced during his tenure at Westminster Chapel, but neither does he prevent you from seeing the incredible blessings of God upon his life and the life of his church because of his passionate pursuit of God's glory, not his own.

You will unquestionably notice—immediately—the way these pages speak to you. The insights from this autobiographical journey into Kendall's life are not only practical, but also intensely personal. Dr. Kendall's stories, illustrating the biblical truths he unfolds and how he lived out those truths in his own life, are in the best tradition of today's contemporary Christian writer. His personal reflections upon his interactions with spiritual giants like Dr. Martyn Lloyd-Jones, Billy Graham, and Arthur Blessitt provide the kind of mentoring that increases faith and inspires passion in our own lives.

Dr. Kendall opened the Word at Westminster Chapel at a pulpit with a long history of faithful, gifted preachers—a role he served worthily, using the classic expositional approach that is so historic in British tradition. This classic value is too often neglected by (sometimes even unknown to) some current messengers of God's Word.

The first decade of my pastoral life, I was greatly influenced by the writings of some of the great expositors of the English pulpit. Among these were G. Campbell Morgan, Reginald E. O. White, and Guy H. King, three preachers of the twentieth century but who evidenced the qualities born of earlier insightful teaching resulting from thorough scholarship. But in this book by Dr. Kendall, what is even more impressive than his preaching style is his passion to lead his congregation into a deeper personal relationship with God Himself.

This is a book filled with the revelations and memoirs of a man who gave himself to the pursuit of God's glory. Dr. Kendall will show you how to "do" spiritual leadership. It's done by pursuing the glory of God with a passionate faith no matter what. You will be blessed and enriched in your own life by what you read.

—JACK W. HAYFORD
FOUNDER AND SENIOR PASTOR, THE CHURCH ON THE WAY
CHANCELLOR, THE KING'S COLLEGE AND SEMINARY

Foreword
by Ernest Paddon

WE COULD NOT have known when Dr. Kendall was invited to preach for us in February 1976 that here was our minister for the next twenty-five years.

His name was suggested to me. I had never heard of him, but in consultation with the deacons and Dr. Lloyd-Jones it was agreed that he should be asked for a Sunday. He did not seem over-excited at the prospect but said he would come.

We had been in an interregnum for three years and could see no leading toward a future pastor. Dr. Kendall was well received and his ministry appreciated. He came again, and it was then that we asked him to consider preaching for a six-month period. We had had different preachers every week for three years and felt the need for consecutive preaching. Dr. Kendall was completing his doctorate in philosophy at Oxford and had promised his family, who were homesick, that they would soon be returning to America.

However, with persuasion he did agree.

We were all very impressed and challenged by his series on Jonah, and as the six months proceeded we increasingly felt that he was the right man. He too became likewise convicted. He therefore agreed that his name should go before the church. There was an almost unanimous call.

I was privileged to sit under his ministry for the whole of that period. It was a vital part of my Christian walk with the challenge to tithe, pray more, and to evangelize. I would never have become a Scripture reader if he had not been concerned about reaching the soldiers in Wellington Barracks when it was rebuilt.

He changed—and so did we. He truly practiced what he preached. He sought to reach every type of person and showed increasing patience and love to difficult people. Sometimes too patient! He always showed himself to be open and honest. There were difficulties but also many blessings. He was faithful in his commitment to Pilot Lights, only encouraging us to do what he himself was willing to do.

Dr. Kendall is a man of great authority and leadership. He has an amazing knowledge of the Scriptures and a willingness to deal with any verse in the passage preached, however difficult it might be. I can never remember hearing a sermon that did not bless me. He was able to preach on familiar verses with a new emphasis or meaning.

Dr. Kendall was not only a wonderful pastor but to me a counselor and friend, and I will greatly miss him. My prayer is that this book will be a blessing to all who read it and that many would understand more of this truly great man. I thoroughly recommend it.

—ERNEST PADDON
MEMBER OF THE CHAPEL SINCE 1946
DEACON SINCE 1960
CHURCH SECRETARY 1970–1990

Foreword
by Bill Reynolds

I FIRST SPOKE with Dr. Kendall in September 1978; I was between churches but didn't want to travel twenty-five miles to church. He replied, "Is twenty-five miles too far to travel to get your soul fed?" Needless to say, I began traveling back to the Chapel and have been there ever since, but now live only eight miles away.

To sit under the ministry of RT has been a real privilege, and I don't think anyone could regularly listen to his preaching without it becoming life changing; it demands that one should seek to live a more Christlike life. I have often wondered if this is one reason why some people do not stay longer at the Chapel, but move on.

RT's preaching has always been born out of experience, not dry dusty academic study. A preaching that is from the heart and shows he knows how people really feel. Preaching that scratches where people itch and makes them want a closer walk with Jesus. His prayers are special, too, especially Sunday mornings, when they regularly make one feel as if he knows one's exact situation.

But in addition to RT's preaching and teaching has been the immense privilege we have had to hear and meet some of God's more unusual sovereign vessels from over the Atlantic: Billy Graham, Arthur Blessitt, Paul Cain, John Arnott, Randy Clark, Rodney Howard-Browne, Charles Carrin, and Jack Taylor, who have all had notable and significant influence on the life and direction of the Chapel in the last fifteen years.

Some evangelicals believe that RT in his pursuit of the glory of God has gone too far, but most of them do not know the heart of this man. Although he wears his heart on his sleeve, I have believed and said to others for many years that the only extreme that RT has is that of balance. RT has been his own man; he has made and kept friends from all spectrums of evangelical Christianity and has not been constrained by any one theological tradition. I believe this has been his genius, and God has blessed his ministry as a result.

This book only traces the rainbow. His preaching on "total forgiveness" means that you will not see the clouds and rain that gave this rainbow its beauty. I count it an honor to be a friend of RT, and I recommend this book to you.

—Bill Reynolds
Member since 1978
Deacon since 1985
Church Secretary from September 1990

Preface

THE AMERICAN EDITION to the book you hold in your hands coincides with the fiftieth anniversary of my call to preach that came in November 1954. I began preaching one week later, and I have not stopped since!

Dr. Jim Packer begins the foreword of his classic work *Knowing God* with these words: "As clowns yearn to play Hamlet, so I have wanted to write a treatise on God. This book, however, is not it." Dr. Packer's statement describes my own feelings about writing my memoirs; this book, therefore, is not that. It is but very selected accounts of twenty-five years of life at Westminster Chapel. I could have written a book four times this size!

I did not come to the title *In Pursuit of His Glory* overnight. A half-dozen titles had been settled on over eight or nine months of struggling. But after several discussions with my deacons and friends, I came to the present title for two reasons. First, it best describes my twenty-five years at Westminster Chapel. Second, it has served as a built-in warning system to be doubly sure I do not write anything— as best as I can tell—that is not designed to bring glory to God. I only know that dozens of pages have had to be shredded that I might have initially wanted in the book.

This book is not a success story, as David Coffey candidly put it to me. For this reason I can only be thankful that my publisher would take it on. I have never really got over being called to be the minister of Westminster Chapel. My vacuum cleaner days gave me such a deep sense of inferiority and unworthiness that I am still in awe that I had the privilege. The fact that I can write an account of this era in my life is almost overwhelming to me. I can only say that God has been incredibly good to me.

I want to thank my friends who have read the manuscript and who have been extremely helpful. My debt to Rob Parsons, Lyndon Bowring, and Robert Amess is so profound that I blush to think what this book would be like apart from them. They have removed their names from the manuscript countless times, but I have put them back in when I felt it was right to do so. I hope they will forgive me for this. I thank Julia Fisher for her encouragement, as well as members of the Chapel such as Ernie and Margaret Paddon and Bill Reynolds. I am so honored that Ernie and Bill would write forewords. You will see how fortunate I am to have people like this over the years to support me.

But to have Pastor Jack Hayford write the foreword to the American edition is an honor that exceeded my greatest expectations.

I would like to thank the publisher of Charisma House and CEO of Strang Communications Company, Stephen Strang, for his role in publishing this autobiography. I would also like to thank Barbara Dycus, Ann Mulchan, Tom Marin, and Lillian McAnally for their penetrating insights. My new (the third and last) secretary Beryl Grogan has typed every word and has worked lovingly and laboriously on this for an entire year. My thanks to my assistant Brian Reed (my fifth and last) who both read the manuscript and compiled the lists of my books and sermons over the last twenty-five years and the index.

My deepest thanks go to my wife, Louise, my best friend and best critic. How I thank God for a wife who has stood by me faithfully during those twenty-five difficult years. The years were harder on her and our children—TR and Melissa—than they were on me. Their reward at the judgment seat of Christ will infinitely surpass any I may receive. We never dreamed that our arrival at London's Heathrow Airport on September 1, 1973, would find us living in England for the next twenty-eight and a half years.

Returning to America after having had the awesome privilege to live in our Mother Country was not easy. To all our friends in Britain, I say, "I thank my God every time I remember you" (Phil. 1:3). You are the best and dearest friends we ever had.

—R. T. KENDALL
MARCH 1, 2004
KEY LARGO, FL
WWW.RTKENDALLMINISTRIES.COM

Chronology

DATE	EVENT
September 1, 1973	Arrived in England to pursue a doctor of philosophy degree at Oxford
Third Sunday, February 1976	Preached at Westminster Chapel for the first time
Third Sunday, September 1976	Preached at Westminster Chapel for the second time
December 16, 1976	Successful *viva* (oral exam) at Oxford
February 1, 1977	Began my ministry at Westminster Chapel
March 1, 1981	Death of Dr. Martyn Lloyd-Jones
May 1982	Arthur Blessitt preached every Sunday night
June 1982	Pilot Lights ministry was born; began giving an altar call
May 6, 1984	Billy Graham visits Westminster Chapel
January 16, 1985	Historic church meeting
October 1990	Met Paul Cain
October 1992	Word and Spirit Conference at Wembley; began the School of Theology
January 1995	Louise impacted by the ministry of Rodney Howard-Browne
October 1995	"Toronto Blessing" came to Westminster Chapel
May–November 1999	Partnership with Holy Trinity Brompton
October 19, 2000	TR and Annette's wedding, leading Melissa to return to the Chapel
June 15, 2001	Word, Spirit, and Power Conference
February 1, 2002	End of my twenty-five years of ministry at Westminster Chapel

Introduction

Personally I'm always ready to learn, although
I do not always like being taught.
—WINSTON CHURCHILL

COME WITH ME on a journey. It is one filled with much joy but also a lot of pain. This is partly because the journey has not led me to the destination I envisaged when I embarked on it twenty-five years ago. It has been mainly a pursuit instead.

Not that I saw this early on; far from it. I had a definite idea what I wanted to achieve when I came to Westminster Chapel on February 1, 1977. But God stepped in at some point in the journey, and, yet, not in the way I had in mind. Whereas I had a definite goal, He had a certain goal as well. I wanted success; He wanted glory—His glory.

Before I move on, I must take you back even further. I was born of Christian parents, Wayne and Lucille Kendall, in Ashland, Kentucky, on July 13, 1935. The population in Ashland then was around 29,000. I was converted on April 5, 1942—an Easter Sunday morning, kneeling at my parents' bedside.

I was named after Dr. R. T. Williams, my dad's favorite preacher. I was given the name Robert Tillman but went by RT ever since I was one hour old. My parents were loyal members of the Church of the Nazarene, a small holiness but non-Pentecostal denomination that had been founded by Dr. Phineas Bresee, a former Methodist. "Keep the glory down" was his cry to early Nazarenes who had been blessed with a great sense of God's presence and power. Our theological hero was John Wesley.

My mother died on April 8, 1953, when I was seventeen. I graduated from high school in May of that year. I had been on the debating team. I also played the oboe in the school band; I equally enjoyed basketball and baseball but was never good enough to make the school teams. My dad remarried in 1954 to Abbie West. Abbie has been a wonderful wife to my father. My dad died April 1, 2002, two months after my retirement from the Chapel. I was able to participate in his funeral. He was a very strong father and drove me to a high level of ambition and perfectionism. His heart was broken when it became apparent I would not have a future in the Church of the Nazarene.

In September 1953 I entered Trevecca Nazarene College in Nashville, Tennessee. In November 1954 I felt the call to be a preacher. A Scottish preacher, John Sutherland Logan, was sovereignly used of the Lord to enable me to see for myself that I was called to preach. My local church back in Ashland immediately issued a preacher's license. On December 2, 1954, I preached my first sermon at the Calvary Church of the Nazarene in Nashville. In March 1955 I became a student pastor. The Church of the Nazarene in Palmer, Tennessee, 115 miles from Nashville, called me to be pastor. I attended Trevecca on Mondays through Fridays and went to Palmer on the weekends, usually arriving there Friday afternoons and often returning Sunday night after the evening service.

On Monday morning, October 31, 1955, driving back to Trevecca Nazarene College in Nashville, I had what I can only call a "Damascus Road" experience, although it was not my conversion. I believe it was my baptism in the Holy Spirit. I found myself praying hard with a very heavy burden and was beginning to wonder if I was saved or sanctified. Two scriptures came to my mind: Matthew 11:30, "For my yoke is easy, and my burden is light" (KJV), and 1 Peter 5:7, "Casting all your care upon him; for he careth for you" (KJV). I began to pray for grace to cast my care on the Lord so that I could say, "My yoke is easy, and my burden is light."

Suddenly there appeared as if before my very eyes the Lord Jesus Himself, interceding before me at God's right hand. I began to weep with joy as I drove. I found myself becoming a spectator; I was carried into the heavenlies. Jesus was praying for me! I couldn't tell what He was saying, only that I felt such love that I was almost overwhelmed. I still wonder how I was able to drive.

The next thing I remember is forty-five minutes later, just before arriving at Trevecca, when I heard Jesus say to the Father, "He wants it." I heard a voice answer back, "He can have it." In that moment I felt a surge of warmth enter into my chest. I could feel it physically although I am sure it was mainly spiritual. There appeared before me the face of Jesus, looking at me with such peaceful eyes. The vision of the Lord lasted for less than a minute, and then I pulled into the parking lot at Trevecca.

I soon began to have visions. I saw that I would one day have an international ministry—not within the denomination of which I had known, for my spiritual experience had changed my theology. For example, I knew I was eternally saved; I even saw that God predestined the elect. I began to be truly convicted of sin and identified with 1 John 1:8, "If we claim to be without sin, we deceive ourselves and the truth is not in us." I thought I had discovered something "new"—that I was the first person since the apostle Paul to see those things! I experienced a real closeness to the Lord Jesus. Four months later, in February 1956, I spoke in tongues—but only once. In May 1956 I resigned my church in Palmer and returned to Ashland, to my dad's dismay, for I also had no plans to return to Trevecca.

In August 1956 I met Henry Mahan, pastor of the Thirteenth Street Baptist Church of Ashland. He held strongly reformed (Calvinistic) views. He was stunned in disbelief when I told him I too believed in these views and that they came by the immediate revelation of the Holy Spirit. He took me in but could offer me no ministry opportunities. I had to place preaching aside, but I cherished his teachings in those days, for they helped to crystallize my understanding of the gospel. Henry became an extremely close friend. I also began working with a new friend, Ed Ketner, who had begun a business selling Stroll-o-Chairs—baby equipment. I learned to sell them and did so for the next two years, from 1956 to 1958. Jesus Himself spent many years in a carpenter's shop. The apostle Paul developed an expertise in making tents.

In January 1958 I entered Olivet Nazarene College in Kankakee, Illinois (near Chicago). An old friend, Harlan Milby, who was a businessman and Nazarene layman, had persuaded me to return to a Nazarene college and to let him set me up selling baby equipment in Illinois. It was at Olivet that I met a beautiful young woman—Louise Wallis, the prettiest girl on campus. Henry Mahan came to see me there, and during that visit led Louise to a saving knowledge of Christ. Louise and I were married at the Church of the Nazarene in Sterling, Illinois, on June 28, 1958. My dad was my best man at our wedding. He now had a hope I would remain a Nazarene.

Louise and I moved to Fort Lauderdale, Florida, in late October 1958. An old friend, Jesse Oakely, had moved to Fort Lauderdale from Ashland where he was pastor of a Nazarene church there. He persuaded us to attend his church, and he got me a job selling life insurance, but later I began selling vacuum cleaners. I eventually became his associate pastor and preached for him on Sunday nights. My new theological views did not threaten Jesse, and he hoped I would have a future in my old denomination.

On July 1, 1962, we moved to Carlisle, Ohio, through the influence of Billy Ball, an old Nazarene friend who had become a prominent minister in the Church of God. I became pastor of the Fairview Church of God. This was a part of a non-Pentecostal movement whose headquarters were in Anderson, Indiana. But this was not a happy time for us. My Calvinism did not sit well there. We gave up this church eighteen months later and moved back to Fort Lauderdale in early January 1964.

Prior to our move to Ohio I had learned to sell vacuum cleaners door-to-door, and I took up this trade again when we returned to Florida. We never returned to the Church of the Nazarene after this incident. I went to Bethany Presbyterian Church and was recommended by their pastor, Donald Graham, to be the interim pastor of the Bethel Orthodox Presbyterian Church in Lauderhill, just west of Fort Lauderdale. I continued selling vacuum cleaners and was able to pay for my own radio program and a new magazine (which was cosponsored by Evangelist Rolfe Barnard) called *Redeemer's Witness*. During those days I developed a good friendship with Dr. D. James Kennedy, senior minister of the Coral Ridge Presbyterian Church in Fort Lauderdale, Florida. Jim actually asked me to lead his new enterprise, later known as "Evangelism Explosion."

In 1966 God gave Louise and me a son, Robert Tillman II, whom we call TR. In 1970 Melissa Louise, whom we call Missy, was born. In 1967 we became Southern Baptists. My old friend Ed Ketner was now pastor of the First Baptist Church of Hallandale, Florida, just ten miles south of Fort Lauderdale. To my surprise but with tremendous wisdom, Henry Mahan urged me to become Ed's associate, so I did. But in a very short time I became the pastor of my own church, the Lauderdale Manors Baptist Church in Fort Lauderdale in the spring of 1968. Thus, after over four years of knocking on strangers' doors selling vacuum cleaners between Fort Lauderdale and Miami, I was back in full-time ministry. Were it not for Henry Mahan's loving care and concern, who knows how long I would have kept selling vacuum cleaners?

After nearly three years at Lauderdale Manors, I felt the need to finish my education and go to a seminary. In the autumn of 1970, we returned to Trevecca so that I could get my BA degree. It was a case of eating humble pie. Upon obtaining my BA degree, we then chose to go to Southern Baptist Theological Seminary in Louisville, Kentucky. I assumed I would need a secular job after finishing Trevecca the following December. But a phone call came from out of the blue. Bob Parker, a man I'd never met, asked me if I would like to be his successor at the Blue River Baptist Church in Salem, Indiana, thirty-five miles north of Louisville.

"Yes!" I answered. "But how do you know me?"

He replied, "I used to get your magazine called *Redeemer's Witness.*"

In January 1971 I enrolled at Southern Baptist Theological Seminary, traveling forty minutes each way virtually every day for the next two and a half years. I was able to preach every Wednesday night and twice on a Sunday at Blue River Baptist Church. Although it was normally a three-year course, I worked hard and completed the requirements for the MDiv (master of divinity) in two years. In the summer of 1973, I picked up the master of arts degree at the University of Louisville. In the meantime, my professors in Louisville recommended me for Oxford.

Louise, TR, Missy, and I first arrived at London's Heathrow Airport on September 1, 1973. For three years we lived at 2 Ramsey Road, Headington, Oxford. An unexpected development occurred soon after we arrived in England. A Southern Baptist church in Lower Heyford, Oxfordshire, comprised mostly of U.S. airmen and their families who were stationed at the Upper Heyford air force base, somehow found out about me and issued a call for me to become their pastor. For the third time in my life I would become a student pastor—this time from January 1974 to December 1976, almost exactly three years.

We could not agree to stay in Headington for another year,

so we took temporary residence at 59 Valley Road, Brackley, Northamptonshire, in the late summer of 1976. There I typed my PhD (doctor of philosophy) thesis, "The Nature of Saving Faith From William Perkins (1558–1602) to the Westminster Assembly." On the third Sunday of February 1976, I had preached at both services that day. No bells rang as far as I could tell, but Mr. Paddon kindly invited me back, and I gave him the September date. On the third Sunday of September 1976, I preached for the second time at Westminster Chapel.

I had arrived at London on the previous Friday before I was scheduled to preach to do some last-minute research at the British Museum. I had not brought any sermon notes; I was preoccupied with my thesis. That Sunday morning on the way to the Chapel, I hurriedly jotted down some notes on Romans 8:28 while riding on the subway:

> And we know that in all things God works for the good of those who love him, who have been called according to his purpose.

Preaching this time did not have the attraction for me that it had the previous February. However, the theme of Romans 8:28 apparently went over well with the people. They had learned only that week that the Rev. John Blanchard, who had been called several months before to speak, had decided to turn down the invitation. After the morning service I returned to my bed and breakfast place on Gower Street and worked on my thesis. I then hurriedly prepared another sermon, this time on Luke 16:19–31, as I headed back to the Chapel on the subway.

After the evening service the twelve deacons asked to talk with me in the vestry.

"Have I done something wrong?" I asked.

"No," said Sir Fred Catherwood. "We want to know if you would postpone your departure for America—for six months."

I replied that it would take an invitation from the queen to persuade my family to stay in England any longer. They asked me please to pray about it. Two weeks later Dr. and Mrs. Lloyd-Jones came to see us in Brackley to persuade us.

My thesis was fully typed and prepared by early October. My *viva* (oral exam) was set for December 16. Nearly forty months of sheer agony were about to be over.

Our years in Oxford were hard. It was difficult for our children, and also for Louise. We never felt we fitted in at Oxford. There I was, an unconfident man in my late thirties from the hills of Kentucky, having to read in the Bodleian Library alongside some of the brightest young minds in Britain who had been trained in the British educational system. Those invited to do research normally had a first-class degree, or at least an upper second. My educational background had not prepared me for what I was up against. In the days when there were only forty-eight states, we had a saying, "Thank God for Arkansas." Kentucky was forty-seventh in educational standards, and Arkansas was below Kentucky. Now I was in Oxford to do a doctorate in theology.

My supervisor was Dr. Barrie White. He was as English as they come and also a scholar's scholar. I was blessed to have him. But his encouragement that I would eventually pass was almost entirely absent. He worked me hard. He put me through considerable anxiety, turning down one essay or chapter after another. He turned down my chapter on the Puritan John Cotton three times before he let it stay. After three years I asked him, "Will I pass?"

"I don't know, Robert." (He loathed calling me by my initials though I told him it was all I'd known since I was born.)

"There surely ought to be a way of knowing by now," I said.

His reply: "It's a wicked world, Robert."

It was on October 6, 1976 that Dr. and Mrs. Martyn Lloyd-Jones came to see us in Brackley in order to discuss the offer of the deacons and members to be their visiting minister for six months.

"You have nothing to lose," Dr. Lloyd-Jones said to

Louise and me. "It will be good for Westminster Chapel, and it will be good for you.

"They need a time of consecutive ministry, and it will be good for you to have only to preach and forget Oxford," he continued. For some reason he stressed that I needed to get away from Oxford.

I looked at Louise and asked, "What do you think?"

"If it's only for six months," she replied.

We agreed. Dr. Lloyd-Jones then urged me to write to the church secretary, Ernest Paddon, immediately and send a first-class letter in order that they would have it for their church meeting the next day. Before they left, Dr. and Mrs. Lloyd-Jones signed our guestbook and wrote, "Visiting this time in the role of ambassadors—successful we hope!" After they left, I typed a letter to Mr. Paddon and mailed it before the last postal collection that day.

I walked into the exam room on December 16, 1976, for my *viva* wearing a junior student's robe, my heart pounding like a riveting machine. There sat Dr. Blair Worden, the Oxford internal examiner, and the well-known Calvin scholar Dr. T. H. L. Parker, the external examiner. Dr. Worden introduced himself and Dr. Parker and began, "This is a good thesis, Mr. Kendall, but do you think Theodore Beza knew he had departed from John Calvin?" I nervously replied that Beza may not have known about this since there were much larger issues that held them together at the time. I realized days later that Dr. Worden's calling my work a good thesis was a signal that I had already passed. But I took no joy until he said, "There are some corrections to be made for the copy that will be in the Bodleian"—a code phrase in Oxford that one had passed. But they said no more and politely nodded as I left the room.

I rushed to the coffee shop in the High Street and phoned Louise: "I passed!" I said, with tears of joy and relief. When Louise got off the phone she said to Melissa, "Now we can call him Dr. Kendall."

Missy looked sad. "I want to call him Daddy."

~

After Christmas in Florida we returned to England, landing at Heathrow on January 31, 1977 to begin our ministry at Westminster Chapel. Instead of having to make our way to a bus and then a train to Oxford as before, we were driven by a Chapel member to central London. We were taken to our new home at Durward House in South Kensington. The deacons had been encouraged over the way this lovely apartment had turned up quite suddenly. It gave us a comfortable feeling from the first few hours. Already we were feeling that London would be a lovely but temporary place in which to live. We loved walking around in the area, and our children were placed in an American school in South Kensington so that they might make the transition to a school in the United States six months later.

The following Friday the four of us went to the Chapel for our first "At Home." (That is the name given to the occasion when the members of the church welcomed the pastor back from his long vacation.) I was a little surprised that we were given this status already. Nobody explained to us the origin of this phrase "At Home." It seemed quaint to us and somewhat inappropriate for Americans who were aching to get back home to the United States after three unpleasant years in Oxford. But it was a delightful evening. The four of us stood in a reception line; we were treated like celebrities. Mr. M. J. Micklewright, the Chapel's most senior deacon, gave a word based on Acts 10:33:

> It was good of you to come. Now we are all here
> in the presence of God to listen to everything the
> Lord has commanded you to tell us.

The following Sunday morning I began a new preaching series from the Book of Jonah. While waiting for my *viva* in Brackley, I outlined eight sermons from the Book of Jonah, two from each chapter. I envisaged that I would preach on something else for the Easter period and then come up with a short series during the remaining time before our departure after the end of July. We let friends know of our availability in America after that time. One church in Florida showed interest, as did also a theological seminary.

But something unexpected happened the week before I preached my first sermon on Jonah. As I began to prepare, thoughts came to me spontaneously that I hadn't counted on. I had never preached on Jonah before, nor did I have any commentaries on Jonah. Why Jonah? I don't really know, but by Sunday morning I had a sermon based on Jonah 1:1–2 and that was as far as I got. I assumed I would finish the chapter the following Sunday. The following week, however, I found that the same exact thing happened again. I had all I needed for the second sermon, which was based on Jonah 1:2–3.

I did not know that Dr. Lloyd-Jones planned to be in the congregation for my second sermon. When the service was over, people rushed back to the vestry, saying, "Did you know that Dr. Lloyd-Jones was in the congregation this morning?" He had sat in the back row behind a pillar to keep me from seeing him. The truth is, I saw him—at least I thought I did, and I wasn't too surprised to hear that it was he. He always sat in the same place, with Mrs. Lloyd-Jones in the seat in front of him. I always knew after then when he was there.

That same evening the telephone rang at Durward House. "Is this the great preacher?" he said playfully.

"Hi, Doctor, how are you?"

"Listen to me," he said. "You're a preacher, a born preacher. Your place is not in a seminary or a university but in a pulpit."

I was flattered and deeply honored. Ernest Paddon later told me what had actually happened the year before, when he invited me to preach the first time at Westminster Chapel. The suggestion that I preach then came from Terence Aldridge, a dentist but also a minister who preached often at the Chapel and who frequented our services at Calvary Baptist Church at Lower Heyford. Dr. Lloyd-Jones had actually preached for us there several times during those three years. So when Terence Aldridge gave my name to Mr. Paddon as a possible Sunday preacher, Ernie immediately phoned Dr. Lloyd-Jones for a second opinion. "Oh yes, have him. Theologian, you know—but have him," he replied.

By Easter I had finished preaching through the second chapter of Jonah. In the meantime the Doctor (as everybody affectionately called him) continued to take his seat in the last row of the Chapel when he wasn't preaching elsewhere. People began coming to me with the word that Dr. Lloyd-Jones was happy with me. By early May there was a move to get us to stay in Westminster. Terence and Joyce Aldridge, hearing of this and knowing we were not wanting to stay in England any longer, came to see us at Durward House. When they signed our guest book, Terence added 2 Corinthians 5:15:

> And he died for all, that those who live should no longer live for themselves but for him who died for them and was raised again.

I took the point. That verse would haunt me for the next twenty-five years, for it cohered with the words of John 5:44, which first gripped me in 1956: "How can you believe if you accept praise from one another, yet make no effort to obtain the praise that comes from the only God?" My old friend Billy Ball brought that verse to my attention. John 5:44 has shaped my thinking for all these years, probably more than any other verse in the Bible.

Knowing that the people were wanting us to stay, I felt I should put certain obstacles in their way to test how much they really wanted us. When I preached I touched on every controversial subject I could think of—sometimes even if the text in Jonah did not call for it (tithing, for example)—that would stop any such move. Not that I was opposed to coming if it was God's will; I simply didn't want trouble down the road over any of my theological views! I wanted the people to know everything I believed, including my views regarding Christ's atonement. We eventually agreed to let the people vote on us at the church meeting in May. We received 92 percent of the vote.

Sir Fred and Lady Catherwood (Dr. Lloyd-Jones's daughter) came to see us at Durward House after the church meeting. Knowing that I wanted a unanimous vote, Sir Fred insisted that this was a very good vote. Dr. Lloyd-Jones phoned later that night. "That's a better vote than Campbell Morgan would have got and a better vote than I would have got," he said to me. Fred urged me to try it for five years. I said to Louise, "Let's stay for one year."

I turned to the Lord, praying as earnestly as I knew how. I remember sitting on the bed in Durward House and asking the Lord for a confirming scripture. All I got was Acts 28:26:

> Go to this people and say, "You will be ever hearing but never understanding; you will be ever seeing but never perceiving."

That seemed to be a green light, but it was also threatening. Could it be that I will preach to people who will oppose me? Does this mean that I will not have great success if we agree to stay on? It hardly sounded like a promise of great revival. But I felt no peace about the church in Florida or the seminary offer.

We agreed to stay. I phoned Mr. Paddon with the news. He seemed delighted.

"Will there be an induction service?" I asked.

"We don't go in for that sort of thing here," he replied.

"Then when do I become the minister?"

"You're it now," he said. That was it.

The following Sunday, the first in June 1977, John Raynar, the chairman of the pastorate committee, publicly announced our decision to the Chapel. They sang, "How Good Is the God We Adore," and I continued preaching in the Book of Jonah, which ended up being twenty-three sermons.

Several ministers were already booked to preach during the summer, so we were asked to take a six-week vacation, the time ministers of the Chapel always took each year. (That was one tradition I never wanted to change.)

The Chapel had rented Durward House for six months only, so we immediately began looking for a place to live. We chose Ealing in order to live near Dr. and Mrs. Lloyd-Jones. They had become good friends during our Oxford years, visiting us from time to time, even doing things with us like seeing a Shakespeare play at Stratford-upon-Avon. We settled on a house that was only an eight-minute walk from 49 Creffield Road, the Lloyd-Jones's home. Our address, which became known as "the other 49," was 49 Hamilton Road. We lived there for more than nine years.

The decision to stay was no small trauma for our children. We managed to get them into Montpelier School in Ealing, but it was not very pleasant for them. The Headington Church of England School in Oxford had been hard for TR in particular. The kids there made fun of his accent and size (a bit larger than most young boys there). One of the hardest moments I can remember was TR coming to me one evening after we had moved to Ealing, crying and saying, "But Daddy, you said we'd be going home." I could not look him in the eyes. During the days at Oxford, TR would say grace before the meal, always with the words, "Thank You for the food, and help Daddy get his PhD so we can go back to America."

When I drove TR to Montpelier that first day, he refused to get out of the car. He previously had to make the change from the Headington school to an American school near Brackley, then to the American school in South Kensington. Now it was back to an English school. Tears rolled down his cheeks.

"I'm not going," he said to me.

"I'm sorry, Son, but you have to go."

He just sat there and watched kids he had never met playing on the grounds.

"TR, look at me," I said. "I am going to be praying for you all day long. I won't stop. At any moment when you feel scared, just remember: Daddy is praying for you at that very moment." He opened the door and walked to the school, never looking back.

Both of our children were very shy. They lacked the confidence needed to make many friends at first. I wish with all my heart I had been there for them more than I was. I am almost ashamed to say that if I could turn the clock back to 1977, I would. I should have more faith in my own preaching generally and Romans 8:28 particularly. I just wish I had spent more time with the children. I put the Chapel first, supposing I was putting God first. I spent more time preparing sermons than being with our precious children. I now believe as I write these lines that I would have preached just as well (probably better) had I spent more time with them. But now all I can do is trust utterly in the truth of Romans 8:28.

Shortly after I accepted the call to be the minister of Westminster Chapel, Edward England, a director of Hodder & Stoughton (a London-based book publisher), came to see me in the vestry. He wanted me to do a book with them. At that time I hadn't even finished preaching on Jonah, but he said that series would do very well.

"How do you know you aren't making a mistake?" I asked him.

"Hodder doesn't make many mistakes," he replied, and I signed a contract for my first book.

My Oxford thesis (which also became a book) was in some ways to do me more harm than good. I remember sitting in the Bodleian Library in early 1976, shortly after I had my greatest breakthrough on Calvin's doctrine of the atonement. My first essay for Barrie White in October 1973 was on Calvin and limited atonement (the view that Jesus Christ did not die for all, but only the predestined elect). I took the view that Calvin believed in limited atonement. But a more careful reading of his commentaries, sermons, and *Institutes of the Christian Religion* forced me later on to adopt a different view. Although Calvin believed in predestination and election, he still held that Christ died for all. I myself struggled a long time to accept the latter. I knew in my gut that this would not thrill the reformed community.

The Doctor had kept abreast with my research at Oxford. When I shared my discovery that the Puritan John Cotton believed in the immediate and direct witness of the Holy Spirit, he was amazed and excited. He asked me to speak on John Cotton at the Westminster Conference in December 1976. When I had shown him John Calvin's view that Christ died for all people, he was surprised but fascinated. He too had always assumed that John Calvin believed in limited atonement, that Christ died for the elect only. What convinced him I had gotten it right on Calvin was the latter's own statement that people are "doubly culpable" if they reject Christ since Christ died for all.

"Read that to me again," he interrupted. I did. "That clinches your case," he said. He knew in advance all I would say at the Westminster Conference when I chose as the subject: "John Cotton: First English Calvinist?" Those present on that evening in December 1976 were stunned. I should perhaps add that I had been invited by the Doctor to speak at this conference months before I was asked to come to Westminster Chapel.

Little did I know that I would still be in England when my thesis became a book. Dr. Lloyd-Jones warmly supported my views both privately and publicly—as all who attended Westminster Chapel in December 1976 can testify. But his approval of my thesis was not sufficient to compensate for the understandable anger that came from certain quarters. I was simply not ready for the long haul ahead.

Westminster Chapel is a Congregational church. It was first built in 1841. In those days it was most certainly a "local church" for people who lived in the area. Today things are different. We have tried very hard to reach the residents near the Chapel but with very modest success. But at the beginning the Chapel existed for local residents. It was built on the site of the old Westminster Hospital. The Rev. Samuel Martin was the first minister. The original building seated a thousand, but because of the Chapel's growth a new building was needed, one that might seat up to twenty-five hundred. That is what exists today. The present building was completed in 1865. The Chapel's original ministry was not only aimed at the residents nearby but also to the poor and helpless in the area.

In 1904 George Campbell Morgan, a Congregationalist by persuasion, accepted the challenge and call to Westminster Chapel. Dr. Morgan gave the Chapel its international reputation. He was a gifted preacher and teacher with a "tall imposing presence and perfect speaking voice," says Dr. Charles James, the late historian of Westminster Chapel.

Dr. Morgan began the Friday night Bible School, which many people attended, for even the top gallery was needed. He founded the *Westminster Record,* which began in January 1905. During the First World War, Dr. Morgan resigned and moved to America, where he worked closely with D. L. Moody. In the meantime Dr. Henry Jowett, who had been pastor to the Fifth Avenue Presbyterian Church in New York, returned home to England to be the Chapel's minister in 1918. Prime Minister and Mrs. David Lloyd-George were present for his first service. Dr. Jowett was the minister until 1922.

Dr. John Hutton, who was Dr. Lloyd-Jones's favorite preacher, became the minister of the Chapel in 1922. As a medical student Martyn Lloyd-Jones attended the Chapel during John Hutton's ministry. The Doctor told me that it was Dr. Hutton who not only influenced him most to become a Christian but also inspired him to become a preacher.

Dr. Campbell Morgan returned from America and began a second ministry at Westminster Chapel in 1933. In the meantime Dr. Lloyd-Jones, who had been a brilliant young physician and assistant to Lord Horder, the king's personal physician, gave up practicing medicine and became the pastor of a church in Wales. In 1938 Campbell Morgan invited Dr. Lloyd-Jones to be his associate minister. In 1943 Dr. Morgan retired, and Dr. Lloyd-Jones became the minister.

Dr. Lloyd-Jones gave up the ministry at the Chapel in 1968 after a serious illness and major surgery. During his ministry the Chapel left the Congregational Union and later became affiliated with the Evangelical Fellowship of Congregational Churches (EFCC) and the Fellowship of Independent Evangelical Churches (FIEC).

The Rev. Glyn Owen became the minister of the Chapel in 1969. He too was a Welshman and was greatly loved by those who remained at the Chapel. But under his ministry a number of people decided to "settle locally." He resigned in 1974 to accept the pastorate at Knox Presbyterian Church in Toronto.

G. Campbell Morgan used to say that Westminster Chapel is not a church but a preaching center. It certainly ceased to be a local church during the twentieth century, and in Dr. Lloyd-Jones's day people traveled in from far and wide. Dr. Lloyd-Jones wanted the Chapel to be more than just a preaching center. Mrs. Lloyd-Jones encouraged people to bring meals such as casseroles to the Chapel to be warmed up after the morning sermon, and many ate together. Hence the Chapel became more of a church fellowship in Dr. Lloyd-Jones's day.

The Chapel had a three-year interregnum from 1974 to 1977. Sixty-six different men preached at the Chapel during these three years. One of these was Rev. Terence Aldridge. As I said, it was he who suggested to the church secretary, Mr. Ernie Paddon, that I be invited to preach at the Chapel. My first time was in February 1976, the second in September of that year. My ministry actually began on February 1, 1977, but our decision to stay came in May.

I was filled with so much excitement. But had God shown me then what the next twenty-five years would be like, I am not sure that I would have agreed to come. I would have certainly asked Him to make me doubly sure that we had no other choice. I was young and naïve. There was a spring in my step. But the thought of occupying the pulpit of G. Campbell Morgan and Martyn Lloyd-Jones—something that I knew would certainly please my father—was handed to me without my lifting a little finger. I really felt I had no other choice.

God only lets us live a day at a time. Jesus said, "Therefore do not worry about tomorrow, for tomorrow will worry about itself. Each day has enough trouble of its own" (Matt. 6:34). One reason God only gives us a day at a time—and doesn't tell us all He knows about the future—is that we couldn't bear such information. So God knew that Louise and I could not have coped had we known in advance all that was entailed in accepting the offer for me eventually to be the minister of Westminster Chapel.

More than anything else during those twenty-five years we prayed for the manifestation of God's glory in our midst. We equally prayed to be open to the way He chose to manifest that glory. And I thought I was so open!

But for the manifestation of that glory to be our equally upholding His honor—and not to see a sovereign demonstration of His mighty power (true revival)—is hardly what I expected. And yet glory, honor, and praise come from the same words in the original biblical language: *kabodh* (Hebrew) in the Old Testament and *doxa* (Greek) in the New Testament. Moses asked to see the glory of the Lord—the *kabodh*, which means "weightiness" (Exod. 33:18), and Jesus asked, "How can you believe if you accept *praise* from one another, yet make no effort to obtain the *praise* that comes from the only God?" (John 5:44, emphasis added). Our twenty-five years have been the pursuit of the glory that comes from Him alone.

I am sorry to tell you that I believed in my heart that I had "arrived" when I first began my ministry at Westminster Chapel on February 1, 1977. Despite feeling very honored and very unworthy, I took myself very seriously. In truth I had not the remotest idea what the journey ahead held and how much I had to learn.

PART ONE

~

The
Early Years

The worst thing that can happen to a
man is to succeed before he is ready.
—Dr. D. M. Lloyd-Jones

1

Dr. Martyn Lloyd-Jones

Under Gamaliel I was thoroughly trained.
—Acts 22:3

I DOUBT IF any minister in the church since the time Timothy had access to the great apostle Paul has been more fortunate than I in having Dr. Martyn Lloyd Jones as a friend, confidant, and teacher. I was indeed blessed to have mentors like Barrie White and Jim Packer when at Oxford, but being with Dr. Lloyd-Jones was spiritual as well as intellectual preparation. For nearly four years the Doctor and I were much like father and son. There was a time when I may have been closer to him than anybody outside his family. There would sometimes be a look on his face when we made eye contact—a tenderness and acceptance—that used to remind me of how my Grandpa McCurley, my favorite relative, loved me. I sometimes have to pinch myself that I, a man from the hills of Kentucky, actually knew him.

Dr. Lloyd-Jones was a genius. Few people excel in the area of both arts and sciences. At best, it is usually one or the other for most of us. But he was equally competent in either. As a physician, he was at the top of his field and would almost certainly have become the king's physician after Lord Horder retired. When he went into the ministry, it soon became apparent he was a Welsh orator of the highest standard. But he never lost his ability to diagnose diseases. Even after he gave up medicine, he read medical journals as a hobby, and sometimes doctors would call on him for help with their most difficult cases.

He had an ability to assess one's intelligence unlike anybody I have met. It may seem strange, but he would almost know a person's IQ or health problem just by looking at them. He studied a person's face. He also thought there was more to phrenology than many who tended to dismiss this study out of hand as an old fad. Until I met him I never paid much attention to whether a person was basically intelligent, but I suspect it was the first thing he noticed. I suspected too that, though loving and tender with most people, he did not always "suffer fools gladly." He also made an acute distinction between being intellectual and being intelligent. "A cockney taxi driver may not be an intellectual but often has more intelligence than many a professor," he would say.

Dr. Lloyd-Jones was the greatest preacher since Charles Spurgeon (d. 1892) and arguably the best expositor in the history of the Christian church. "I always felt I understood Paul," he once said to me, but it was not until he felt he understood Romans 6 that he began his historic series on Romans.

I myself was forced to take a different approach when it came to dealing with a particular book in the Bible, for had I waited until I felt I understood it all I would never have started any book! I only know that I in no way compared with him, and I continue to be baffled that God would put me in his old pulpit. The one consolation I had is that the Doctor himself stated again and again that God put me there. "To prove my point," he once said with a grin, "Maynard James in his book on spiritual gifts said I have the gift of wisdom. Well then, I say God put you where you are and it is my wisdom saying this." He knew how incapable and unqualified I felt, and so he resorted to this to help me to believe what seemed to be almost overwhelming.

What perhaps meant most to me in those days was his endless patience. Even if I returned a week later—whether with the same feeling of inferiority, the same old weakness, or a complaint about low congregations—he listened lovingly as if he hadn't heard me speak about it before.

Soon after we moved to Ealing, he suggested Thursdays as the locked-in weekly date when we would be sure to meet. This gave me three days to prepare for my "tutorial." I used to travel from Ealing to Oxford on the train every Monday morning and start my preparation for the three sermons the following weekend: the Friday Bible study and the Sunday morning and evening services. I would arrive promptly at 11:00 a.m. I once arrived at five minutes to eleven.

"You're no Englishman," he said to me.

"What do you mean by that?" I asked.

"No Englishman would ever arrive early," he replied. I never arrived early after that!

Mrs. Lloyd-Jones would have coffee and KitKats ready. She would sit down only for a minute or two, then close the door as we would begin. We would usually chat about things generally, from how things went at Westminster the previous week to national politics. Some may not realize that the Doctor was a "political animal" and a consummate politician right down to his fingertips. I have often thought that, had he gone into politics, he could have been prime minister. Eventually I would turn to my preparation, usually beginning with the Sunday morning sermon, then to Sunday evening, and then the Friday Bible study.

Sometimes tears would fill his eyes when I finished. "Very good, really good, you're going to have a great Sunday morning." Other times he would say, "Now look here, take that out; it is distracting from your theme, and all they will think about is that when the sermon is over." Sometimes, although rarely, I would make a case for leaving something in. "Very well then, but don't make so much of it." He loathed the use of alliteration as sermon outline headings, so I dispensed with that for a long time. I never consciously uttered anything in the pulpit if I thought he would seriously disapprove.

There was one unforgettable exception: my view of the faith of Christ, that it is Christ's very own faith that justifies us once we put faith in him. On the Fridays in those days (1977–1981) I preached on Galatians. Galatians 2:16–20 has much to say about the faith of Christ. Only the King James Version makes this very clear. At one stage, I temporarily convinced him when I quoted what he himself had said from his volume on Romans 3. He never was completely convinced but graciously said, "You go on." He would often say this to me, "You go on," when we did disagree. He barely left the door open to the possibility I may have got it right that we are justified by our faith in Christ in order that we may be justified by His faith (who believed perfectly on our behalf).

The one subject that upsets many people in the reformed constituency but that did not upset him was my view of the atonement. He encouraged me no end to preach my view that Christ did not die for the elect only but for all.[1] His first comment to me when I shared with him that Calvin himself did not believe in limited atonement—sitting with us at 2 Ramsey Road—was, "You know, I only preached limited atonement once—when we came to Romans 5:15—and I was in great difficulty when I did so." Mrs. Lloyd-Jones used to say, "I never believed in limited atonement, and I never will."

When he learned that Oxford University Press had decided to publish my doctorate of philosophy thesis, he decided to read it again. One weekend when he did not feel well enough to go out, he began checking my footnotes. "You've got me to reading Calvin," he said. "You've left a lot out that would prove your thesis to the hilt."

When he quoted a passage from the *Institutes* or from a commentary, I would interrupt him. "I know all about those statements, Doctor."

"Then why don't you use them when your thesis comes out as a book?"

I replied that the Theological Monograph Committee wanted to print the book "without any changes" and that I didn't want to argue with them. He said this was a pity because biased readers of my book would not recognize how absolutely right I really was in interpreting Calvin on faith and the atonement.

He used to get annoyed that I always wanted to have something fresh or original every time I preached. It was my pride. He warned me that a man's strong point is usually his weakest, and that I must abandon trying to say something no one had said before every time I preach. He said it would lead to my making extreme statements. I listened to him and began to realize that the people need to be fed from the plain, simple exposition of the text and that they would not know whether something was all that fresh. "Your job is to make it interesting for them," he would say, "without trying to be original all the time."

But there was one verse I did succeed in changing his mind on:

> What good is it, my brothers, if a man claims to
> have faith but has no deeds? Can such faith save
> him?
>
> —JAMES 2:14

It was because of James 2:14 that I was loath to begin the Book of James. I simply did not know what it meant. Even when I finished James 2:13, I was no closer to the meaning of that problematic verse that caused Martin Luther to dismiss James as "an epistle of straw," sadly. But something happened. I was on a flight back from Israel. Out of the blue I recognized that the "him" referred to in James 2:14 refers not to whether the person himself—who claims to have faith—is saved but to the poor man who needs to see the works of the man who claims to have faith. Indeed, the grammar and the context bear this out. In other words, James never changed the subject at all from the poor man of James 2:6: "You have insulted the poor"—*protchon,* "poor man," accusative masculine singular in the Greek. "Can faith save the poor man?" is what James asked, which causes the succeeding verses to make sense. They also show that James does not contradict Paul and that Martin Luther missed it by focusing on whether the person who claims to have faith is truly a justified man. The truth is, James was not questioning that person's being a Christian at all! James only questions whether his witness to the poor man was effective if he did not show works. I shared this with the Doctor the following Thursday. "You have convinced me," he said. But that sort of thing didn't happen very often.

He asked me early on to let him appraise my preaching invitations, which I gladly did. This began when I had taken an invitation in Wales, which he said I should never have accepted. When he heard about it, he asked to know who was inviting me, if only to spare me taking invitations that would not be best for me and the Chapel. But I also turned down preaching at the Keswick Convention during my first year, as the Doctor was not happy about Keswick at all. He was especially unhappy with the Keswick message.

One of the greatest things he did for me was to introduce me to a Bible reading plan created by a Scottish preacher named Robert Murray M'Cheyne. I began using it immediately and kept it up consistently if not rigidly for the whole of my twenty-five years at the Chapel. It is a tough plan, and I do sympathize with those who begin it and give up on it. I have never been sorry I kept it up. It was one of my greatest sources of strength during those twenty-five years.

The Doctor introduced Louise and me to homeopathy, Marmite (a yeast spread for crackers), and routes in central London I'd never come across. "I know my London," he

used to say. "I could be a taxi driver in London." He loved
driving in London but not long journeys. Such a journey
would be heading for Fred and Elizabeth's beautiful home at
Balsham, near Cambridge, which he adored. Though hardly
a Tory in his politics (he loathed the *Daily Telegraph*), he did
have a secret wish to live in a palatial country home. God gave
such to the Catherwoods, and the Doctor loved being there,
especially to edit his old sermons for books. It was there he
introduced me to Marmite.

"This is very good for you; it contains vitamin B," he said.

"Then why aren't you having any?" I asked.

"It doesn't agree with me," he replied. We both almost
fell on the floor laughing. As for homeopathy, he and Mrs.
Lloyd-Jones used it all the time.

In September 1977 I drove Dr. Lloyd-Jones to Chipping
Norton where he was to preach at the Cotswold Bible
Conference. We stopped for tea on the way. I began to discuss
my plans to preach through Hebrews 11.

"I need a good definition of faith," I said to him. "Can
you help me?"

He laughed and said, "I would never think to do anything like that."

"But can you still help me to come up with a good definition of faith that will carry me right through Hebrews 11?"

He smiled, and we paid the bill for the tea and carried
on to Chipping Norton.

The next day the phone rang. "Believing God—there's
your definition," the familiar voice declared. He began to
quote various passages showing that faith is, simply, believing
God. "Not believing *in* God," he stressed, but "believing
God." I knew that definition was unimprovable. Those sermons were published by Hodder & Stoughton as *Who by
Faith*. (The reprint is called *Believing God*.)

One day the Doctor asked me my opinion on the Puritan
Thomas Goodwin's view of the sealing of the Spirit, based on
the King James Version's translation of Ephesians 1:13: "In

whom ye also trusted, after that ye heard the word of truth, the gospel of your salvation: in whom also after that ye believed, ye were sealed with that holy Spirit of promise." I told him I agreed with Goodwin, that I had already read it in the course of my research at Oxford. Goodwin's view, breaking with Calvin and every single Puritan that I know of, was that this sealing of the Spirit—the highest form of assurance—follows conversion generally and does not refer to conversion itself. In other words, it is usually subsequent to conversion, which the King James Version certainly suggests.

But the Doctor asked, "Would you mind reading it again?" Certainly. I returned the following Thursday. It was one of the few times that he had an agenda and brought up Thomas Goodwin's view of Ephesians 1:13 as soon as we finished coffee and KitKats. "Well," he began, "what did you think?"

I merely replied, "That is exactly what I myself believe."

Tears filled his eyes. "That's the greatest thing I have ever heard you say," he said.

"I'm an eighteenth-century man," he used to say. By that he meant that he was a Calvinistic Methodist. He loved the two great men of the eighteenth century, George Whitefield and John Wesley. He accepted Whitefield's Calvinism and dearly loved John Wesley's view of the immediate witness of the Holy Spirit, although he did not agree with Wesley's doctrine of sanctification. By saying he was an eighteenth-century man, he meant emphatically that he was not enamoured with the preaching of the nineteenth century, especially in the Church of England, and was not particularly fond of the arid and scholastic teaching of the seventeenth-century Puritans, except for Thomas Goodwin. I used to feel that this matter was far more important to him than some of his followers realized.

Our first Thanksgiving in London was in November 1977. We pulled off a real coup for our friends Harlan and Olive Milby, who now live in Nashville, Tennessee. The Milbys paid every penny of my Oxford tuition for three years.

I don't know how we would have managed financially apart from them. So when they happened to be in London at such a special time, I wanted to do something that showed a measure of appreciation. Joining the four of us were Dr. and Mrs. Lloyd-Jones with both daughters and sons-in-law. I was told that it was the only time that the entire Lloyd-Jones family could recall meeting together on such an occasion outside their own homes. We had brought a sugar-cured Kentucky ham for the occasion, to be served alongside the traditional turkey dinner. When the Doctor tasted the ham he said, "This takes me right back to Wales when I was a child. This is what the poor were served." I explained to him that it was a delicacy to us. It was the first occasion our new china could be used—all for the most important people of our lives.

I will always believe that Dr. Lloyd-Jones was attracted to me mainly because of my Nazarene background rather than anything else he knew about me. Having read a biography of Phineas Bresee, the founder of the Church of the Nazarene, he seemed thrilled to know that I had been brought up in the Church of the Nazarene. Again and again he said to me, both when we were in Oxford and after I became the minister at the Chapel: "Don't forget your Nazarene background. That is what has saved you." By this he meant that I had a tendency to be too academic and cerebral but that my background would keep me from being too intellectual. As a matter of fact, when he and Mrs. Lloyd-Jones came to see us in Brackley, knowing I agreed to take his advice, his final words to me as they left were: "Preach like a Nazarene."

Had it not been for Dr. Lloyd-Jones's teaching on the "immediate and direct" witness of the Holy Spirit—he insisted on those very words—I would never have survived at the Chapel. All in the Chapel who were present in the Doctor's day not only knew his views (even if some didn't agree) but also knew how important such views were to him. Therefore when I have stressed an openness to the Spirit it was apparent to them that it was not novel teaching. But for

Dr. Lloyd-Jones, then, I would not have made it through.

On December 20, 1977—his seventy-eighth birthday—he phoned to say he was coming over to give me something. I had no idea what he meant. I then saw him walking to 49 Hamilton Road with a book in his hand. It was his own book: *The Christian Soldier* (an exposition of Ephesians 6:10–20). He had written inside: "To R. T. Kendall, the first man I have addressed as 'my minister' since 1926, and with increasing love and esteem, and with warmest good wishes for Christmas and the New Year and always." Mrs. Lloyd-Jones also signed a card "our fondest love." The Doctor repeated this the following Christmases 1978, 1979, and 1980. He truly seemed to take pleasure in calling me his "minister." It humbled me and thrilled me more than anything else he could say.

One day the Doctor had something particularly on his heart for me. He began, "I hear you visited someone."

I replied, "Yes, Doctor. It was a deacon, and he had had a heart attack."

"Listen to me," he interrupted. "I never visited. Campbell Morgan never visited. If you do it, you're finished." Then he added, "The people who choose Westminster Chapel for a church don't need or expect to be visited."

He used to say, "Westminster Chapel runs by itself." I think that may have been true in his day. And I took his point to a large extent, but I felt the need to visit people at times. The trouble, of course, is that others would hear about it and expect the minister to visit them too, even if, because London is so vast, it would take the better part of a day to call on only one person.

Dr. Lloyd-Jones warned me early on that I would soon lose my voice if I didn't stop shouting when I preached. He urged me to start out in a very, very low key: "The text to which I call your attention is found…," and then build up. He used to say: "Remember Abraham Lincoln: from the log cabin to the White House." He felt I began too often with the White House and ended up with a log cabin. I remember that at his eightieth birthday party he began with his "least favorite" of the desserts and ended with his very favorite. "From the log cabin to the White House," he said to me with a big grin. The "White House" to him was almost anything that was chocolate!

The trouble was, however, I began trying to sound like him a bit, though I never tried to imitate him. I once asked Sir Fred Catherwood, "Why did you all really call me?" He replied that I was "the only man who came to Westminster that didn't try to imitate the Doctor." But I was slipping into this. I once got an anonymous letter that said, "What has happened to your style? You no longer sound like the man who first came to us."

I thought about this a lot and decided that I should share it with the Doctor. He replied, "Very well." That is all he said. But it seemed he took the point that perhaps I should be more like I was when I first began. He had only my best interest at heart and genuinely wanted me to succeed in his old pulpit. I think I was more myself during the first six months than at any time after that until the 1990s.

He gave me practical advice all the time, such as how long to pray in the Sunday mornings, how long to preach. I never tried to preach as long as he did, certainly not on Sunday nights. I knew I did not have the ability to hold people's attention for that long. He always said one thing, however, about the main difference between the Sunday mornings and Sunday evenings at the Chapel. He felt I should keep Sunday mornings much the same, but if I would make any changes, such could come on Sunday evenings. "Flash all you like on Sunday evenings," he once said. I nearly fell to the floor laughing. The Doctor did not realize how flash could be taken these days!

The Lloyd-Joneses always celebrated Thanksgiving Day with us. Louise knew exactly what he liked to eat—mostly desserts and always chocolate. "I could live on sweets," he once said to me. But I will never forget what he said as they were leaving the last time they ever had a meal with us. As he was walking toward the door, he stopped and said, "There is only one thing I ever wanted in life." And then he was silent.

"Go on," I said.

He couldn't speak. All he could do was nod toward Mrs. Lloyd-Jones as she was putting on her coat. He adored Bethan Lloyd-Jones beyond the ability of words to describe.

If there was a tendency for me to try to be more like him at one stage—and this had to be dealt with—I must add that the help he gave was worth more than gold. I would not take anything in the world for what I learned from him about expository preaching, sermon delivery, and common sense. He always said that I prepared far more carefully than he ever did. If so, it is because I lacked the confidence he had, and neither did I possess his brilliance. In other words, I had to work twice as hard to be at home in his old pulpit. I doubt if the Doctor was ever as intimidated by Campbell Morgan as I was by the Doctor. But Mrs. Lloyd-Jones shared with me a surprising word after he died. Knowing as she did that people said of my own ministry "it surely isn't like it was in the Doctor's day," she said to me: "They said the same thing about Campbell Morgan and Martyn." "He's no Campbell Morgan," they would say. It made me feel better, of course. But the truth is, I am not like those who have preceded me. I have had to be at home knowing that God chose to put me where I am because this is the way He made me. And, yet, the hardest thing I've had to do is to come to terms with being myself. The funny thing is, the Doctor, as well as Mrs. Lloyd-Jones, used to say I always reminded them of Campbell Morgan. I never was sure if it was a compliment, but the Doctor used to say, "You're the most like Campbell Morgan of anybody I've met."

I once asked Dr. Lloyd-Jones if he would allow his mantle to fall on me. "It already has if I had any," he replied. "Have you noticed that they all refer to you as my successor?" I didn't know what to say, but a few days later he brought up the subject. "You know that you hoped my mantle would fall on you? I have been thinking lately. My ministry in Westminster was a wilderness ministry. But I think you are going to take the people over into the promised land." If only. He had such high hopes for me.

When the Lloyd-Joneses visited us at 2 Ramsey Road in Oxford, I shared with him a dilemma that had bothered me since early 1964, when I left Carlisle, Ohio, for Fort Lauderdale, Florida. I brought it up again at 49 Creffield Road.

"You still are bothered with this?"

"Yes."

He asked me to get on my knees.

"I believe what I preach," he said, and he laid his hands on my shoulders. He prayed that this matter would be resolved. It was a very moving moment, and I treasure that moment beyond words to describe, but nothing happened.

In 1980 David and Margaret Newbon, who had become members of Westminster Chapel shortly after I became the minister, kindly looked after our little house in Fort Lauderdale. They used it as their home in America since they did much business there. They arranged for Dr. and Mrs. Lloyd-Jones to spend a month in our home the following winter, but these plans were never to be fulfilled, for during 1980 the Doctor became unwell.

I usually chauffeured him to Charing Cross Hospital where he underwent a series of tests. He was anxious to get the all-clear sign so he and Mrs. Lloyd-Jones could go to Florida. I will never forget sitting with him, waiting for his name to be called. It was the strangest feeling to hear a nurse call, "Mr. Lloyd-Jones? Mr. Lloyd-Jones? Is David Lloyd-Jones here?" It made me see how the great Doctor was being treated just like any other patient in the waiting room.

When we returned to the hospital several days later, Dr. Lloyd-Jones received an ominous word. When we got into the car he was quiet. Driving to Ealing on Cromwell Road, he broke the silence with a phrase that surprised me. "As Karl Barth said, 'I have had a good life.'" Then he said, "I will tell you everything." I was pretty sure that day he and Mrs. Lloyd-Jones would not be traveling to Florida. The Doctor later went into the Charing Cross Hospital for several days, a stay that would be repeated.

In every relationship there are always times of stress and testing. People ask if the Doctor and I ever had serious quarrels. Yes, but we always made up. I remember a day I plucked up the courage to call on him when our relationship had been under a strain. I took a small branch from a tree in front of 49 Creffield Road, just before I rang the bell. When I walked into the room, he quickly perceived it as if it were an olive branch. He stood. He hugged me and literally kissed me on my left cheek. "We have a gracious God," he said. That is the kind of man he was.

Soon after this incident Dr. Lloyd-Jones phoned to see whether I would ask the Rev. David Gardner to come with me to his home and pray for his healing. David Gardner is an Anglican clergyman who faithfully attended the Westminster Fraternal every month. I brought David along to 49 Creffield Road. Together we anointed the ailing Doctor with oil, along the lines prescribed in James 5:13–16. The Doctor was grateful, and we did not stay long that day.

Not all our prayers are answered in the way we want, and the Doctor's illness worsened. The time had come when he was not up to any more two-hour sessions on Thursdays. I visited him from time to time, and we spoke on the telephone, but the era of being mentored by him as before was now virtually over. Hearing my discovery regarding James 2:14 turned out to be our last Thursday session.

He was also losing his appetite. In November 1980 Louise had prepared a turkey Thanksgiving dinner for just our family. It was the first Thanksgiving in London that the Lloyd-Jones family was not able to share with us. So Louise prepared two plates of food for Dr. and Mrs. Lloyd-Jones, including Louise's special chocolate mixture he loved and a piece of pumpkin pie for Mrs. Lloyd-Jones. That evening he phoned. There was silence on the phone, and yet I knew it was he. I heard a whimper, as if he were crying. He finally spoke up. "I never respected you more than I do now," he said. He said that he wanted to affirm me "as a man." He knew he was dying, and I can only believe he wanted to give me this word as a memory. We learned later he barely touched the food Louise had prepared. And when I learned he didn't even eat the chocolate, I knew he was a very ill man.

The last time I saw him alive was when I called on him after the Sunday night service on February 22, 1981. He was a shadow of himself and could not speak at all. But he took a pen and wrote me a note: "Don't pray for my healing, pray that I will be ready for this glory." It is a priceless note I keep in my old Bible, the one which he had also signed four years before, adding, "How unsearchable are His judgments, and His way past finding out!"

On Sunday morning, March 1, 1981, St. David's Day, his daughter phoned. "Dad's in heaven," were her words. She asked if I would like to come over and see him before they took him to the funeral home. I hurried over without shaving and saw his body lying on the bed where he had died a few hours before. I knelt beside him, sobbed like a child, then prayed and thanked God for him.

That morning I announced to the Chapel the passing of a great man. Most, however, had already heard the sad news as the Sunday program on the BBC had been playing one of the Doctor's sermons. All felt it was beautifully significant that God took his beloved servant home on St. David's Day, the most important day of the year to the Welsh. I thanked God for him in my morning prayer, then did my best to preach from James 4:10, the sermon I had prepared from the series that had begun in the autumn of 1979.

The Westminster Fraternal met the next day, March 2. The Rev. John Caiger was to chair the meeting but was late. After several minutes I decided to open the meeting, to pray, and read some scripture. I chose Joshua 1:2–10, which begins with the words, "Moses my servant is dead." Exactly one year later, in consultation with Mrs. Lloyd-Jones, I renamed the Institute Hall, which had been the venue for the Fraternal meetings and the Westminster Conferences, as Lloyd-Jones

Hall. I had the privilege of announcing this to the Fraternal on the first anniversary of his death. I remember saying, "Short of renaming the Chapel itself, this is the best we could do." Everyone seemed to appreciate our decision. A lovely plaque still hangs near the spot where Dr. Lloyd-Jones chaired the meetings.

On Wednesday, March 4, I went over to 49 Creffield Road to pray with Mrs. Lloyd-Jones. In my prayer I recalled 2 Peter 1:11, which refers to an abundant entrance into the kingdom, and remarked, "What must it have been like last Sunday morning when the Lord and the angels welcomed the Doctor home?" It was a moment I will never forget. As I sat on the platform that day at his memorial service in Westminster Chapel on April 6, 1981, and saw the church packed with people who honored and loved this great man, I thought to myself, *What a privilege and what a heritage to be in this pulpit, which was his and mine.*

As I look back on those Thursdays and contemplate his wisdom, I still find it so amazing that God gave the Doctor to me as long as I had him. I felt, however, that I still needed him after he went to heaven. I had to accept, nonetheless, that God's timing was perfect in taking the Doctor home. I now must apply what I had learned. The greatest thing he ever said to me was this: "The worst thing that can happen to a man is for him to succeed before he is ready." It would be that comment, more than any other he made to me, that would refine my outlook and expectations in Westminster Chapel without him.

---

1. The view that Christ died only for the elect is called "limited atonement." It is the third point of the five points of Calvinism based upon the acrostic TULIP: total depravity, unconditional election, limited atonement, irresistible grace, and perseverance of the saints.

    My own view is that Christ died for all, which breaks with traditional Calvinism, but that His intercession at God's right hand is limited to the elect only. In other words, Christ died for all but does not pray for all, but only the elect. "I pray for them. I am not praying for the world, but for those you have given me, for they are yours" (John 17:9). This makes me a "four-and-a-half-point" Calvinist.

2

The Honeymoon

What we expect is always greater
than what we enjoy.
—WILLIAM SHAKESPEARE

IT DIDN'T SEEM like a honeymoon at first. I was too anxious to prove myself. But when I look back I do see it as a honeymoon. For one thing, the Chapel seemed very happy for my family and me to have a six-week vacation each summer. They treated me as they did the Doctor. This pattern had been a long tradition. Louise and I especially looked forward to this, for we took TR and Missy to the United States every summer—and I fished a lot! Never in our lives did we dream of living outside the United States. Oxford was to be the exception. But now here we were in London.

A lady once asked me in the vestry, "Dr. Kendall, what is bonefishing?" I replied that knowing the answer to that question was a requirement for membership in Westminster Chapel! I have described bonefishing in some detail in the introduction to my book *Worshipping God*. In short, it is sport fishing. You don't eat bonefish; they are too bony to mess with, in any case. It combines hunting and fishing in the shallow waters near the shorelines in the Florida Keys and Bahamas (but bonefish have also been discovered in the Indian Ocean). I began bonefishing in Key Largo in 1964, and didn't catch my first one until August 10, 1965. I would go to Key Largo weekly (at least) when we lived in Fort Lauderdale, Florida. I have introduced bonefishing to dozens and dozens of my friends.

So we went to America annually and always headed for the Florida Keys. In 1979 when vacationing with David and Margaret Newbon, we first attended the Island Community Church in Islamorada, Florida. The pastor in those days was Bruce Porter. He befriended us and introduced us to his members. As a result, some of them opened their waterfront homes to us, even providing us with a boat. Our relationship with these lovely people has continued during the years. The present pastor, Tony Hammon, is not only a friend but also a bonefishing partner! Nearly every year we have shown slides of our vacation, and especially catching fish, at the "At Home" in September. Not all have appreciated my enthusiasm for catching fish you don't eat, but they were compensated at times by pictures of Disney World and other things!

On the first Monday of June 1977, I was made a member of the Westminster Fraternal. Dr. Lloyd-Jones chaired these monthly meetings, which were open to ministers who were generally reformed in theology but especially sympathetic to the Doctor's separatist ecclesiological (that is, church doctrine) views. As I understood it, before 1966 many Anglican ministers attended. But owing to a public meeting with John Stott sponsored by the Evangelical Alliance in 1966, apparently a watershed for many reformed ministers, only Anglicans willing to come out of the Church of England attended. I was not around in those days, and I am unqualified to discuss it very much. I only know that Dr. Lloyd-Jones never inquired of my own ecclesiological views, neither did any of the deacons bring this sort of thing up when they interviewed me. All knew I was utterly devoted to the Doctor, and that, no doubt, was enough.

I recall a helpful conversation I had with the late Dr. Robert Strong in 1964 when he was the minister of the Trinity Presbyterian Church of Montgomery, Alabama. At the time I was totally independent insofar as a denominational affiliation was concerned. I was a member of the Thirteenth Street Baptist Church in Ashland, Kentucky. Henry Mahan is still the pastor there. That church ordained me to the gospel ministry in 1964. Dr. Strong, knowing I was an independent Baptist at the time, shrewdly observed: "You're not an independent. You don't have that kind of personality." That really gave me pause. I never forgot it. I hadn't thought of one's personality in connection with one's theological views. At any rate, ironically, I became a Southern Baptist in 1966 at the suggestion of Henry Mahan who himself had come out of the Southern Baptist Convention! My church at Lower Heyford where Dr. Lloyd-Jones preached several times was a Southern Baptist church. I believe Dr. Strong was basically right. One's personality is not disconnected from one's doctrinal views. The truth is, I have never been an isolationist or much of a separatist.

I never felt totally at home in the Westminster Fraternal, and yet I felt at home with Dr. Lloyd-Jones personally. He was ever so warm and gracious. I loved his own comments. But I wondered if some of his followers really appreciated what meant most to him. Dr. Lloyd-Jones was a genius at chairing discussion meetings and was unexcelled in wrapping things up after a two-hour discussion—on any subject. I was helped again and again. All of the ministers in those days, as far as I knew, accepted me. They also knew that I was not a proponent of limited atonement, but knowing that the Doctor accepted me was apparently good enough for them— at least then. I was often invited into their churches, and some of those pastors even became my good friends.

During my first year I was invited to speak in Swansea by the Evangelical Movement of Wales, an invitation the Doctor told me to take "with both hands." But the feeling I had during the monthly Fraternals was that I was sometimes like a fish out of water. Some of the dear brothers seemed so narrow. And yet the reformed community warmly accepted me in those days as can be seen in the July 1977 issue of *Evangelical Times*. A verbatim question-and-answer interview with editor Bob Horn appeared. I was treated with great respect. My books, including *Calvin and English Calvinism to 1648*, were given highly positive reviews. Other journals and Christian magazines (including those that did not necessarily represent the reformed perspective) showed the same enthusiasm for me and my coming to Westminster Chapel. At times I almost felt like a hero.

After I finished preaching from the Book of Jonah in September 1977, I turned to Hebrews 11, the "faith" chapter of the Bible. I reckoned at the time I would not be staying much over another year. My family were all homesick, and I did not want to embark on a series that would last more than a year.

In the autumn of 1977, I went to hear Dr. Carl F. H. Henry speak to a group of church leaders at All Souls, Langham Place. Dr. Henry is the founder of *Christianity Today* and a man whom I had admired for many years. He is often called "the dean of American evangelicals." He seemed pleased that I had come to hear him, and after the meeting we found ourselves walking together toward Oxford Circus subway station. "What are you doing for supper?" I asked. He had no plans, so I invited him to ride to Ealing and have a meal with us. I rushed to a phone to warn Louise that I was bringing the great Carl F. H. Henry home for dinner. "Who's he?" she asked, but she learned thirty minutes later!

Sitting at the table Carl noticed that we did not have any china, only plain, ordinary dishes. He insisted that we do what he and his wife, Helga, had done: buy a set of "Old Country Roses" bone china pattern made by Royal Albert. We have always been glad that we made this purchase at the near beginning of our ministry in London and when the prices were reasonable. We have added to our set over the years, and we always remember that it was Carl Henry who persuaded us to get that china—incidentally, the very same china that we used for Dr. and Mrs. Lloyd-Jones when they visited us.

Carl Henry became a summer preacher over the years and endeared himself to our people. I had the privilege of introducing him to Dr. Lloyd-Jones, whom Carl interviewed in honor of the Doctor's eightieth birthday. But the memory that stands out most was when I drove him to the Chapel one afternoon and I asked him, "Carl, if you had your life to live over, what would you do differently?" He waited for a moment before he answered. I remember exactly where we were when he spoke to us—as we passed Buckingham Palace: "I would remember that only God can turn the water into wine." It was a comment I would reflect on many times over the ensuing years.

I began preaching from Revelation 1 on the Sunday evenings. Dr. Lloyd-Jones expressed surprise that I chose this. But I assured him I would not be going beyond the first chapter of Revelation. In the autumn of 1978 I began preaching from Jude on Sunday mornings. That too lasted for a year. I preached on 1 Samuel in the evenings. I always had the Doctor tutoring me from week to week. I began Galatians in the autumn of 1977 at the Friday Bible study series. Those who attended did not meet in the auditorium at first but in the Institute Hall (now Lloyd-Jones Hall). We only had about a hundred, if that many, but Dr. Lloyd-Jones thought I should have the Friday meetings in the Chapel, so we moved the venue. The crowds stayed much the same, but many of those who came were interested mainly in my interpretation of the Law. I learned later that those studies were attended by men like Michael Eaton (now in Nairobi), Robert Norris (now pastor of Fourth Presbyterian Church of Washington, DC), and Colin Dye (now pastor of Kensington Temple).

"The Doctor never taught us your view of the Law," a number of long-standing members said. I told the Doctor they had said that. He had been their teacher for years, and most of them were privileged to hear his lectures on Romans. He smiled as if he understood what they meant when I told him they said I was giving them something new. Only a few perhaps knew that he was spoon-feeding me week after week. "It is clearer to me now than it was then," he said, referring to his own exposition on Romans 7. He admitted he taught me things he himself hadn't preached in the 1960s. But I never once told them that. He appreciated my not claiming that all I was teaching on the Law literally came from him.

I was invited to join the Council of the Fellowship of Independent Evangelical Churches (FIEC). Sir Fred Catherwood, a godly and outstanding man, was the president, and he thought it would encourage them if I came on it. He put me on the finance committee. My views on tithing were becoming widespread, and Fred thought I could do some good in this area.

When Bob Horn interviewed me in the *Evangelical Times,* he asked me what problems I saw in British evangelicalism. I replied that I wasn't qualified to answer, but I did wonder about two things: British evangelicals don't seem to tithe, and I thought some might be weak in the area of evangelism. I had the feeling that those observations were accepted at the time as being fairly accurate. Apparently Dr. Lloyd-Jones did not preach on tithing, but he never hinted that I shouldn't. As for evangelism, it was well known that the Doctor's Sunday evening sermons were very evangelistic. But he may have been one of the exceptions in the United Kingdom in those days.

One of the more painful dilemmas I faced in those early days was whom to invite to preach when I would be out of the pulpit. It was an assumption that I alone would do the preaching throughout the year. Like it or not, if there ever was such a thing as a "one-man ministry," we were it. The only time I could invite anybody to preach was during our summer vacation period and the Sundays after Christmas and Easter, when the minister usually took a break. The reason for the dilemma as to whom to invite was the person's preaching ability, theological aptitude, and cultural adaptation. Dr. Lloyd-Jones used to say that not inviting those you may personally prefer, as in the case of close friends, was part of bearing the cross.

I will never forget the pain I felt when one of my closest friends wrote to us soon after I became the minister of the Chapel. He came straight to the point: "When are you going to have me preach for you?" I was sobered. I knew in my heart that I could not have him. There was no way under the sun, no matter how hard he tried, he would fit in at the Chapel. I could have had him at any of my previous three churches. But I could not have had him in London. He was not one of those who could bridge the cultural gap. I feel guilty even in saying this, lest I seem to betray my friends. But there is no other way to put it. The cultural gap is so wide that few Americans successfully cross it. I myself had three years of living in Britain before I preached here with much acceptance. Those who come straight from the United States and show cultural and theological sensitivity to the typical membership of our congregation are exceedingly rare. Even Billy Graham had lived in Britain for a good while before he was widely accepted.

I discussed this matter often with Dr. Lloyd-Jones. He claimed he faced the same thing in his day. He would repeat that you can only invite those you believe God leads you to invite, not those good friends you want to please. Even more painful than hurting my old friend was having to turn down two professors apart from whose recommendations I would not even be in London at all. Now with the Lord, they were the ones who put me in Oxford. The problem in having these men preach, however, was mainly theological. They could not have preached in a manner that cohered with the theology of the Chapel. I simply could not invite them to preach for me. I took this hard, and they probably did as well.

But there was one deep regret that I felt as I wrote these lines about the early years, and it was the way I would get embarrassed over my dad when he would visit us in London. Talk about being "American"—and being Kentuckian on top of that! My dad and Abbie first came to see us in London in the autumn of 1977. My dad's uninhibited ways embarrassed me to the limit at the time, but now I am ashamed that I worried so much. The people actually loved him dearly.

Back in 1956 I had taken a stand against some of my old theology as a result of my baptism in the Spirit. I agree that the baptism of the Spirit doesn't necessarily change everybody's theology, but it did mine. My father was unhappy with my doctrinal discoveries and was devastated that I would not be remaining a Nazarene. He was totally convinced that I was right out of God's will and that the devil had got in. It wasn't until 1977 that he changed his mind, and that was because I was in G. Campbell Morgan's old pulpit. Campbell Morgan had been one of my dad's heroes. When he learned that I was actually in Dr. Morgan's pulpit, he instantly affirmed that God had been with me after all!

When he visited us in London he was proud of me. But he needed reassurance that the people were proud of me, too. So he would go up to anybody—not knowing whether they were even members and sometimes taking no account of their age—and ask, "What do you think of my son?"

A typical reaction was, "Oh, yes, well, Mr. Kendall, we think he is fine."

"How do you like his preaching?"

"Yes, very good, yes."

Some of these people interviewed by the minister's father were bowled over. They were lost for words.

One day Dad walked into the old church parlor.

"Where's the boy? Where's the boy?" Dad inquired.

"Sorry?" replied Sir Fred Catherwood.

"Where's the boy?"

"The boy?"

"Where's my son?"

"Oh, you mean Dr. Kendall."

"Yes, where's my boy?"

I can laugh at that now. I only wish I had been able to do so then.

Before I came on to the FIEC Council, I was invited to give the Bible readings for their annual conference in 1979, which was in Bristol that year. I preached three sermons from Isaiah 58:1–12. Never before had I been received so well outside Westminster. The Rev. David Mingard, the General Secretary for the FIEC, reckoned that my preaching at that conference gave them an impetus to be more evangelistic. It was a wonderful feeling indeed to be accepted by fellow ministers in Britain. Little did I know that this joy was simply part of our honeymoon period.

For a good while I was younger than any of my twelve deacons. I had a superb relationship with every single one of them. When they detected discouragement in me owing to the lack of numerical growth, they were immensely supportive.

We made the decision to redecorate the sanctuary and do some long overdue work on the cherished Willis pipe organ. The money came in without any trouble. I used to dream of pastoring a church with a pipe organ. My wishes were more than fulfilled. We were told that the Chapel organ is one of the finest in London. As for the redecoration, the lacework banisters were trimmed in gold and white and the ceiling was painted a deep sky blue. People were proud of our "new" look. Even Dr. Lloyd-Jones, skeptical at first, gave his approval. I also thought it might draw more people. It didn't.

But they were happy days. Louise and I felt deeply loved. TR and Melissa made some friends of their own age. I had not only a great relationship with the deacons but also with nearly all the people. Finances were on the increase. I assumed many of the people began tithing. There was also a feeling that something great was on the way. Revival? We thought so. Therefore I announced that we were in a "pre-revival" situation. If that was really the case, it was to last for many years. For true revival was continually postponed. Was

I searching for *His* glory or my glory in my wish for revival?

Our first baptismal service, April 8, 1979, included seven different nationalities. The first person I had the privilege of baptizing was Jay Michaels, a Los Angeles Jew. He was the right-hand man of Mark McCormack, the famous entrepreneur who has managed many Wimbledon players. Jay had been invited by his London secretary to the Chapel. I was not aware until later that he was almost immediately converted. The night of his baptism was a most glorious occasion. It also included the baptism of a Japanese banker whom Sir Fred Catherwood had influenced for Christ.

I made a small mistake that night. I said, "This is the first baptism service at the Chapel in seventy-five years." The next day Dr. Lloyd-Jones slapped my wrist. "How dare you say that—we baptized people all the time." I apologized; he accepted. He knew what I meant; he sprinkled believers, and I baptized believers by immersion.

Although a Southern Baptist, I felt it wise not to divide the Chapel on secondary issues. I never wanted to "Americanize" Westminster Chapel or turn it into a Baptist church. The preaching of the gospel was paramount, and I did not want anything to militate against what seemed to me to be the main purpose for which God had raised up the Chapel. It is a commitment I have kept. Whatever changes we have made during those twenty-five years, the preaching generally and biblical exposition particularly had been central. We did not insist that a member be baptized by immersion (although they usually asked for it). And as in the case of Dr. Lloyd-Jones's latter years, those who believe in infant baptism would sometimes go to another church for this rite, but still remained with us.

Jay Michaels remained a dear friend. He arranged his travels to be in London on a Sunday whenever he could. He joined us on our vacation in Florida when he could. He took our family out deep-sea fishing, and I was present when he caught his first bonefish! There was one other fringe benefit to his friendship: he always got Louise and me center-court tickets at Wimbledon and invited us back to the marquee for gourmet food and meeting a number of players and famous people. Jay went to heaven in 1982. I miss Jay, and I miss the tennis.

One of my disappointments after my London publisher, Hodder & Stoughton, asked to do my sermons on Jonah was the Doctor's refusal to write the foreword. Mrs. Lloyd-Jones urged him to do it, but to no avail. His reasons were three-fold. First, he said, people would see me as "the Doctor's man" at the Chapel. Second, "no minister of Westminster Chapel needed someone to write his foreword." Really? I did. And still do. The third reason: I had not "earned my spurs," as he put it.

I think it was very humbling for Westminster Chapel to have to pick me. If there is a pervading sin in the Chapel—no one's fault in particular—it is that they have taken themselves very seriously. I think, too, that there were a lot of naturally cautious people around when I arrived. These people deeply loved God and did not know they were smug. They were very conscious of the Chapel's great history and good location (being a block or so from Buckingham Palace). Some seemed to think there was a divine aura over the place and that it was special. This may be true, in that central London needs places where the gospel is upheld and Christ is honored. But the Chapel was very middle class then, and those who weren't middle class sometimes felt unwelcome. So there was a feeling that the pulpit must be protected alongside the church's rep-utation. I can appreciate this, but I think they were overly concerned. I believe some thought God humbled them by sending me. Perhaps it is God's sense of humor.

Dr. Lloyd-Jones seemed to appreciate it when I would call at 49 Creffield Road after the Sunday evening service. He wanted to know how the evening service went, what the crowds were like, and how I felt about the day genuinely. It was a wonderful privilege. I would stay for only fifteen or twenty minutes, but it was a nice way to end the day. I would then go home and eat Indian food with Louise and the children.

While in Oxford, we learned to love Indian food. This appetite continued in London. We would order take-out food from the local Indian restaurant virtually every Saturday night. We never went out socially (nor would I take preaching engagements) on Saturday evenings. We would switch off and watch television and get my mind off the next day. We learned to love British programs, but we also watched American programs such as *Starsky and Hutch, Dallas,* or *Kojak* (so did the queen!) whenever we could. To this day my favorite food is Indian, but so too with many Brits! Some of the culinary pleasures we would greatly miss are onion bhajees, Bombay potatoes, brinjal bhajees, and tandoori chicken tikka masala.

But I would miss preparing sermons more. Knowing you are going to preach at Westminster Chapel makes you want to do your best. As I said earlier, Dr. Lloyd-Jones warned me that my desire to always be fresh could also be my downfall. I have taken this warning on board. I still hunt for something fresh when I prepare, but recognize that the pursuit of the glory of God is more important than new insight. The irony is, once I have become willing to give up looking for fresh things to say, the more such insights come. I only pray now that I have not allowed anything to go into print that does not glorify God's name. I can't very easily stop recordings from going out. They have often been turned into books, which I can edit. But the unguarded comments have emerged, and one doesn't know for weeks or months how foolish a comment was. Dr. Lloyd-Jones never allowed any of his tapes to be played by anyone when he was the minister.

The Westminster Record was barely ticking over when I came on the scene. We ran my sermons on Jonah, Jude, and the general epistles of John and James. Subscriptions were less than half what they were in the Doctor's day, and though they increased slightly at first when I came, they diminished eventually. The cost of printing and posting far outweighed what came in by subscriptions. My sermons simply did not read well, and I had to live with that fact. I tried the best I could to keep the *Westminster Record* afloat, but we eventually turned it into tape recordings of my sermons, calling it the *New Westminster Record*.

There is no way to exaggerate the giant shadow the Doctor cast over the Chapel in our earlier years. For at least ten years it was as though the Doctor resigned only weeks before, when in fact it was in 1968. The respect people felt for him as a result of the authority that emanated from his oratory and leadership was most profound. Whatever I did or said would be set against a frame of reference: What would the Doctor do? What would he say? What would he think? Not that people seriously compared me to Dr. Lloyd-Jones. He was beyond being compared with. But people still thought of him whenever I would say something they hadn't heard him say or suggest something he would never consider. Thus, Mrs. Lloyd-Jones was so gracious at this point by saying, "You're just going through what Martyn went through after Campbell Morgan." But I always knew I was just fortunate to be there at all and had no thought of being "my own man" in those days.

The Friday Bible studies were the hardest on me emotionally, although I had the Doctor working with me all the way to Galatians 5:16. I dreaded seeing only sixty or seventy on most occasions. Many pastors brought their members with them on Fridays in the Doctor's day, but I inherited little of that. Some of the ministers who did come did not remain, as they had difficulty with my view of the Mosaic Law. They did not realize it was Dr. Lloyd-Jones who shaped my thinking on this!

I chose the Book of Galatians for the Friday Bible studies only because for some reason this is what the people asked me for. Some felt they were becoming woolly on justification of faith, and since it had been nine years since Dr. Lloyd-Jones left, the time had come for a fresh look at justification and the Law. This I was happy to do, especially since I was well acquainted with Calvin's and the Puritans' teaching on the Law. But I still listened carefully to Dr. Lloyd-Jones.

By the time we reached Galatians 5:16 we had passed the

controversial section. I therefore had the full benefit of my own research at Oxford plus the Doctor's distilled views— "clearer" to him in the years 1977–1980, he admitted, than when he lectured on Romans in the 1960s. Dr. Lloyd-Jones was unhappy with both Calvin and the Puritans generally when it came to the Law. Although Calvin rejected the notion of coming to assurance via one's sanctification and keeping the Law, he did believe that the Christian was to be under the Law. The Puritans did follow Calvin on the latter, but they also stressed that keeping the Law is the way we know we are justified by faith. It was at this point that the Doctor disagreed with the Puritans. The Law not only does not justify, he would say, neither does it sanctify; and if our gospel is accused of being antinomian (literally, "against law"), it is probably because we have not preached the gospel in the first place.

He was adamant that the Christian is not under the Law at all. He went further than I did; he didn't even like those churches that had the Ten Commandments printed out on the walls for all to see. I was afraid then to repeat all he actually said to me about the Law. He did believe that the Law served to prepare the sinner to come under conviction of sin, but once that sinner came to Christ he was only under the "law of Christ," as in 1 Corinthians 9:21. My own view, as I show in *Just Grace*, is that we are not assured of salvation by the works of the Law, but that they are nonetheless evidence that we are truly walking in the Spirit.

I always took questions at the close of the Bible study. This is something Dr. Lloyd-Jones didn't do. He told me I shouldn't, that I would be sorry if I kept it up. On this the Doctor was probably wrong. I did keep it up, and the people seemed to appreciate this part of the series as much as any of it.

There were some bright spots during my early days, but I was not to appreciate some of them until later. For example, Michael Eaton, who came out of the Church of England in 1966, was a steady member of the congregation for a year or so. He had been pastor of the Nairobi Baptist Church and was then in a transition period. He took on board virtually all I taught—from the view that Christ died for all, my position on the faith of Christ (Gal. 2:16–20), and all I taught regarding the Law. Afterward he took a church in Johannesburg, South Africa, and later revealed to me that his whole life and ministry was changed by my lectures on Galatians and James, especially James 2:14. He is now a theologian of world class and kindly credits me with much of what he writes and preaches. This goes to show that one may be doing more good than is apparent at first. I thank God for Michael. I must add, moreover, that Dr. Eaton has vastly outgrown me and is now my teacher!

I had the privilege of giving the first address for the end of the year service of the London Theological Seminary. I had a lovely relationship with the tutors, especially Hwell Jones, Graham Harrison, and Andrew Davies—all able and godly men. Andrew and I used to play squash fairly regularly at the Oxford and Cambridge Club until I pulled a leg muscle and had to give it up. Reformed men all over Britain were my friends. I remain particularly fond of Erroll Hulse and often remind him of Charles Wesley's word to George Whitefield: "Friends at first are friends at last."

Sir Fred got me into the Oxford and Cambridge Club in Pall Mall. I used to go there on Sunday afternoons and work on my evening sermon. I also took a lot of friends for lunch, especially mid-week. Eventually the annual dues got so high I had to forfeit my membership. But it was there one afternoon that Edward England asked me to do my second book for Hodder—my sermons based on Hebrews 11.

Louise and I attended more cultural events in the earlier days, for some reason, than we did in our latter years. We often went to the Royal Albert Hall, thanks to Howard and Rosemary Curtis, who let us use their box seats. We also did more socializing, taking meals with members and friends. We would occasionally go back to Oxford and keep in touch with Regent's Park College. Once I was invited to speak there at one of their chapel services.

I took a train every Monday in those days to Oxford. I began my sermon preparation on the train and continued it either in Regent's Park Library or the Bodleian. Our friend Phil Roberts, now president of Midwestern Baptist Theological Seminary, was a research student at Regent's, and I often had lunch with him. It was fun to be in Oxford when there was no anxiety over whether I would eventually pass. I also kept up my relationship with Barrie White.

In those early days of ministry, Barrie and Margaret White came into London one Sunday morning to hear me. When Dr. White came into the vestry he said, "Don't you think you should call me Barrie?" I found it a struggle, but perhaps not nearly the struggle he had in trying to call me RT. So, I called him Barrie, and he called me Robert.

One of my greatest encouragers in those days was Norman Stone. He worked with the BBC (he was one of their top producers). He has a personality triple plus and gathered many young people around him. The son of a Baptist minister, Norman was sound theologically and helped keep many on the straight and narrow. His kindness and attention given to our son, TR, was so great that I almost come to tears when I think of Norman and his loyalty to our family. He later married Sally Magnusson and moved out of London. But he as much as anyone contributed to our honeymoon era.

I did a great deal of traveling in my early years, mostly to FIEC and other churches that had long ties with Westminster Chapel. These were small churches and very kind to me. I was elected president of the FIEC and was privileged to address the annual assembly of the Free Church of Scotland in Edinburgh, and was received very warmly. I have always felt a debt to Scotland since the day John Logan had influenced my life. Although my Calvinism did not totally measure up to the standards of some reformed people in Britain, I never felt anything but warm acceptance from them wherever I went.

I will never forget a service in a church in Leighton Buzzard. John Sloan, one of our deacons, came to hear me. He said to me afterwards, "You say you don't preach with unction. You had it tonight." He was one of my greatest encouragers. Another memory I cherish that came time after time in those days was old Mr. Micklewright, then in his eighties, coming into the vestry on a Sunday night to say, "Well, I got saved again tonight." What he meant was that the gospel was refreshing to him and his assurance was renewed. He lived until he was ninety-seven. The only time I interrupted a summer vacation was when I preached at his funeral in August 1994. His daughter Betty was in charge of our book room.

After Dr. Lloyd-Jones died, I visited Mrs. Lloyd-Jones weekly when she was in London. She spent a lot of time at Fred and Elizabeth's home at Balsham, near Cambridge. Fred had become a member (and was eventually vice president) of the European Parliament. Mrs. Lloyd-Jones made rock cakes (with a special Welsh recipe) and always had them ready with tea. Mrs. Lloyd-Jones was an extremely shrewd, compassionate, and very godly woman. I would ask her again and again about the Welsh Revival. In 1904, she was six and living in London. But her father put her on a train at Paddington for Wales—taking her out of school! He was criticized for this but replied, "Bethan can always go to school, but she may never see revival again." She never did. And how she cherished those months in Wales at the height of the revival!

Louise visited Mrs. Lloyd-Jones often as well and continues to treasure the wisdom given on how to deal with problems as a pastor's wife. I used to take my friends to meet Mrs. Lloyd-Jones and would ask her to tell the same old stories. People like Joyce and Billy Ball, O. S. Hawkins, and Pete Cantrell regarded meeting her as the high point of their visits to London.

I developed a close friendship in those days with Harry Kilbride. We first met in Bristol where I gave the Bible readings at the FIEC Conference in 1979. Harry was also a speaker at that conference. He was the pastor of Lansdowne Baptist Church in Bournemouth. I always said that Harry was the best preacher in Britain. If anyone could have filled Westminster Chapel, Harry could. For much of 1980 to 1985 we met on Mondays, usually at Basingstoke, for several hours. "Iron sharpens iron," and Harry was good for me; during those years he was my closest friend next to Louise.

A strategic pivotal turning point in my spiritual journey emerged quite unexpectedly as I was preparing a Christmas sermon in December 1981. It was on Zechariah and Elizabeth, from Luke 1. The thrust of the message was "being ready for answered prayer," for Zechariah wasn't nearly ready at all.

> But the angel said to him: "Do not be afraid, Zechariah; your prayer has been heard. Your wife Elizabeth will bear you a son, and you are to give him the name John."
>
> —LUKE 1:13

Zechariah had no idea that his prayer—put to God many years before—was to be answered after all. He had given up. From this came two points.

First, any prayer prayed in the will of God will be answered. So says 1 John 5:14, "This is the confidence we have in approaching God: that if we ask anything according to his will, he hears us." Second, the shape answered prayer takes is determined by our readiness at the time. Zechariah wasn't ready and paid dearly for it: "And now you will be silent and not able to speak until the day this happens, because you did not believe my words, which will come true at their proper time" (Luke 1:20). I have since preached this sermon in many places around the world. It became the basis for my book *Ready for God?* (Scripture Union, 1995), published in America as *When God Shows Up*.

But my point in relating the above is this. I used the same theme in my Palm Sunday sermon in the spring of 1982, where Jesus wept over Jerusalem because the Jews were not ready for their answered prayer for the Messiah to come. As a consequence of this—"because you did not recognize the time of God's coming to you" (Luke 19:44)—Israel's temple would be destroyed. I applied this to the possibility of God showing up at Westminster Chapel but His presence not being recognized, so we miss entirely what God might have wanted to do in our midst. It was that very Palm Sunday sermon that, more than anything else, made me open to the ministry of Arthur Blessitt, who came to us soon afterward. The whole time I listened to Arthur, despite his unconventional manner and dress, I kept thinking of the Jews not recognizing the time of their visitation. Had it not been for the insights of Luke 1:13–20 and Luke 19:37–44, I would never have dreamed of trying to persuade Arthur to preach for us in May 1982.

I began my series on 1 John in January 1982. I finished preaching through James a few weeks before, and 1 John posed a greater challenge yet. We now had no plans for returning to the States. TR and Melissa were becoming very British. Louise was regularly involved in the ladies' meeting and the Sunday Bible class. God gave me some insights on 1 John that made me feel He was truly with me. I would always ask myself, *What would the Doctor say?* I missed him more than words could express. I had to be on my own from the time he became seriously ill, but even during this time—until he was utterly unable—I could call him. In truth I did feel lonely. But in other ways I could identify with the apostle Paul and say, "The Lord stood at my side" (2 Tim. 4:17).

PART TWO

~

Taking Risks

*If I'd thought about it
I never would've done it,
I guess I would've let it slide.
If I'd lived my life
By what others were thinkin'
The heart inside me would've died.*
—From "Up to Me" by Bob Dylan

3

Arthur Blessitt

His word is in my heart like a fire,
a fire shut up in my bones. I am weary
of holding it in; indeed, I cannot.
—JEREMIAH 20:9

ONE DAY IN 1979 my secretary Pam Harris phoned to say that a Mr. Graham Ferguson Lacey wanted to meet me and asked whether I might come to his home around the corner from the Chapel. Graham was known in London as a "boy wonder" in finance. He was only about thirty years old at the time. I met him on a Friday afternoon, a couple of hours before our Bible study. I could not have known then that this meeting would turn out to be important for me and the Chapel. Just as I was leaving, Graham commented that Arthur Blessitt was staying with him for a day or two. I was fascinated, having met Arthur and also having heard him preach in Miami, Florida, back in 1969. His impact on me was deep, and I asked if I could see him. There he was when I came out of Graham's office.

Arthur Blessitt is sometimes regarded as the "father" of the Jesus movement in California in the 1960s. He began a coffeehouse, called His Place, on Hollywood's Sunset Strip. He erected a large wooden cross and hung it on a wall inside the coffeehouse, so that people coming in would know why they served only coffee and orange juice. Arthur said later that if he knew he was going to have to carry it he wouldn't have made it so big! But one morning at five o'clock God told him to take the cross down and carry it on foot around the world. He has led countless thousands to Christ, leading many to go into the full-time Christian ministry and reaching out to all kinds of people. He has even been sought after by heads of state. He has spent time with Yasser Arafat and has stayed in Prime Minister Begin's home. He also appears in the *Guinness Book of Records* for the longest walk in human history.

I asked Arthur if he had any plans for the evening and whether he would want to follow me to our Bible study. He looked at Graham to see if they had any plans.

"No, why don't you go?" Graham replied.

Arthur did not remember me nor, as far as I know, had he ever heard much, if anything, about the Chapel. He was just going along with me to a Bible study. I will never forget the place in the Bible where we were: Galatians 4:26, "But the Jerusalem that is above is free." (He found out later that night that his wife was pregnant with their sixth child. When he was born they named him Jerusalem.) At the close of the study, I said, "We aren't going to take questions tonight. I have always wondered what it would be like for Arthur Blessitt to speak at Westminster Chapel. Come on up, Arthur—take ten minutes." He took thirty. He could have spoken for an hour! Some of our deacons were almost in tears. It was a fantastic night.

The next day I got in touch with Arthur to see if he would spend some time with Louise. Louise had been struggling with homesickness. We had abandoned sunny Florida for London, and I think it had rained every day for six weeks. Arthur said yes, and Louise went to see him at Graham Lacey's home. They met for an hour on the Sunday morning before the service. She told me afterward that Arthur prayed that there would be a definite sign in the upcoming service that would encourage her, not only to believe it was right to be in London, but that things would get better.

Nothing apparently happened until after the sermon. I had chosen to close the service with the hymn "In Heavenly Love Abiding." When we came to the third verse, "Bright skies will soon be o'er me where the dark clouds have been," Louise turned and looked at Arthur. He waved at her with a big smile. God had stepped in.

Arthur had told me after the Friday Bible study that he once met Dr. Lloyd-Jones in Manchester. "I looked forward to hearing what this great man of God would say to me," he said.

"And what did he say?"

Arthur replied that Dr. Lloyd-Jones had only one comment: "Don't let anybody change you." I repeated this to the Doctor.

"Oh, yes," he said, "I was very taken with that man."

Calling Arthur up to the pulpit is something Dr. Lloyd-Jones would not have done. But it led to the best thing I ever did, as far as I am concerned, during my twenty-five years at the Chapel.

I was elected president of the FIEC in 1981. In the autumn of 1981, I chaired an FIEC committee meeting, which met to discuss who should be the speaker at the following year's annual conference, to be held in 1982 at Westminster Chapel. Several names were thrown around as to who would be suitable.

I spoke up. "Would you like to fill Westminster Chapel next year?"

"Yes, of course," they replied. "Do you know how to fill it?"

"Yes," I said.

"How?" they asked.

"Arthur Blessitt."

Silence. It took three further committee meetings

before I got it through, but they all eventually agreed. Best of all, Arthur said yes.

The 1982 FIEC Annual Conference was held in April. I chaired the meetings. Arthur first spoke to the pastors and church leaders on a Tuesday afternoon. Only a hundred or so were expected, so we planned to meet in the Lloyd-Jones Hall. But we soon realized we had to move into the Chapel. Over two hundred turned up. It was an exciting afternoon. Peter Collins, one of our deacons who took time off work to be there, came up to me and said, "Luis Palau is coming in 1983, Billy Graham in 1984. But what if God wants to do something in 1982?" He will never know how deeply that comment impacted me. It is what got me to think about a way that I could get Arthur to stay around for a while.

Before the Thursday night service Arthur sat with me in the vestry. He casually said, "Now when I give the invitation..."

I interrupted. "Arthur, we don't do that here."

"You don't?" he quizzically asked.

"No," I replied. Then I saw the look on his face. So I said, "But if you feel led to give an invitation, go ahead."

He shot back, "I can tell you right now, I do." He was true to his word.

When we walked up into the pulpit the place was filled to overflowing, with people standing in the aisles. I don't know where the people came from! The members of the FIEC Council sat somewhat nervously on the platform. When I introduced Arthur, I jokingly said that when I first suggested him as a speaker, three of the Council members put nitroglycerine tablets under their tongues!

Arthur preached on "Do We Still Need the Cross?" It was brilliant. He preached for an hour. Then came the moment when he asked people to receive Christ. He put it like this. "If you want to receive Jesus, stand—right now." In a few seconds to my right there stood Beryl Denton, the daughter of two well-known members of the Chapel and a close friend of Melissa. I was thrilled beyond words. Others stood, eventually dozens, without any pressure. They all were asked to go back to the church parlor. They couldn't all get in. In the meantime, the new president of the FIEC, to whom I had turned over the gavel, said to the congregation, "You may not believe it, but this is an FIEC meeting." I wasn't sure how to take that comment.

But the next morning I found out. The FIEC Council assembled for their own quarterly meeting. Some were angry with me. "I felt betrayed," said one. "You told us Arthur isn't a charismatic."

"He isn't," I replied.

"He sure sounded like one to me," the man said.

I didn't believe Arthur was a charismatic. Arthur is Arthur. He goes to all places. He is a Southern Baptist. He believes in all the gifts of the Spirit, yes, but so do I. Did this make me a charismatic?

My relationship with the men on the Council was never to be the same again. I had not meant to offend them. I was stunned that morning. I sincerely believed they would be as thrilled as I. If anything, I thought I would receive a hero's welcome when I walked into the Council that morning. Was I ever wrong!

The Rev. Omri Jenkins, general secretary of the Evangelical Missionary Fellowship, had arranged for me to speak for one of his missionaries in Malaga, Spain, the following Sunday. I boarded a plane for Malaga after the Council meeting. I was sorry for the way my brothers felt, but I began thinking of only one thing for the next several days: how could I get Arthur to stay a while in London? I do not believe there was a time in my life—ever—when I was so full of conviction and excitement. I knew that I should persuade Arthur to stay in London for several weeks. My motive? To get close to Arthur personally—he was so much like Jesus, and the thought was not far from my mind that God might send genuine revival to the Chapel through him.

As it happened, we already had Arthur booked to preach on the last Sunday of April 1982. I tried without success to get in touch with him before then. He showed up just before the service. He was wearing jeans and an open-necked sports shirt. But this didn't bother me. In the vestry I put it to him: postpone your visit to Norway and preach on Sunday evenings for us the whole month of May, which happened to be a five-Sunday month. He asked, "If I were to agree, are you going to handcuff me or let me be myself?" I assured him that he could be himself. We went to the platform, I told the congregation what I had asked Arthur to do. We all prayed. Arthur, on his knees, turned to me and asked, "Are you ready?"

I replied, "I'm ready."

He agreed. The greatest turning point for the whole of my twenty-five years in London was now at hand.

I don't think I was ever so filled with anticipation in my life as I was at the thought of having Arthur Blessitt be with us for the five weeks of May, making it six Sunday nights in a row. Arthur had unbreakable commitments in Los Angeles and had to commute for the first three Sundays. I would always worry that he would miss a plane or something would make him late. But he always arrived at the last minute and sat near the back of the congregation on Sunday mornings to hear my preaching on 1 John.

His sermon on the last Sunday in April was on "The Glory of God." One of our deacons said to me later, "I could have walked up and hugged him that night." For an aristocratic Englishman that was indeed something! At that stage I detected no opposition to Arthur at all among the Chapel members.

But after the first Sunday night in May I noticed the first beginnings of trouble. One of the deacons, who had been a great supporter from the first day I arrived, left the Chapel somewhat upset. "I won't be back until he's gone," he said to me. He was the only deacon who felt that way then, as far as I could tell. I was surprised that this man reacted as he did. He was, and is, a very good man and possibly the most forward-thinking deacon we had. I wish now that I had gone to him first—before I invited Arthur. I have always wondered whether, had I done so, I would have carried him with us and avoided a major controversy. I can't prove that, of course, but it is what I've always thought about. I simply announced to the deacons what I had intended to do—to ask Arthur to stay—and there was not a single objection.

Arthur asked whether anybody in the Chapel could play a guitar. I knew no such person. He then publicly asked if anyone did, and a young man came up to Arthur afterward to say he could do it. Arthur hated our organ! I personally love the organ, but I had promised not to handcuff Arthur. The following Sunday night this young man led the congregation in singing "He Is Lord." That was the first chorus ever sung at the Chapel in my day. I thought the chandeliers might fall! This began a new era in the Chapel—singing choruses and having people sing from up front, whether it was a trio or whatever.

Each Sunday evening Arthur preached with power. For weeks after he left I listened to the tapes again and again. He is an exhorter rather than an expositor, and his preaching was largely anecdotal. But what stories they were! I couldn't imagine anyone not being thrilled from head to toe—and most people were. But then I heard this comment more than once: "He is fine for Speakers' Corner but not Westminster Chapel." This disturbed me. Was I to believe that this great depository of biblical truth called Westminster Chapel could not have had a John the Baptist or an Elijah? And, yet, the overwhelming majority were behind Arthur's visit—including eleven of the twelve deacons.

On the third Friday evening I asked Arthur to speak to our young people in the church parlor. Our young people's meetings in those days always followed the Friday Bible studies. Arthur attended our Bible study, and then I introduced him to thirty or forty young people who gathered to hear him. I asked him to fire us up on witnessing to the lost. The idea was that we would head for Page Street as soon as he finished. The only way we knew how to witness in those days was to take our six-question survey to the council apartments on Page Street. We only went there because you could never get into the luxury apartments around the Chapel. Arthur finished speaking after about forty-five minutes, and we all headed for Page Street.

Little did I know that my own life was about to be changed—for ever. We walked through the Chapel yard, and I turned right at the entrance next to the zebra crossing in Buckingham Gate. But Arthur didn't make a right turn. He saw three young people standing there and went up to them faster than a speeding bullet. He began to talk to these young people about the Lord. I was agitated. I looked at my watch as Arthur went on and on. Finally, he asked them whether they would like to pray to receive Jesus, and two of them did. I looked at my watch again. When they finished praying, Arthur whipped out more literature from the hip pocket of his jeans and began follow-up. I gently whispered, "Arthur, we need to get to Page Street." He just nodded and continued to show these two young people what had just happened to them and what to do from now on, since they were Christians.

Finally, he finished.

"Arthur, we need to hurry to get to Page Street."

But he saw another young man walking toward the Chapel. I recognized him as one who used to attend. In several minutes Arthur had him on his knees to receive the Lord Jesus Christ. After follow-up with that young man Arthur turned to me. "Dr. Kendall, I don't know where this Page Street is, but you don't need to leave the steps of Westminster Chapel. You have the whole world passing by here."

I died a thousand deaths. I knew in a flash what I had to do. In that moment I had what was like a vision; it was of a pilot light that stays lit in an oven day and night. I turned to Arthur. I said to Arthur, "Couldn't we have coffee here on the porch of the Chapel for passers-by?"

"I like it," Arthur replied.

In that moment I committed myself to be an evangelist in personal witnessing. I had always felt I paid my dues by being faithfully evangelistic in my Sunday night preaching. I rationalized that there weren't many ministers who preached the gospel to the lost every single Sunday night of the year—which I did, and have continued to do so for those years at the Chapel. But I now knew I had to do more. The pursuit of God's glory would prove to be painful.

Arthur met with all who wanted to come on each of the last three Saturday mornings in that month of May 1982. Nearly a hundred would turn up each week, but many were not our own people, which worried me a little, but never mind. I was ready to do whatever God called me to do. After he spoke each Saturday for an hour we took to the streets. I remember the first person I spoke to—a lady from Birmingham with an elegant fur coat (despite the warm weather). She was either going out of or coming into the St. James Hotel (as it was then called) next door. I was so full of joy that she listened. When I asked her to pray to receive the Lord, she did! Was she saved? I don't know. Neither do I know if those Arthur witnessed to that Friday night were truly saved. Seed was being sown, in any case, and these people may be converted later if not already.

After two more weeks, the deacons asked to spend some time with Arthur. He doesn't like confrontation but agreed to meet with them. The one deacon who said he wouldn't come back until Arthur was gone apparently had made some of the other deacons uneasy. They simply asked to have time with him to ask questions. It was hard for Arthur, but the deacons had not heard the likes of Arthur before. They believed in him but wanted to understand him better. Their main concern was whether his method of calling people to stand gave adequate faith, or trust, in the Holy Spirit to do His sovereign work. I sympathized with the theologically minded deacons. I was partly responsible for the way they felt. I too felt the meeting was important, and Arthur knew this or he wouldn't have turned up at all. Arthur doesn't claim to be a theologian. And there were admittedly a few times during the month of May when one could feel he put on some pressure for people to stand up.

I had promised not to handcuff Arthur, and I kept my word. I also felt that to sort him out to our refined theological taste would unwittingly quench the Holy Spirit who was, after all, working mightily through Arthur.

Many Calvinists today would criticize the great George Whitefield for exactly the same thing. Whitefield once had a trumpeter stationed out of sight over a hill to be ready to start blowing his trumpet on signal. The signal was "Stop! Gabriel, stop—don't blow your trumpet!" Mr. Whitefield was preaching on the Second Coming of Christ, which would be introduced by the trumpet of God. At that moment Whitefield shouted, "Stop!" the trumpet player began playing there in the fields. People shrieked and some fell to the ground. Did any of them receive Christ? Probably. But it was a rather questionable thing to do.

Whitefield was severely criticized by John Wesley for allowing people to fall, laugh, cry, and in some cases, bark like dogs. Wesley said this was of the flesh and should be stamped out. Whitefield agreed that not all that happened was the direct result of the Spirit but of the flesh. But he took the view that if you stamp out the flesh you will quench the Spirit as well.

That was precisely my view of Arthur's method. I was prepared to let him be himself. I have never been sorry.

A funny thing happened immediately after we left the deacon's apartment that night. We had left the deacons to discuss matters on their own, and as we were heading out toward Kensington High Street, we turned back and looked up at the same apartment. Arthur said, "Let's pray for them." Both of us lifted our hands toward the apartment and prayed aloud and earnestly for those men. While our hands were in the air a taxi pulled up. The driver thought we were hailing him! Arthur went to the cab driver and tried to explain that we didn't need a taxi but were praying. He at once proceeded to present the gospel to the taxi driver—who bowed his head and prayed to receive the Lord several minutes later! I have wondered many times about that cab driver and wonder if he will be in heaven one day. I would not be surprised if he is.

Arthur's six-week visit to the Chapel was like the earth-quake that rolled the stone away on Easter morning. Inviting him was truly the best decision I made during our twenty-five years. It set us free, broke us loose from doing things as they had always been done. Even if I had already had the vision that Arthur gave us—which I didn't—I doubt very much that I would have had the courage to initiate the changes that came.

But one thing was certain: we weren't turning back. The eleven deacons, their unease notwithstanding, believed God had sent Arthur to us. They still said so at that stage. Therefore, either God sent Arthur to us or He didn't. If He did, then why?

There were essentially three things Arthur began: first, widening our musical taste by singing choruses; second, getting us out on the streets witnessing; and third, giving an appeal at the end of his sermon. Believing as I did that God sent Arthur, I was not about to reverse what, it seemed to me, had been handed to us on a silver platter. I would have been irresponsible before God to say, "Well, Brothers and Sisters of the Chapel, wasn't that a good time we had over these six weeks? But now we will go back to business as usual." It is my view that, had I done that, I would be out of the ministry today; God would have sidelined me for not being obedient to the heavenly vision.

And yet, I was very anxious if not troubled the week following Arthur's departure for Norway. Three big things were to come up on that first Sunday night in June 1982, being without Arthur. The first was my new series on the life of Joseph. The second was whether we would immediately carry on with singing choruses, and the third was would I really—*really*—give an invitation for people to respond to my message? Never before, as far as I know, had an appeal been given at the Chapel at a regular service by its pastor. Would I, or wouldn't I? I can tell you, I wrestled all week long.

There was one thing of which there was no doubt: I

myself would be out on the streets the first Saturday in June 1982. I called a dozen people into the vestry on the previous Sunday in order to see how many would join me. Most said they would try to be there. Had none turned up, I would have gone out by myself! That is how deeply I felt.

The Pilot Lights were born on the first Saturday of June 1982. Six people turned up, including one of our deacons, Bob George, and his son Malcolm. Bob's wife, Cath, prepared drinks or coffee for passers-by every Saturday from the earliest days until her death in 1993. Mr. George would often call to mind a question I had asked the congregation a few years before: "How many of you have never led a soul to Christ?" Bob George was shaken. "I realized I had never led a soul to Christ in my life," he said. He was sixty at the time. I can tell you, the Pilot Lights was the excuse he was waiting for. He vowed to make up for lost time in his senior years and never missed a Saturday morning until 1997, when he was unable to drive into London. He has led not dozens, but hundreds, to the Lord. Are they all saved? I am sure some of them are, and one even went into the Anglican ministry. Even if it could be proved that most were not truly converted, I am prepared to argue that Mr. George still had more genuine converts through his efforts than hundreds and thousands of Christians who never manage to talk to either friends or strangers about the Lord at all.

A few years later Derek Temple, now a deacon, began coming out as a Pilot Light. Mr. George's mantle surely fell on him! He too has led hundreds to the Lord in recent years.

On the first Sunday evening of June 1982 I began the series of sermons on the life of Joseph (Genesis 37–50). I never dreamed it would become a book, but a few years later these sermons became *God Meant It for Good*. What never ceases to amaze me is that my first "altar call" at Westminster Chapel came after the inaugural sermon in this series. I have personally regarded the success of *God Meant It for Good* as God's seal on my giving an appeal after each sermon on the life of Joseph.

All week long, then, I walked the floor in our Ealing house

over whether I would, at the end of the day, actually give an opportunity for people to respond to my sermon. Arthur had done it for the previous six weeks, usually with dozens coming forward. I was not a hundred percent sure I'd do it, all the way to the very end of the sermon. I was so nervous. Never before had it been done, as far as I know, in a Sunday service. (Dr. Lloyd-Jones would not make an appeal lest he compete with the Spirit's own work. But he always told me he had "no problem at all" with the way he had seen me do it after he himself preached at Lower Heyford.) When I finished the first sermon on Joseph, we prayed as usual. And then I did it—I actually gave an opportunity for people to walk forward. Seven came. We have done it ever since. I never exert pressure or manipulate the congregation. We simply give people an opportunity to do what they want to do, not what they don't want to do.

Louise, however, was a bit nervous about my starting the Pilot Lights. She wondered if it was really necessary to take to the streets the way Arthur does. But one morning, to my surprise, Louise said, "I'm going to be a Pilot Light today." Really? Yes, but she asked the Lord for a sign if it was all really of God!

Tony Gaylor suggested that she stand outside St. James's Park subway station. Immediately, a young man with a Che Guevara T shirt walked over to Louise. With her hand shaking like a leaf, she handed him a tract, "What is Christianity?" He looked at her as tears filled his eyes. "I'm an atheist, I'm a Marxist," he said to her, "but five minutes ago I was in a church and said, 'God, if you are really there, let me run into someone who believes in you.'"

In late July 1982 we took our annual vacation in Florida, one of the most memorable we had ever experienced. Old friends from our former church in Fort Lauderdale opened their home in Tavernier for us to stay in for a whole month. Jack Brothers, the legendary bonefish guide, gave us the use of his boat while he fished in Canada for two weeks. That was the summer we really got to know Rev. Bruce Porter, the pastor of the Island Community Church in Islamorada,

Florida. Bruce invited me to preach for him.

Just before I got up to preach, Bruce told me there would be a famous fisherman in the service: Don Gurgiolo.

"Are you serious?" I asked.

"Yes, but why do you put it like that?" Bruce replied.

"Because Don Gurgiolo is the guide who first took me bonefishing in 1965, and I haven't seen him since," I said.

I stood up to preach, thanked Bruce for the warm welcome, and then told the story of my first bonefishing trip with Don Gurgiolo. (This is the same story as recounted in the introduction in *Worshipping God*.) Don was very pleased that I remembered him and immediately invited Bruce, TR, and me to go out the following day on his big boat for deep-sea fishing. Don seldom took people bonefishing any more but had moved to fishing for sailfish and blue marlin.

The next day we left early in the morning to fish with Captain Don Gurgiolo on his forty-foot boat, Gonfishin V. I had learned, in the meantime, that Don was in deep trouble with the law. He had been arrested for selling cocaine, and his trial was coming up shortly. I had one thing in mind from the moment he invited us to be his guests: to lead him to Christ. I am almost ashamed to say that, had this fishing event taken place one year before, this plan to see Don converted would not have entered my mind. But Arthur Blessitt's influence on me was potent, and I was full of determination to talk about Jesus to nearly everybody I met.

After some two hours of trolling for fish, I decided to catch a better kind of fish—Captain Don himself. I climbed up into the crow's nest and began presenting the gospel. He kept saying he wasn't good enough. But I just kept preaching. There wasn't anything better to do, since we hadn't caught any fish. I was given grace to help Don see that Christ died for sinners, for the ungodly; that all the fitness God required was to feel one's need of Him. Don gave in and prayed the sinner's prayer. He wept. We all wept. He recalls the place—near the Gulf Stream, twenty miles east of Islamorada in six hundred feet of water.

Moments later Don said, "You'd better go down and get your rods ready—we're coming into fish." He knew what he was talking about. We filled a big box with many pounds of good eating fish, some of which we took home with us that night.

Don's trial came up just before we returned to England. He was convicted of a felony, dealing in drugs, and was sentenced to prison. He and I exchanged letters faithfully over the next few years. He spent five years in prison. During that time he grew in grace, received the gift of tongues, was healed miraculously and instantaneously of arthritis, and emerged from prison a beautiful Christian man indeed. Don and I became very close friends. He kept in touch with me continually until he died suddenly of a heart attack at the age of seventy-one in 1999. I can never forget that, but for Arthur Blessitt, humanly speaking, Don would not have been led to the Lord—at least by me.

During the same summer of 1982, I introduced O. S. Hawkins, then the pastor of the First Baptist Church of Fort Lauderdale, to bonefishing. We went to Bimini for a couple of days. As we sat under the swaying coconut palms on a moonlit evening, OS said, "Kendall, how can you sit here in Bimini and be so calm when your church back in London could be falling apart after your having a man like Arthur Blessitt?" I only replied that I knew I had done the right thing and that God would see me through any difficulty. But had I known what would follow for the next four years, I doubt if I would have been so calm.

The first day back after vacation I found one of our deacons at our door in Ealing. He came to share with me his concern that there might be trouble brewing in the Chapel. He wondered if it might be a good idea to backpedal a bit on street witnessing and chorus singing—at least for a while. I assured him that this would not be necessary, that God was with us, and that we should not be too worried. He seemed relieved, if not pleased, that I was at peace.

On our first Sunday back after our summer vacation in 1982, I went into the pulpit for the first time without a robe, known as a Geneva gown, which Dr. Lloyd-Jones always wore. I had followed the Chapel tradition by wearing it both services every Sunday from the first day. I was always self-conscious in it but assumed it was a harmless tradition to uphold. But I felt more and more that it fed into my pride. I am aware of the argument that the robe "covers the man," as if he would be less visible, but it did more to inflate my ego than keep me humble, if I'm honest. I do not deny that for some it would be an act of humility to wear it, but for a man from the hills of Kentucky it was probably otherwise.

When the twelve deacons came in for prayer on that first Sunday morning after vacation, one of the deacons spoke up. "Did you forget your robe?"

"No," I replied. Nothing else was said. We prayed and went into the sanctuary. After the morning service an eighty-year-old lady, Miss Hilda Rogers, walked by the vestry door to ask, "Where was your robe?"

I replied, "I decided not to wear it any longer."

"Good," she said. "You should have thrown it away a long time ago."

That was a surprising comment—especially coming from her! But it told me that not wearing it was not going to be too controversial. Most of the young people never liked it, and some were not surprised that I abandoned it after having had Arthur Blessitt with us.

A few weeks later—still in the autumn of 1982—a man came into the vestry with his wife after a morning service. He felt he should lovingly warn me that Westminster Chapel was now very unsettled, that the "quality people" of the Chapel were very unhappy. He was referring to the fallout of Arthur's historic visit in May.

"What is it we are doing you don't like?" I asked.

"The whole package," he replied.

He apparently meant our witnessing in the streets on Saturdays, singing a chorus or two on Sunday nights, as well as my allowing people to make a public response after my sermon on Sunday evenings. There was also uneasiness with the type of people (not always middle class) who were coming into the services as a result of the Pilot Lights ministry. There was even fear that the finances of the Chapel would suffer. The type of people now coming could hardly pay the bills.

In the meantime, my preaching on 1 John continued on Sunday mornings, with the life of Joseph on Sunday evenings and Hebrews on Fridays. I made sure that at least one chorus— or something not in our hymnal—was sung every Sunday evening. The morning service stayed much the same as before. The crowds did not increase greatly, but they certainly did not decrease. People who were unhappy with the Sunday night changes began leaving the Chapel, but more were coming in all the time. And finances were up! All the concern about finances, considering "the type of people" who were coming along, turned out to be unwarranted. I never knew where the money was coming from. But catering for all kinds of people— whatever color, class, or appearance—was being blessed by God.

Revival did not come. But there was, nonetheless, a good feeling in the Chapel. We were loosening up. A friendlier atmosphere was apparent. Visitors were commenting on how they were feeling welcomed. I can't say that my preaching noticeably improved, but it was not worse! I was relishing the insights I was given week after week on 1 John, the life of Joseph, and Hebrews. If anything, my sermon preparation was yielding more fresh thoughts than ever.

A new criticism was beginning to come through, however. "Where are all these people who are presumably converted on the streets?" In other words, what results were to be found from the Pilot Lights ministry? Word would leak out that people were praying to receive Christ almost every week. But where were they? True, quite a number of people were turning up—including tramps and beggars. But they weren't around long enough to ask for membership in the church.

One Saturday morning, just before we were to leave our home for our Saturday Pilot Lights ministry, I shared this burden with Louise. I asked her to pray with me that someone from the immediate area would pray to receive the Lord—not only to encourage all of us but to help stem the criticism that the Pilot Lights ministry was doing the Chapel little good. An hour or so later, a rather impressive lady of middle age accepted one of my tracts. She allowed me to pray for her, but she did not accept Christ. Still, she came to church the next day. The following Saturday she came by the steps of the Chapel on purpose—to talk with me. She then prayed to receive Christ. She came forward the next day after the evening sermon. I later baptized her. She became a member. Her name was Barbara Arnold (she is now in heaven). She lived one hundred yards from the Chapel.

God knew how to encourage us in those days. They were very hard times. I found it difficult to smile when I was on the steps of the Chapel on Saturdays. I was self-conscious that Dr. Lloyd-Jones probably would not have done this. I sensed that a growing number of people were unhappy. Although the congregations were not going down, they were not rising much either. I could almost hear Dr. Lloyd-Jones saying, "What you are doing won't make one bit of difference." I feared he might be right. But I feared disobeying God more. God would give us what I can only call "tokens" now and then that kept us reassured we were pleasing Him. Moreover, old Mr. Micklewright would remind me of one particular question Dr. Lloyd-Jones would always ask when a minister did something risky or different: "What has it done to his preaching?" In other words, if it doesn't hurt his preaching, don't worry.

During those days one of our deacon's wives, Margaret Paddon, led Michael Gough to the Lord. Michael was living on the streets behind the Army and Navy store. He had been rejected by both his natural parents and his adopted parents. He had no job, no home, no friends, no family, and no money. And he was angry with God. He agreed, however, to come to Chapel the next Sunday. The Paddons invited him to sit with them in church and to eat with them. They were so kind to him. They nurtured him. He was shortly converted and became a Chapel member. He attended every single service. He found a job and a place to live. Less than a year later he developed a heart condition. He was scheduled for open-heart surgery. Two days after the operation, one of our members, Tony Gaylor, knocked on my vestry door. "I've got bad news," he said. "Michael Gough died a half hour ago." I broke down and wept. My last memory of him was seeing him sitting with the Paddons the previous Sunday morning in a three-piece suit he had bought and wore every Sunday. Mrs. Paddon spoke eloquently of him at the memorial service we held in his honor at the Chapel two weeks later.

The autumn of 1982 was fraught with difficulties and anxiety. I felt so lonely. Some of my closest friends and supporters were distancing themselves from me, criticizing all I was doing—from Pilot Lights and calling people forward at the end of the Sunday evening sermon to singing choruses. One thing that didn't help was the lack of good musical and singing talent, or so it seemed. When a solo or trio would sing without great ability or sensitivity to where we were at the time, the people became restless. When I would prepare to give people an opportunity to confess Christ publicly, my head would literally break out in a sweat. Sometimes the only person to walk forward was a senile old man who did nothing but count his change during my sermon—then walked forward at the end of the service! One needed more "success" at a time like this, and I seemed to get little of it.

Until I invited Arthur Blessitt—we had no trouble at all in the Chapel. None. The people loved us, the deacons loved us. During our first five years I had three books published (*Jonah, Calvin and English Calvinism to 1648*, and *Who By Faith*). I had preached through Hebrews 11, Jude, James, 1 Samuel, and Galatians. No problems arose from my preaching, teaching, or writing. There was great unity despite our not needing to use the galleries for congregations. But soon after I invited Arthur, I knew in my heart the honeymoon was over.

4

Tracing the Rainbow
Through the Rain

*Remember that by the time the
arrows of the enemy strike you they have come
under the permissive will of God. Do not resist or
you may be resisting God's grace and God's will.*
—ANONYMOUS

MY FIRST WORDS in my journal on January 1, 1983, were
these: "Ambitious in love." If I had a New Year's resolution
it was that. I have always been an ambitious man. This no
doubt was instilled in me by my father. But surely it would be
right to channel that ambition—toward love. I determined
that all I lived for and dreamed of would be motivated by a
drive to love—wherever it led me.

Sitting on the first floor of our Ealing home I was feeling
the need for an assistant. Dr. Lloyd-Jones used to have an
assistant, but the position of assistant was more for the assistants than for the Doctor. They didn't do much more than
teach a Bible class on Sunday afternoons. But I needed help.
I asked Louise to pray with me, claiming the promise of
Matthew 18:19 ("I tell you that if two of you on earth agree
about anything you ask for, it will be done for you by my
Father in heaven"), that God would send us an assistant.

A half hour later my secretary Pam Harris phoned to say that the choir of Dallas First Baptist Church would like to sing at the Chapel some time next year and would I please call a Jon Bush if I was interested. I remember phoning Jon Bush at 1:30 that day to say that, yes, the choir would be welcome to sing as long as they didn't expect too much in the way of big crowds. I then said, "How do you know about that choir?" He said that he had spent a year at First Baptist Church in Dallas as part of an arrangement they had with Spurgeon's College, where he had been a student. My mind began to work overtime. I thought to myself, *Here is an Englishman who will not be too entrenched in tradition if he has had a year in a church like that!* I inquired as to his future plans. He said he was open to whatever the Lord was leading him to do. I then asked him, "How would you like to be my assistant?" He was very positive, and we eventually took him on. He later revealed to me that on the very day we talked, knowing he would be trying to contact me, he said to his wife, "I wonder if Dr. Kendall needs an assistant?" He came to us when the Chapel was approaching our most volatile period. I don't know what I would have done without him.

One day Michael Leviton, one of the top solicitors of BP Chemicals, came to see me. He asked whether I would be open to having a lunchtime service at Westminster Chapel. I replied that I had not been inclined to this sort of thing because Dr. Lloyd-Jones used to say that lunchtime services "would not work in Westminster." I agreed with this, and I certainly didn't want to start something that would be seen as a failure! Then I was smitten inside. I felt convicted. I suddenly spoke up: "We'll do it. My fear of failure means I must do it—even if it fails." It was only my pride that kept me from saying yes.

Michael seemed delighted, and we agreed to start meeting in the Lloyd-Jones Hall on Thursdays beginning May 3—even if nobody came. On May 3, 1983, thirty-five people, almost entirely people working in the area, turned up. Soon after that we began the lunchtime services. Chris Porteous got involved and did much to spread the word around central London. We never looked back. Our numbers generally ranged from fifty to eighty, depending on the weather or subject or guest speaker, and we never were sorry we did this. Although we didn't need the extra space, we moved these services into the main auditorium to make it easier for people to come in.

Hodder & Stoughton approached me to see if I would like to do another book with them. Yes. I felt a book burning inside of me I wanted to call, *Once Saved, Always Saved*—not a book of sermons. I sat at my old typewriter, which I had used to type my doctor of philosophy thesis, and typed every word of it. I finished it in the summer of 1983. I wrote it not to change anybody's mind, but to encourage those who wanted to believe it but were afraid it was not true, for it was what I always preached at the Chapel, and with full and enthusiastic acceptance.

On June 12, 1983, I went to All Souls, Langham Place, for the induction of their new rector, Richard Bewes. I regarded it as an honor to have a relationship with All Souls, which we playfully referred to as "the other place." I first met their former rector and now rector emeritus, the Reverend John Stott, in 1977, shortly after I accepted the pastorate at the Chapel. John graciously invited me to have lunch with him and the staff at All Souls when Michael Baughen was the rector. John was the only minister in London to reach out to me in those days. Louise and I invited John and Michael to lunch at our home in Ealing back in 1978, and there has been a plan ever since 1983 to meet for lunch with John and Richard at least once a year.

During this time I was privileged to be invited to the European Congress on Revival, led by Manley Beasly of Texas and Ron Owens. These meetings were held in various places on the continent, like Interlaken in Switzerland and Innsbruck and Salzburg in Austria. It was a pleasant respite for Louise and me during these days. Ron Owens is a great singer and composer. He and his wife, Pat, came to the Chapel a number of times and were always very much appreciated. The meetings in Europe were mostly attended by Americans but also by pastors in Europe. It was there that we met some ministers from the Soviet Union.

On June 28, 1983, Louise and I celebrated our twenty-fifth wedding anniversary. Three days later the deacons gave a surprise party for us at John Raynar's place and presented us with lovely gifts. It was an encouraging time for us. Later in the summer I began a new book; it would be called *Stand Up and Be Counted*, a smaller book that sought to give a biblical and theological rationale for calling people to confess Christ publicly. I wanted to show that a Calvinist could give an "altar call," which I preferred to call a "public pledge." Billy Graham kindly wrote a brief foreword.

On Monday, November 7, 1983, I woke up on the Operation Mobilization ship *Logos*. I spent the night there in order to address the staff and missionaries who lived on the ship. It was berthed in Ipswich, and that day I was to meet a man who would one day be perhaps my closest friend—Robert Amess. He was a pastor in Ipswich at the time, came to hear me, and then took me out to lunch. I didn't see him again for a good while, but I knew at once that we had "hit it off."

We began Evangelism Explosion (EE) at the Chapel in 1983. This is the best tool for leading a person to Christ on a one-to-one basis of any I know. I recommend it most warmly. I had learned EE personally from its founder, Dr. D. James Kennedy, many years before. But I had to brush up on it in order to be allowed to teach it in the UK. I drove to Vic Jacopson's home in Southampton and took the test. I passed—just barely! But I was able to announce the following Sunday that I had been "certified," and the place fell apart. It was the first time I found out that in Britain to "be certified" means that you are declared officially mentally ill!

A bit of a controversy emerged in 1983 over the organist's preludes and postludes in the Sunday services. We had not said a word for years about this, but after a while there was an increasing unease with the organist playing secular, though classical, music before and after the services. It was felt by some, nonetheless, that Beethoven or Mozart created a great sense of worship. I assured them that in Westminster Abbey many would agree, but this was Westminster Chapel.

The following year, 1984—a year that would live in infamy—started with visiting Terry and Wendy Virgo in Hove. We attended their service, and I preached on Hebrews 4:16. It was one of our first experiences in a truly charismatic church, which included an hour of worship interlaced with people prophesying. Peter Lewis had introduced me to Terry several months before when Terry addressed the Westminster Fraternal. What impressed me most was Terry's lovely spirit, and this made me want to get to know him.

During 1984 the Pilot Lights ministry continued with modest progress alongside Evangelism Explosion. These two evangelistic enterprises were better attended by our people than we had expected, despite the success we had hoped would follow. And yet there were a lot of people in the Chapel who were opposed to both. While this would not have meant the majority, it nonetheless included too many who didn't believe we should be involved in these outreach programs. The feeling was that the pulpit is the ministry that God has ordained; He uses preaching—full stop. Any kind of evangelism that involved lay people was probably not of God! For this reason, some people who enrolled in EE could not even find prayer partners. (EE encourages each person to have a prayer partner for the duration of the course.) They were met with negative reactions of people who said they couldn't pray for something they didn't believe in. The same was true regarding the Pilot Lights ministry. Some thought it was almost a disgrace—and certainly an embarrassment—that their minister would be on the streets of Victoria doing "personal work."

And yet there came an opportunity early in the year that would end up opening more doors for me to preach than anything that had yet come along. At a time when some reformed churches were distancing themselves from me, on January 13, 1984, I was to meet a new friend—Clive Calver, the visionary leader of the Evangelical Alliance. He came to invite me to a meeting that would take place in October, to be called Leadership '84. He could not have known how lonely and isolated I felt. But he was very friendly and most anxious to have me come. I accepted.

Monday mornings are historically tough for preachers, especially if one has had a bad Sunday. I was seemingly having a lot of these in those days. I remember one Monday morning in particular when I woke up depressed because I felt I had preached so poorly the evening before. I decided to reach out to a friend who I thought might make me feel better. When I explained how badly I preached, his comment was: "This is a sign of God's judgment on Britain, that there isn't much good preaching around." I told him that his comment made me think of a story attributed to John Bunyan. A woman came to him fearing she had committed the unpardonable sin, and Bunyan became convinced she really had. That is how my friend's comment made me feel!

Dr. James Dobson has a helpful theory about preachers and Mondays. He says that many preachers think it is the devil attacking them on Mondays to get vengeance over their faithfulness on Sundays. The truth is, says Dr. Dobson, it is often nothing more than the loss of adrenaline: the body loses adrenaline when you are so keyed up on a busy day, and you feel depleted the following day. That loss of adrenaline plus a friend's unhelpful comment when I was already feeling like a broken reed certainly seemed like a satanic attack!

BILLY GRAHAM

On January 25 I received a phone call that would lead to the high-water mark for 1984 and one of the greater moments in our history.

"Mr. Kendall?" the voice inquired.

"Yes," I replied.

"This is Billy Graham."

I was so embarrassed that I didn't recognize his voice at first, although I should not have been completely surprised that he phoned. Some weeks earlier, Dr. Walter Smyth, the executive vice president of the Billy Graham Evangelistic Association, came to the vestry for lunch. I asked whether Billy could preach for us on May 6, the week prior to Mission England. So Billy rang to say that May 6 was a definite possibility. We talked for about fifteen minutes. "Call me Billy," he said. He was interested in my next book, *Stand Up and Be Counted*, and was curious as to how things were in my church. Dr. Lloyd-Jones had refused to back Billy in any of his meetings in the past. I assured him that he would be welcomed at Westminster Chapel, but that what we were doing was like turning a battleship around in the middle of a river. "I can well believe it!" he said.

There was, however, mounting opposition in the Chapel to Billy Graham's visit, although most were thrilled at this prospect. On Saturday, April 14, over one hundred turned up to give out leaflets advertising Billy's May 6 meeting. We were hoping to fill the Chapel with local residents and, therefore, refused to advertise his visit in Christian magazines. We even asked permission to put loudspeakers outside, so that any who couldn't get inside could hear Billy, but the city of Westminster would not approve it.

On Friday, May 4, the side doorbell rang, and I rushed to answer it. There stood Billy Graham, his closest friend, T. W. Wilson, and Maurice Rowlandson. Had I not been expecting him I would not have recognized Billy, with his crumpled hat and glasses. He came into the vestry to spend nearly two hours with me while TW and Maurice stayed outside the closed door.

"You are here because of Arthur Blessitt," I began.

"So I've heard," he replied.

What I meant was that Arthur's visit in 1982 had freed us from the past in such a manner that I could actually invite Billy to preach at Westminster Chapel.

We discussed his preaching for us the following Sunday evening. He was thinking about "loneliness" as a subject. He wanted to know how to give the invitation. I assured him he could do what he was used to doing. "Do it your way," I insisted.

We talked about Arthur, Dr. Lloyd-Jones, Billy's wife, Ruth, and his own sinus condition. I told him I could wallpaper the vestry with pictures of him and the pope because of what people had been sending in recent days! He laughed. He said he agreed with my view of Hebrews 6:4–6 and that there was nothing he had read in *Once Saved, Always Saved* that he disagreed with. He asked me to send him all my books and back copies of the *Westminster Record*. He returned to his sinus condition. He was understandably preoccupied with this. As a matter of fact, he was taken to the hospital after he left me. There was to be a lot of concern over whether he would be fit to preach on the Sunday evening.

But before he left he brought up other things. "I can't preach nearly as well as these English preachers. My gift is giving the invitation," he said, adding—as if one could really believe this—"I'm not a good communicator." Then he talked about being attacked by fundamentalists and what he had learned from Bob Jones. He discussed his membership at Dallas First Baptist Church, being in Russia, and his appointment with a doctor on Harley Street as soon as he left me. I then walked with him, TW, and Maurice to his waiting car.

As they drove off, I walked back to my vestry in disbelief. I couldn't take it in: *I have spent nearly two hours with Billy Graham,* I kept telling myself.

I hurried home to tell Louise and to write down in my journal every word I could remember that we had just talked about.

Louise asked, "What was it like to be with Billy Graham?"

Tears filled my eyes. "He is so simple and uncomplicated," I said.

It was most extraordinary. It was one of the great privileges and moments in my whole life. Maurice Rowlandson phoned later to say that Billy was "thrilled to bits" with our time together, which to me was the icing on the cake.

On May 5 an article on "Conversion" I wrote for *The Times* was published, which related to Billy's visit to the Chapel but also to Mission England. An article I had written for them a year before, on the subject of eternal punishment, had been rejected, so perhaps they were glad at last to have something by me that they apparently liked. *The Times* had always carried the times of our services, and I was glad for a good relationship with this newspaper.

My dad and Abbie came to London for the Billy Graham visit. Dad joined the Pilot Lights on the Saturday and was utterly at home talking to passers-by about the Lord. He and dear Mr. George got along so very well. There was a good feeling all around that Billy would be with us the next day. Walter Smyth and Maurice Rowlandson phoned during the day to assure me that, despite Billy being in hospital, he would definitely be at the Chapel on time on Sunday evening!

The next morning, however, confusion about his pending visit persisted. It was announced on the radio that Billy was in hospital and would not be at the Chapel. Elizabeth Catherwood phoned from Cambridge to sympathize and say how she felt for me in my disappointment. But I assured her that the media had got it wrong; they had jumped to conclusions, but Billy would be preaching that evening as scheduled. Billy, in fact, phoned me. We talked on the phone for twenty-five minutes. He said he would be present, bringing two nurses and a doctor! He added that a nurse had read my article in *The Times* aloud to the other nurses in his hospital room.

Billy arrived at 5:30 p.m., an hour before the service. One of the sweetest things that God did was to let our verger, Fred Jinks, be present in Castle Lane to welcome Billy before anyone else did. Fred was privileged to tell Billy that he had been converted at the Haringey Crusade in 1954—on the very first night of the mission! Billy said that it was the first time he had met anyone who had been converted on the first night of that historic series of meetings.

With an hour in the vestry there was time to get photos with Billy—including one with my dad. My dad carried that photo of Billy, himself, and me for many years. Billy had a touch of laryngitis, so I did most of the talking. He seemed to love my favorite sermon illustration—about the Holy Spirit and bonefishing! The deacons—all twelve—came in at 6:25, each meeting Billy. All of them were cordial to him. When John Sloan, one of our treasurers, offered him an envelope, Billy gave it back. "I haven't taken an honorarium in over twenty-five years," he said. Jon Bush, my able assistant who had worked hard for weeks to get things ready, led in prayer. The deacons went out. Billy and I stayed behind for a few moments, and the two of us prayed alone.

The church was full. Despite rumors that Billy wouldn't be there, people were in the overflow rooms. My guess is, had there been no announcements on the radio about his being in hospital, there would have been chaos inside and outside the Chapel.

We began the evening with "And Can It Be?" I offered Billy a hymnbook. "I don't need the words for that one," he replied. During the offering he said to me, "I feel the presence of the Holy Spirit." I introduced him by saying that Billy Graham is the nearest we in America have to royalty. He preached for about fifty minutes on "Loneliness." It was a very moving and relevant message. Perhaps eighty came forward. We went to the rear halls where he met with those who came forward and led them in a prayer of commitment. I then walked with him to the door and to his waiting car. I kissed him on the cheek. It was a magnificent evening and a very bright spot in an unforgettable year.

On February 28, 1984, we had our first church members' banquet. This would be an annual occasion that would last for several years. The emphasis was to be on evangelism, to stress the need to reach the lost by whatever means. Our first speaker was O. S. Hawkins. He was joined by Pete Cantrell of Oklahoma—and, lo and behold, Arthur Blessitt turned up! It was a wonderful night. OS was at his best, Arthur greeted the people briefly, and all felt the occasion was worth all the effort—including the delicious food.

Another verse that was becoming special to me in those days was 1 John 4:16. We had begun 1 John in early 1982. We reached this verse on April 1, 1984. God used this powerfully in my own spiritual development—that I must "believe the love" (King James Version) God has for us or, as the New International Version puts it, "rely" on His love. I began pairing two verses every morning as I started my quiet time— Hebrews 4:16 and 1 John 4:16, the former with reference to obtaining "mercy" each day, the latter regarding affirming God's love for me—and rejecting any thought to the contrary. It is so comforting to rely on His love, refusing to believe otherwise, which is exactly what God wants us to do. My "discovery" of 1 John 4:16, I wrote in my journal on April 11, was like a "tower experience," a phrase Martin Luther used to denote his own breakthrough regarding justification by faith alone. This verse was important because I was beginning to feel attacked more and more. I needed to feel that, even if the best of people were doubting me, God didn't. For by the middle of 1984, nearly half of the deacons were opposing my ministry.

While word was reaching us right, left, and center of older and faithful supporters leaving us—even encouraging and recruiting members to start attending other churches— God sent new friends and supporters to the Chapel, among them David and Doreen Jermyn. They began attending in 1980 but did not make themselves known. But during the early months of 1984, they began to surface and show warm encouragement to Louise and me. David is a self-made businessman and also a magistrate. A few years later they asked for membership. One day David would become a deacon and one of our treasurers while Doreen became active in the ladies' ministry, helping Louise.

Another happy development came about in 1984: my relationship with Southern Baptists was being strengthened. O. S. Hawkins phoned me to say he had been elected president of the Pastors' Conference of the Southern Baptist Convention and that I must speak at it the following year in Dallas. In the meantime, Dr. W. A. Criswell, the venerated pastor of America's largest church, First Baptist Church of Dallas (membership 25,000), had been friendly with us. He first came to the Chapel to hear me preach on July 3, 1983, then again on Sunday morning June 10, 1984. I called him to the platform for him to participate in the dedication of Justin Sloan, the infant son of Stephen and Gillian Sloan. It was a sweet moment. Taking little Justin into his arms, he began, "Will he be a doctor, will he be a lawyer...?" The Criswells afterward joined Louise and me in the old apartment on the Chapel premises for lunch. Louise prepared a shepherd's pie for them. Dr. Criswell later wrote that it was the best meal he ever had in his life. But he has been notorious for exaggeration!

I did have this dilemma, however: was I going too fast or not fast enough in making any changes in the Chapel? On July 4, Terry and Wendy Virgo came to our home in Ealing for supper. Terry hinted that I was not going fast enough! He gave us an illustration of a plane in World War II in which the pilot radioed that they might have to return to base because rats were eating into the wiring and would soon cause the plane to fall. Suddenly the pilot came up with a surprising decision: "Put on your gas masks, we are ascending higher," thus killing the rats by the freezing temperature. I have thought of that story ever since. Perhaps I will never know for sure whether we have been too slow or too fast in departing from the old ways.

Our summer vacation in 1984 was spent in the home of Meint and Linda Huesman in Key Largo, Florida. They have a lovely home on Largo Sound—the place where I first began bonefishing in 1964. It was like a dream. Little did we know what friends the Huesmans would turn out to be, not to mention the fact that one day we would become next-door neighbors when we retired to Florida in February 2002.

On July 18, 1984 I flew to Los Angeles and appeared on Trinity Broadcasting Network's *Praise the Lord* with Arthur Blessitt. Arthur interviewed me for forty-five minutes on live TV that went all over the U.S. to perhaps six million viewers. I then preached briefly my sermon "Are You Ready for Answered Prayer?" based on Luke 1:13 and Luke 18:1. Afterward we went out to a Japanese restaurant—my first time to have sushi—with Paul and Jan Crouch, the founders of TBN.

Throughout the whole of 1984, Tony Gaylor, one of our most faithful members, looked after our family in a most caring and loving way. Virtually every Sunday that year he invited the four of us to Sunday lunch after the morning service. Knowing as he did the stress Louise was under and the difficulty of either going back to Ealing or bringing in the necessary food, he insisted week after week that we join him and his friends—usually a dozen or more. May God continue to bless Tony for this kindness to us.

On Tuesday, October 9, I took the train to Weston-super-Mare. I spoke to 1,500 church leaders at *Leadership '84* on the subject of "Evangelism and the Local Church." I had unusual help from the Lord. The people there seemed to love me. This event, more than any other, would open new doors for me at a time when they were being closed elsewhere. It was there I first met Gerald Coates and Roger Forster. I was interviewed on a closed-circuit TV network with Arthur Wallis. A new breed of people would be coming into my life.

The following week I went to Westminster Central Hall, joined by Terry Virgo, to hear John Wimber. The emphasis was on signs and wonders. I thought John Wimber was extremely good. His emphasis on the kingdom of God seemed to cohere with my view. I wrote in my journal: "Is God leading me in this direction? I should wish so."

Another bright spot in this difficult period was that Dr. Charles James, a physician and former deacon but now a minister, asked if he could join me on the streets as a Pilot

Light on Saturdays. Yes! He said he wanted to learn how to do this so that his church could engage in the same kind of ministry. But I think he did it also, if not mainly, to encourage me and make a statement to his Chapel friends, some of whom were not happy with some of the changes at the Chapel.

A few weeks later the Christian magazine *Today*, featuring me, was released. It had my picture on the cover with the headline "Man in a Minefield." This piece came at the exact time our problems came to a head. But despite all the trouble that followed Arthur Blessitt's visit—and losing a good number of people—we survived.

I come now to the most difficult and delicate part of this book. I have written and rewritten this section. At one stage I took almost an entire chapter out, deciding to say nothing. But some of my friends have pointed out that to omit this part of the story is to leave a huge gap that would thus not give a true picture of our twenty-five years. Some said it would even be like looking at this era with one eye shut.

In truth, Westminster Chapel has been a place where I have felt the greatest sense of God's presence and power. And yet it is also a place in which Louise and I have experienced some of the darkest moments of our lives together. It is therefore a place that in many ways has made us, but it would also be true to say almost broke us. I developed high blood pressure; Louise developed asthma. I have no desire to revisit those times, both for my sake and the sake of others, save to testify to the sustaining power and presence of God in one of the most difficult periods of my life: in other words, to proclaim that the pursuit of His glory dare not be limited to times of ease and apparent blessing. Each of us must hold on, even at those times when His glory seems a distant thing.

As I have written this book I have constantly sought to be governed by its very title—*In Pursuit of His Glory*. To "tell all" could possibly be written in such a manner as to make myself look good and others not so good. My first premise in *Total Forgiveness* is that you do not tell how people have wronged you if you have totally forgiven them.

But one very prominent church leader, knowing a little bit of what happened, was shocked when I told him I had decided to leave the entire story out. He insisted that it would surely be to God's glory for many people, especially church leaders and pastors who also have had difficulties in their churches, to know that I struggled and came through. I therefore must say something, he urged, if only to encourage fellow ministers who have had some opposition from their members. It was also pointed out that I would not be suddenly revealing what certain people did, since it has been in the public domain for many years.

Another trusted friend urged me to write in such a way that the very people involved would actually be blessed by what they read—even knowing that they themselves were being referred to. I have therefore prayed—and prayed hard— that I could touch upon our darkest era briefly in a manner that does not violate the principles of *Total Forgiveness*, and one that indeed would honor these men and honor God. I equally faced the temptation of trying to make myself look good by saying absolutely nothing so people could say, "How wonderful you are to say nothing at all."

What happened was this. Obviously, not everyone loved Arthur Blessitt or his ministry as much as I did, and severe trouble followed his departure. Many left, but many stayed despite being unhappy with Arthur and the changes I felt must be made, such as singing choruses as well as hymns, giving an appeal for people to come forward at the end of the Sunday night services, and our Pilot Lights ministry on the streets near the Chapel. I received a letter from a person who even thought I had abandoned my principle of "waiting for Isaac" and opted for Ishmael after all—a perspective that is made clearer later in this book. But some stayed because they felt they must preserve the Chapel's honor by praying for a ministry that would truly glorify God.

The people who opposed our ministry in those days, an era that began in April 1982 and lasted until the middle of

1986, were among the most talented and godly people we had in the Chapel. I used to confide in some of them as one does to closest and highly trusted friends. They were in pursuit of God's glory every bit as much as I. So these people, who believed they were led by the Holy Spirit, eventually concluded that the issue was essentially theological rather than with our changes. They therefore instigated a process that nearly broke Louise and me and could have driven us away from England forever. It was hard for them to do this, but they felt that they had no choice before the Lord.

I have tried to get into their skins and to enter their thinking in order to understand the reasons for the action they took and why they took it. I have concluded that it was because we were leading Westminster Chapel into unexplored waters and in a direction that did not befit the Chapel's culture and reason for existence. In a word, they believed we were going against the purpose for which God raised up the Chapel in the first place.

Using my book *Once Saved, Always Saved* as the main evidence, they accused me of a heresy, namely one that is called "antinomianism." This word (which translated literally means "against law") is normally used to describe one who teaches that, since we are eternally saved and not under the Law of Moses, it does not matter how we live. I waited almost fifteen years before I wrote a book (*Just Grace*) that people can read if they want to see my views on the Law. As for *Once Saved, Always Saved*, what probably saved me from being disenfranchised was partly that the members of the Chapel actually felt that my teaching made them want to live in a more godly way than ever.

Although my opposition originated as a reaction to the changes in the Chapel after Arthur Blessitt's visit, then, some believed that the Holy Spirit now presented them with this theological reason to oppose the ministry. They concluded that my preaching on Galatians (from 1977 to 1981) was not sound after all. It was their duty before God to warn the members in order to safeguard the pulpit and theological reputation of Westminster Chapel. They believed they were doing what they did as a mandate from God and that they were in pursuit of His glory.

The matter was largely laid to rest at a historic church meeting on January 16, 1985. Old Mr. M. J. Micklewright stood up to remind the members that Dr. Lloyd-Jones always said that if the gospel we preach is not accused of being antinomian, it is probably because we haven't really preached the gospel! Opposition still remained for another eighteen months, but eventually most of these people went to other churches.

The leadership of the FIEC were asked by some of these people to examine my teaching. The dear men on the FIEC theological committee were made to read my books and listen to countless tapes of my sermons. They concluded that there was no charge to answer. Whatever strain there may have been on my relationship with the FIEC, I will always be indebted to them for their reply. Brian Edwards, the highly esteemed pastor of the Hook Evangelical Church for many years, was put in the middle of this. He was brilliant and has remained a precious friend to me.

The people who opposed me in those days probably have suffered as much as Louise and I did. I am sure that it was the greatest trauma of their lives as well. Total forgiveness does not only mean that I forgive absolutely those who I feel sinned against me, but that in return I humbly ask for their forgiveness for anything that might have hurt them. This I gladly do.

Louise, TR, Melissa, and I have survived. If you are going through anything that sounds like what I have just described, God will see you through it. Try hard not to vindicate yourself, and don't use your pulpit or platform to preach at your opposition (I did this too often, I'm sorry to say), but forgive them totally by sincerely praying that God will bless them as you yourself would want to be blessed. And you too will survive.

5

Paul Cain

Anyone who receives a prophet
because he is a prophet will receive
a prophet's reward.
—MATTHEW 10:41

I BEGAN MY book *The Anointing* with a reference to two men who had the most influence on me at Westminster Chapel: Dr. Martyn Lloyd-Jones and Paul Cain. Some would have thought Arthur Blessitt would be included in this short list. But though having Arthur was my most strategic influence, the influence on me by Paul Cain was even more profound. This is because it truly paved the way for our openness to the Holy Spirit in a deeper manner.

It all began October 21, 1990, when Wyn Lewis, the pastor of Kensington Temple, phoned me at the Chapel on a Sunday afternoon. He asked, "Do you still want to meet Paul Cain?"

I immediately replied, "Yes."

Wyn gave me Paul Cain's number, adding, "He can see you tomorrow."

Because of David Pytches' best-selling book *The Kansas*

City Prophets, Paul Cain, though he is from Texas, became regarded as a Kansas City prophet almost from the moment his name was known among certain Christians in Britain. John Wimber brought Paul to London in the summer of 1990 and introduced him at Holy Trinity Brompton. The word about Paul's prophetic gift began sweeping the charismatic world, and I too began to hear about him. What I heard made me think he was of the devil. The idea of publicly calling people's names, addresses, dates of birth, and who their dearest relations were—even if Paul had never been told such information by anyone—to me smacked of the occult. I said so. I sincerely believed I was doing God's will in trying to warn people like Clive Calver that people like Paul Cain must be avoided, if only because of some of Paul's strange connections over forty years before. I said this to Wyn Lewis when he joined Lyndon Bowring (executive chairman of CARE) and me one morning at breakfast.

"Would you like to meet him?" Wyn asked.

"I'd be willing to meet him," I replied. "Do you really know him? I thought he came in from out of the blue."

Wyn said he had known Paul for over twenty years. So Wyn got in touch the following October.

The next day, October 22, I phoned Lyndon. "Are you free for lunch?"

"It would be very hard to get free," he said, but when I told him I was having lunch with Paul Cain, Lyndon said, "I'll be there."

When I put the phone down, Louise and I prayed together, claiming Matthew 18:19, "Again, I tell you that if two of you on earth agree about anything you ask for, it will be done for you by my Father in heaven." I simply prayed, "Lord, if this man is not of You, help me to see it, but if in fact he is a man of God, don't let me miss seeing this."

Paul was staying in the Tower Bridge Hotel. He and John Wimber were having public meetings in the London Arena. Word was out that Paul had prophesied that revival would come to London in October 1990. It was shown later that Paul merely said—it was tape-recorded—that "tokens" of revival would come to London in October 1990. I had no intentions of going to any of the meetings but was very happy to meet Paul Cain for lunch.

Lyndon and I waited on the ground floor near the elevator. I had no idea what Paul looked like, so I began to size up every man who walked out of each elevator in the Tower Bridge Hotel. I began to pray hard in my spirit not to be deceived.

Once I met him and looked into his eyes, I knew that this man was certainly not occultic. Within an hour, I felt he was a genuine man of God. By five o'clock, four hours later, I felt I was singularly blessed to be in his company—as if I had met Samuel or Elijah.

Our earliest moments, however, were tense. He was taken aback when I disclosed that I was not really and truly convinced of him or his gift. This seemed to throw him because, he told me later, he felt the Lord had shown him that I would be the brother he never had! "It had been years since I was so excited to meet someone, although I had never heard of you or Westminster Chapel," he later said to me. This is why he was so shocked that I wasn't very forthcoming at first. But I thought he would have already known this by discernment! I made the same mistake almost everybody makes; they think he knows everything in everybody! I also learned later that during the same hour John Wimber ran into Reed Grafke, Paul's assistant, in the hotel parking lot, where John told Reed there was somebody he wanted Paul Cain to meet—meaning me. Reed replied, "They are having lunch together at this moment." He and John bowed their heads and prayed for us there in the parking lot.

Lyndon had to leave around three o'clock, but before he left, Paul told something about me to both of us that Lyndon knew to be exactly true. Lyndon and I looked at each other; tears filled our eyes. He and I both knew that Paul focused with astonishing accuracy on my motivation and heart of hearts. For the next two hours Paul and I shared together things that were mutually precious. But what put the seal of God on the occasion, as far as I am concerned, was that Paul revealed to me something of my own thorn in the flesh in such a manner that I knew God was making me see I was to take Paul Cain seriously—very seriously indeed. Had I not been forced to meet someone else in the vestry at the Chapel at 5:30 that day I suspect we would have remained together for the rest of the evening. Never had I been so excited to have met someone. I couldn't wait to tell Louise.

The next evening, Lyndon and I went to the London Arena to hear Paul speak. I'm sorry, but I was not impressed. I can only say that I thank God I had the privilege of meeting him privately before I heard him exercise his gift publicly. His preaching did not particularly bless me, and his calling out certain people from the platform in an auditorium filled with several thousand people left me with questions. This negative reaction to Paul's public ministry has helped me to be patient with others who find this kind of public prophesying difficult. Had I not been personally convinced by four hours of intimate conversation I fear I would never have wanted to see him again. I can only say that God was gracious to let me have an opportunity few people get.

The next day, Wednesday, October 24, was Louise's birthday. We had already decided to go out for breakfast for the occasion but wondered if Paul would like to join us. We headed for the Tower Bridge Hotel, and Paul met with us. He began revealing things to Louise about herself and our children. At noon we headed back to Westminster—the three of us. I brought him to our apartment in Victoria, then showed him the Chapel. We stood in the pulpit with no one present. It was precisely then—he revealed later—that Paul saw revival in Westminster Chapel "like in Jonathan Edwards'" day.

Before I knew what I was doing—that is, in a sense, because I knew exactly what I was doing—I asked him to speak at Westminster Chapel the following Friday immediately after our regular Bible study. The next day, however, I couldn't believe what I had done. I had all but vowed in 1986 "never again" to invite anybody to speak who is controversial, neither would I take any more risks. I felt I had paid my dues, thus showing God and man what I was utterly willing to do— if only by having Arthur Blessitt. Surely God would never ask me to put my ministry and reputation at risk ever again. Could He not just sovereignly send revival without my having to go to any more effort or bear any further stress? Then I woke up the next day, realizing I had just invited the very man who was arguably the single most controversial person alive to speak at a public meeting at Westminster Chapel. *What on earth have I done?* I asked myself.

On the evening of Friday, October 26, I conducted the Bible study as usual. We were in Hebrews, chapter 12, verse 2. Just as when I first invited Arthur Blessitt at a Friday Bible study, we dispensed with the question time. I then introduced Paul Cain. He spoke for ten minutes on "Intimacy With God." It was brilliant. I had no idea what he would do. But had I written the script, knowing the people as I did, I could not have improved on what he did and said.

We got in our car to go eat somewhere. Before we had come to the end of Castle Lane, a hundred yards or so from the Chapel, he looked at me and said, "May I share something with you?"

I swallowed. I thought to myself, *Here it comes. He is going to reveal all my sins and weaknesses and the reason we aren't seeing revival.* But that wasn't it. It was about Louise.

"Your wife is in a borderline clinical depression," he said to me, but hoped it was revealed in sufficient time to avoid the worst.

"Is it my fault?" I asked.

"Not intentionally," he wanted to assure me, but he felt that Louise was overwhelmed with all that was entailed in what she was called to be and to do at the Chapel—plus having to be my wife. I accepted all he said, but also hoped this meant she would be instantly healed because of Paul coming into our lives. She wasn't. Paul only gave a diagnosis.

In early January 1991, Paul phoned to say that John Wimber wanted Louise and me to attend the annual Vineyard Conference in Anaheim, California, later that month. We agreed to go. I asked the deacons to lay hands on us. Just before they prayed, Ernie Paddon felt he had to read out 1 Thessalonians 5:19–22, "Do not put out the Spirit's fire; do not treat prophecies with contempt. Test everything. Hold on to the good. Avoid every kind of evil."

Louise and I had four enriching days in Southern California. There we met John Wimber for the first time and several international leaders. We met Mike Bickle, the pastor of the Vineyard Church of Kansas City, and two of the "Kansas City Prophets," Bob Jones and John Paul Jackson, who prophesied to me for about twenty minutes. I also met Leonard Ravenhill, whose book *Why Revival Tarries* had impacted me twenty-five years before. Paul and I had a lot of quality time together. One of the memorable moments of the week was hearing Mike Bickle tell his favorite Paul Cain stories. They sounded as if they came out of the life of Elijah or Elisha or the Book of Acts. It was at this conference I met Dr. Jack Deere, the brilliant scholar who had once been on the faculty at Dallas Theological Seminary.

The following Sunday all twelve deacons listened intently as I reported the events of the week, reading word for word from my journal. There was a strong feeling that the trip was indeed worthwhile, and there was a great sense of expectancy that Paul Cain would return to London and speak to us again at the Chapel.

My greatest fear, however, was that I would endure another upheaval and that the Chapel would be split again. I did not feel able to bear another era like that, which had lasted over four years. A few days later, as I walked from our apartment to Victoria Street, I felt that the Lord gave me Revelation 3:7–11, which includes a promise that one would be kept from tribulation because "you have kept my word and have not denied my name" (v. 8). I somehow knew in my heart that Paul Cain's visits to Westminster Chapel would do us no harm.

Paul Cain's biography will probably be written by someone in due course. In a word, it is generally like this. His mother was pregnant with him, had cancer in both breasts, and other tumors throughout her body. The doctors told her she would not live to see her child. But an angel of the Lord appeared to Mrs. Cain and said, "There is a boy in your womb; you are to call him Paul. He will bring My Word to the nations." Paul's mother lived to the age of 105. In the years between 1949 and 1951, Paul, then in his early twenties, had a healing ministry. For two years, "Virtually every person I prayed for was healed," says Paul. Then the anointing largely left, except for a measure of a rather extraordinary prophetic gift. Paul has seen extraordinary miracles and believes this anointing will return to the church generally one day. As for his prophetic gift, John Wimber told me personally he has never known Paul to get it wrong and that Paul had ministered to at least three hundred families in his own church in Anaheim, California. I would have to say I know of some instances when Paul did, in fact, miss the mark, but they are not too many.

Paul began to say he wanted to be under my own ministry. I had lovingly chided him that he was upholding a defective theology.

Sitting in a restaurant in Victoria Street I said, "Paul, you need my theology, and I need your power."

He said, "You have a deal."

In that moment there was born—in my mind—the need to bring the Word and the Spirit together. He represented the Spirit, as it were, and I the Word. This vision sealed our relationship.

When we were together in California, I put to him something that I feared would immediately ruin our friendship. I told him that I was on record for calling the Charismatic movement "Ishmael." My reasoning was this: for thirteen years Abraham really believed that Ishmael was the promised child, but Isaac instead was promised. I regarded Ishmael as being like the Charismatic movement. Some thought it was the ultimate revival, but something greater is coming—namely, "Isaac," a revival that will shake the whole world. Paul looked at me and said, "I have been preaching that very message for the last fourteen years to charismatics."

Paul began to hint also that he would like to be a member of Westminster Chapel. I had to tell him it was, sadly, out of the question. We required that people come regularly for six months before they are even considered. "And how could you be a member of the Chapel when you don't live over here?" I asked. His reply was that Billy Graham was a member of First Baptist Church of Dallas, but didn't live there. He then asked, "What if I listened to six months of your tapes?"

In March 1991, he and Reed Grafke suddenly came to London for nearly three weeks. As he was driving in Fort Worth, a "healing presence" came into the car, as he put it. He began to intercede for his sister, who was at Mayo Clinic (she was suddenly healed at the precise time), and the Lord said, "Go to London immediately." As it happened, I had twelve preaching engagements in the next two weeks. Never in the whole of my ministry at the Chapel had my calendar been so full. Normally I would only take one preaching engagement in the week, or two at the most. But the result was that Paul, Reed, and I drove all over southern England, and he was able to hear me preach a dozen times and decide for himself if he wanted to embrace my theology. He said, "I want to be a member of Westminster Chapel as much as I have wanted anything in my life."

When Paul first delivered a full sermon to the Chapel, he preached on prayer. All loved it. Then he gave us a prophetic word, one from the Old Testament (Isa. 58:7–11) and one from the New Testament (Rev. 3:7–11). I was amazed at the latter, as it was the very passage I had been given—that which gave assurance in advance that Paul's association with us would do us no damage. That Sunday morning and evening he gave out many words, which many still remember. During these days in March 1991, Paul spent an evening with our deacons and their wives, answering every single question they asked. I then called the whole church together for him to address everybody who was a member. The people became very fond of him. Less than a year later, I put his name before a church meeting. He was accepted unanimously. I had been a little nervous. I feared that someone would stand up and object. David Jermyn teasingly wrote me a note immediately after Paul was voted in: "Wherefore didst thou doubt?"

In October 1992, Paul and I held our first Word and Spirit Conference. It was at Wembley Conference Center and was sponsored by a group of eleven churches in north London called Beulah. Lyndon Bowring chaired the meetings. Graham Kendrick led the worship and introduced a hymn he wrote for us, "Jesus, Restore to Us Again," a marvelous piece of work that shows the need to bring the Word and the Spirit together. The meeting was attended by fourteen hundred church leaders. I preached a sermon on "Scripture and the Power of God" from Matthew 22:29, and Paul preached on the importance of the Word being the basis for any healing or prophetic ministry. Having been so seriously criticized by some people for his lack of education and solid theological background, I think Paul wanted to prove he was orthodox. It may or may not have been a wise choice. He and I each preached three times in one day, and it almost totally exhausted him. His prophetic gift hardly functioned at all.

I suspect that what has been remembered most from that conference was not Paul's ministry but my own address on Ishmael and Isaac. I spent thirty-five minutes unpacking what I briefly referred to earlier—that much in the twentieth century that has preceded was but "Ishmael," but "Isaac" is coming, and the impact will be as proportionally greater over the Charismatic movement as the promise of Isaac was over

Ishmael. People were all, generally speaking, stunned. A stony silence followed. Some felt it was an important statement, among these being Colin Dye, the new minister of Kensington Temple. I am grateful to Lynn Green of YWAM who came to the platform and asked the congregation to weigh this matter carefully.

My address at that conference ended up getting me into more trouble than any talk I have ever given—bar none. It infuriated a number of charismatic leaders. One man called for a conference to "sit in judgment" on what I had said. Evangelical noncharismatics were unhappy with my message because I had, after all, extolled the Charismatic movement to a great degree. I said that most churches in England worth their salt were charismatic, as were most of the good hymns and choruses being written. Three months later, I was to receive a letter that devastated me. The chairman of a well-known Bible convention wrote to cancel my giving the Bible readings scheduled for 1994, citing the reason as being my Word and Spirit address. He referred also to my relationship with Paul Cain. Thus Paul's influence on me did me no harm in my own church, but not so outside the Chapel! The dear brother who wrote explained that it was not an easy letter for him to write. He was gracious, for he is a godly man. He did what he believed he had to do. But I grieved for a long time that I would have to miss the privilege of preaching again at that convention.

Indeed, I have been licking my wounds for years as a result of my Ishmael/Isaac statement. It remains to be seen whether I got it right that night. But I actually preached this for many years before then, even sharing this idea with Dr. Lloyd-Jones before he died. I predicted the birth of Isaac and world revival. It is such a stupendous claim that I now blush to have said it, especially since it can't be proved. But neither am I sorry. Many felt I left my calling of being a Bible expositor and crossed over into Paul Cain's territory.

In March 1993, Paul gave a word to me privately and then—at my request—to our twelve deacons. His word was this: "Isaac will be an ugly baby. He will look like Ishmael. He will burp like Ishmael, need diapers changed like Ishmael, and will be messy. But as an ugly baby can turn into a beautiful child, so Isaac will turn out to be the most handsome person imaginable." I don't know how deeply the deacons were impressed or what they actually thought. But they all remember it, and it would serve to give enormous encouragement to them years later.

Not only did Paul not cause any division, but he actually united the Chapel at a time in which great crisis was averted. Jackie Pullinger gave an address to the Chapel in 1991, which went deep with us. She urged us to reach out to the poor. "So many churches want to reach students," she said, "but who will reach out to the poor?" We perhaps took it too seriously. Because of this, I allowed tramps and beggars of all shapes and sizes to come to the back halls to be seated and fed. But this was beginning to offend some of our families, who didn't want their children eating next to people smelling of urine and who were very dirty. Most of all, they never attended the services. They only came into the lunchtime period after the Sunday services and demanded to be fed. "You are not reaching the poor," Paul said to us. "You are reaching the professional beggar. They will destroy your expository ministry. Westminster Chapel is not called to be a rescue mission." That word saved us from a very big split—and came in the nick of time. I marvel at God's providence that Paul was on the premises at that exact time. It did a lot to open people up to prophetic ministry who had not been so sure of such.

One evening Paul and I were watching his favorite American program, *Columbo,* on television, when the phone rang. It was Benjamin Chan, ringing to see if we would like some of his mother's Chinese food the next day. "Yes," I said. I put the phone down and turned to Paul. Almost before I could speak, he began: "This couple had a son—William—now with the Lord. He died of a hole in the heart.

William—that doesn't sound very Chinese, does it, but they now have a son they call Wing Yung." I was amazed. Benjamin and Fong Hah Chan had hoped for a clear word by which they could know for sure that their son William was in heaven.

One of our members, Elizabeth Campbell, was converted the night T. W. Wilson, Billy Graham's personal assistant, preached for us. The same evening George Beverly Shea sang for us. But Elizabeth's husband, Sam, was not happy with his wife's conversion. Two years later he became seriously ill. Benjamin Chan went to the hospital to see him and led him to the Lord. Weeks later Elizabeth began to doubt whether her husband, Sam, was really saved since he was so ill and heavily drugged. In desperation she turned to a Bible on her table, and her eyes fell on the words "Samuel with the Lord." She told this to Louise, but added that she was doubting it all since she realized "it was a children's Bible and not a proper Bible." Louise tried to reassure her, but Elizabeth always doubted. The next time Paul spoke at the Chapel, knowing absolutely nothing of this story, he looked down at her and said, "Elizabeth"—and then gave her address—"it was at this address God spoke to you, but you are afraid it wasn't really the Lord. I can tell you it was the Lord." Elizabeth wept with joy. Had he not given the address of her apartment she wouldn't have been so persuaded. She does not doubt any longer that her husband, Sam, is in heaven.

In 1995, Paul preached a sermon on worship. It was one of those rare sermons I have heard in my life that have had the profoundest impact on me personally—and certainly the Chapel itself. He spoke of the "hydrological cycle" (I had never heard of this), moisture ascending upwards to form clouds that bring down the rain. He said that our worship and praise were like the moisture that forms clouds, and that if we wanted to see the blessing of God we must see the importance of worship. I was sobered but thrilled. Until that day I think that, if we are truly honest, we found worship rather boring if not unnecessary. People normally came to us because they want preaching and teaching—not worship. But that sermon changed us. Never would we be the same again. Our worship did not improve overnight, but we eventually gave it such focus and emphasis that we now give almost as much time to praise and worship as we do preaching. It all began with Paul Cain's sermon on worship.

When Paul Cain visited us in February 1995, he publicly endorsed the current move of the Spirit, which was being called the "Toronto Blessing" (the name coined by the *Sunday Telegraph*). However, the full blast of the Toronto Blessing had not come to the Chapel. I don't know why, but it didn't. But on February 20, 1995, while talking to Paul Cain and Louise in our family room, I heard the nearest to an audible voice I had known in nearly forty years: "The last shall be first." I also thought I knew what it meant: Westminster Chapel would be the last church in London to experience the Toronto Blessing, but somehow, eventually, we would actually be taking the lead in experiencing this strange phenomenon. The Toronto Blessing came to us on the night of October 22, 1995. I know that the measure of the Holy Spirit's power increased after Charles Carrin's visit to the Chapel in November 2000.

In February 1996, Paul and I held our second Word and Spirit Conference. This time it was held at the Chapel. We invited Dr. Jack Deere to join us, Dave Pope led the worship, and Lyndon Bowring chaired the meetings. It was the first time some had the privilege of hearing Jack. Many had read his books *Surprised by the Power of God* and *Surprised by the Voice of God*. He has a cessationist fundamentalist background, but he was taught to see that God also moves today through signs and wonders. His ministry was well received. The Chapel was filled from top to bottom.

That conference, however, was difficult for me. Only a few knew how the enemy was attacking. But the highlight of those two days for me was not from the ministry, strangely enough. It came from Ian Coffey, who traveled up from

Plymouth to be present at the conference. He came into the vestry on the second morning of the conference to pray with me. He could not have known how profoundly a part of his prayer affected me: "Lord, here is a man whom You have entrusted with Your Word." That was basically it. It was as if Michael the archangel had assured me that God was pleased with me. I have always wished I could operate more in the realm of the miraculous—like Paul and Jack. But Ian's prayer was so anointed by the Spirit that I somehow was able to accept my gift as it is and accept the limits of my own anointing.

Our third conference was called "Word, Spirit, and Power." This too was a highly successful one-day affair and was held on June 15, 2001. Paul Cain was present—but barely. He was quite unwell and just barely managed to speak at the evening service. We brought two new speakers who were well received—Jack Taylor and Charles Carrin. Graham Kendrick led the worship, and Lyndon chaired the meetings. Over fifteen hundred were registered even though we had but two months to prepare for it.

On the Saturday following the Word, Spirit, and Power Conference, Paul was feeling slightly better. He gave a brief greeting to a meeting in the Lloyd-Jones Hall that was open to Chapel members only. He took several questions, some of which pertained to the issue as to who would follow me after February 2002. Paul stressed—and repeated this to the congregation at the Sunday services—that the Chapel must not go back to the way it was. He endorsed the way God was at work in the Chapel.

What to me was perhaps most striking was that, by June 2001, the Chapel had moved so far from what it used to be that Paul Cain was now—truly—a comfort zone! Nobody would have dreamed in 1991 that ten years later this same Paul Cain—whose presence nearly scared everybody to death—would one day be a figure welcomed by nearly everybody. The most conservative people wanted to know, "What does Paul Cain say about what is going on in the Chapel now?" They literally wanted him back to see if he would regard the current move of the Spirit as being truly of God. He did.

In May 2000, I had shared a conference near Chattanooga, Tennessee, with Jack Taylor and Charles Carrin. In October 2000, I invited Charles Carrin to come to the Chapel. He possibly made the greatest lasting impact at the time—in terms of manifestations—of anybody we have ever had. Manifestations of falling and laughter came to be expected in our services, especially during the prayer ministry on the Sunday evenings. Charles's high Calvinistic background (he said he had once been an eight-point Calvinist!) together with his most extraordinary testimony of discovering the Holy Spirit through the laying on of hands by a Spirit-filled prisoner (whom he was supposed to be counseling) endeared him to us. But the manifestations, which continued, understandably made some people uneasy.

This is why they needed to know what Paul Cain thought. Thus the man who was once feared was now eagerly sought after by some of the most conservative people in the Chapel! It shows how we can move out of our comfort zone to the area of the scary and unknown, only to find that this too will one day become a comfort zone.

As I wrote these lines, I sensed the sweet presence of God in the Chapel, which was experienced mostly on Sundays, especially in the evening services that culminated in our time of prayer ministry. We were indeed the last church in London to embrace what was once called the Toronto Blessing. The "last" may indeed in some ways have became "first." It all started with Paul Cain. If I thought I had been brave in inviting Paul to the Chapel, I had no idea who else was just around the corner. For it was Paul Cain who made us open to one even more radical than he: Rodney Howard-Browne.

6

Rodney
Howard-Browne

He that believeth on me, as the scripture hath said,
out of his belly shall flow rivers of living water.
—JOHN 7:38, KJV

ON THE EVENING of May 31, 1994, Lyndon Bowring, who is executive chairman of CARE (Christian Action Research and Education), and Charlie Colchester, executive director of CARE and former churchwarden of Holy Trinity Church, Brompton (HTB), were sitting with me at a table in a Chinese restaurant in Soho, London. As we were waiting for our food to be served, Charlie spoke up. "Have you guys heard about this Toronto thing?"

Lyndon and I looked at each other quizzically. We hadn't.

Then Charlie continued, "Well, I don't know where to begin. The oddest thing has been happening at our church at HTB. People are falling on the floor and laughing—I've never seen anything like it in my life." He continued, "Last Sunday night we left the church at eleven o'clock with about fifty bodies on the floor. I hated to go home and leave them, but we had to leave. I've never seen anything like it. What do you all think of this?"

If you had put me under a lie detector and asked me if I believed this movement was of God, I would have had to say no. Lyndon and I looked at each other, and neither of us was very impressed. But Charlie was so full of it, and the way he put it to us left me thinking about it all evening. We left the restaurant to go and see the film *Schindler's List*, playing in Leicester Square. Then afterward we went to St. Ermin's Hotel and discussed the evening. I found myself thinking more about our conversation than I did the movie. I was really taken by what Charlie said but still did not believe it was of God.

For one thing, I didn't want to believe it was of God, because if God was going to do something great, He would have done it with us at Westminster Chapel first! After all, we had borne the heat of the day; we had paid the price; we had been out on the streets; we had witnessed to tramps, to beggars, to tourists, and anybody with whom we came in contact. Holy Trinity Brompton is up-market; they are largely posh and Anglo-Saxon. Here we were trying to reach *all* of London. If God was going to do *something*, it would not be in a church like HTB. So I reasoned.

In the meantime, I had just had three hundred cards printed up for our new Church Prayer Covenant. One of the petitions of our new Prayer Covenant that was to be introduced in just four or five days from then was, "We pray for the manifestation of the glory of God in our midst *along with an ever-increasing openness in us* to the manner in which You choose to manifest that glory."

I introduced this the following Sunday and explained the reason for this particular petition. Sometimes God turns up in strange ways. I knew a little bit of church history. I knew about the Cane Ridge Revival—how strange things happened there. I knew that people would fall, and sometimes they would laugh and do odd things. This happened again in the Great Awakening in Jonathan Edwards' day. It happened in Whitefield's day. It will be recalled that John Wesley criticized Whitefield for allowing this sort of thing to go on, but John Wesley eventually came to accept that you have to put up with these things. So I explained in unveiling this petition that we must allow for God's unusual ways, and then used, as an example, what was going on at HTB, but added, "I don't happen to believe this is of God, but we must be open to the sort of thing God can do." So I told everybody publicly that what was going on at HTB was not of God, and I was only trying to be honest.

A couple of days later a group of ministers were meeting on the premises of the Chapel. I went in to say hello to some of my friends, and there was Lyndon. He introduced me to Bob Cheeseman, who was pastor of a church near Richmond. This man had just got back from Toronto, and his face was aglow. I looked at him and said, "Tell me more about it."

He replied. "All I can tell you is, I've never felt Jesus so real in all my life. We just got back from vacation—usually I will take a novel on vacation, but this time I only wanted to read my Bible. I've never had anything like this happen to me in my life."

It was the glow on his face that impressed me most, and how he wanted to talk about Jesus that gave me pause. Then I turned to him. I said, "Look, would you like to come into the vestry and pray for me?"

He said, "Sure, I'd love to."

So I said, "Well, I'm going back into the vestry, and when you're finished out here, you come in and pray for me."

He said, "Great."

As I went back to the vestry, I remembered that a close friend of mine was coming for coffee. He was already there waiting for me. I explained to him that somebody who had just got back from Toronto was going to come in and pray for me in a few minutes. Then I said to my friend, "You've heard about this Toronto thing?"

He said, "No, what do you mean by that?"

I said, "You mean you haven't heard of this Toronto thing? People falling down and laughing and all this?"

"No," he said.

(But the following week the *Sunday Telegraph* gave this phenomenon the name "Toronto Blessing.")

I said, "Well, I don't think it's really of the Lord, but I have to say that this guy I just talked to was so full of joy and with a glow on his face that I have said to him that he could come in and pray for me."

He said, "No problem."

A few moments later Bob Cheeseman knocked on the door, and when he came in, he recognized my friend! They knew each other really well. I said to my friend, "Well, I didn't really know who this man was—I'm glad to see *you* know him!"

I said to Bob, "Explain to my friend what happened to you in Toronto." So he explained to him how he went there and was prayed for and blessed, how it changed his life, how it had spread into his church, and how he was just full of blessing.

I said, "Well, look, I want you to pray for me."

My friend spoke up. He had no conditioning for this sort of thing whatever—he is a Reformed Baptist preacher, well known in London and throughout England. He said to me, "Well, he can pray for me, too, if he likes."

I said, "Fine."

But as Bob began to pray there was a knock on the door, and it was Gerald Coates! Gerald was one of those ministers already present at the meeting on the premises and was simply calling into my vestry to say good-bye. I said to Gerald, "Bob is going to pray for me."

Gerald said, "Oh, I want in on this!" So Gerald came in, and now Bob and Gerald were going to pray for me, and just to be polite and courteous, my friend, who happened to be there, was going to let them pray for him.

They started praying. In less than a minute my close friend, who had no idea what was going on and had not even heard of this phenomenon until a few minutes before, fell forward, face down on the floor. There he was, before my eyes, flat out on the floor, head down—and I was sobered. I had never had anything sober me like that in years. He lay there for about ten minutes. Finally, he got up and I said, "What happened to you?"

He replied, "All I know is, I fell, and I couldn't stop it." He told me later that for about a week he felt an unusual sense of the presence of God, unlike anything he had known in years.

Next they began to pray for me—all three of them! Before they started praying, I took off my glasses because I thought I would be next on the floor! They prayed, but nothing really happened to me. It had happened to my friend instead, but that was the first real turning point in my thinking.

A few days later I got a phone call from Mr. Kenneth Costa, a merchant banker and the present churchwarden of Holy Trinity Brompton. He called me to see if I had any sermons on 1 John 4:1–3:

> Dear friends, do not believe every spirit, but test the spirits to see whether they are from God, because many false prophets have gone out into the world. This is how you can recognize the Spirit of God: Every spirit that acknowledges that Jesus Christ has come in the flesh is from God, but every spirit that does not acknowledge Jesus is not from God. This is the spirit of the antichrist, which you have heard is coming and even now is already in the world.

As it happened, I did have sermons on this passage, and he sent a courier across London to pick them up. In the meantime he asked if I would have lunch with him at the Savoy (no less!) the following Friday, because he wanted to discuss my sermons on this and get my opinion on what was going on in his church. He was slightly troubled by the manifestations, and he seemed to have some trust in me as a biblical theologian. The fact that he turned to me made me naturally appreciative of him, and the fact that he was concerned about a text like 1 John 4:1–3 told me that he had not lost his head!

I went to that lunch fully loaded and equipped to explain to him how he must be careful of all this. I was going to persuade him to distance himself from all of it, although I could not forget what had happened to my friend when he was unexpectedly prayed for and brought to the floor.

During that lunch, Ken Costa began to explain to me what was going on. He said that he himself had been touched. He told about having to address a group of men, and as he began to address them, he started laughing and could not stop himself. He'd never had anything like that happen in his life. He then expressed the need for sound doctrine, sound teaching, and good preaching.

He said, "RT, your day is coming because this sort of thing is going to need sound preaching to undergird it and to make it sound. So be ready—your day is coming!" That, of course, caused me to stop and think.

Before that luncheon was over, I had a strange feeling that I might have been on the wrong side of the issue from the moment I first heard of it. I remembered reading that in Jonathan Edwards' day there were those ministers—supposedly "sound"—who opposed Jonathan Edwards. I remembered that often the very ones who opposed what was going on in the Welsh Revival as well were sound and orthodox. I wondered if I was going to succeed those who opposed Jonathan Edwards and those who opposed Evan Roberts in 1904. I feared that I might be getting on the wrong side, all because of my pride and my anger that this sort of thing could happen at Holy Trinity Brompton and not at Westminster Chapel. I felt that God had betrayed me and let me down—that we indeed should be the ones to be blessed if God was going to do anything big in London. But it was obvious by this time that something was happening. Ken Costa is a man of integrity. I knew that he would not defend anything that was not truly of God and that he only wanted help.

So, then, it was Ken's sincerity, combined with my friend falling on the floor unexpectedly, that made me think that I was on the wrong side of the issue.

Later that afternoon I said to Louise, "I think I've been

wrong. I have a deep-seated fear that this thing is of God."

She said, "Well, I am interested to hear you say that."

I then said to her, "I believe I am going to have to change."

The following Sunday morning, June 19, 1994, after wrestling with this for a couple of days, I went into the pulpit and, before the morning prayer, reminded my people that I had, sadly, previously made the point that what was going on in various churches, especially Holy Trinity Brompton, was not of God. I said to them, "I'm afraid that I was wrong. Today I have to climb down. I believe that what is going on at HTB *is* of God." I reminded them of what I had said so many times over the years: "What if revival came to All Souls, Langham Place, or Kensington Temple, but not to Westminster Chapel? Would we affirm it?" They all knew this had been my theology, that revival might not come to us but might come elsewhere. Mind you, I always thought it would come to us. I never dreamed I'd really have to eat those words! But I realized now that God was doing something else-where, and He had bypassed Westminster Chapel—and by this time, I was beginning to be very, very scared that we could miss it entirely. I then became worried that it would not come to us, but I also worried that it would! I said to the people, "I believe something has happened that is of God; it is going on at Holy Trinity Brompton, and I would not blame anybody if they wanted to go there and investigate it." We then bowed our heads and prayed for Holy Trinity Brompton and Sandy Millar, their vicar. On that day I nailed my colors to the mast.

I learned later that there was a "pre-history" of the Toronto Blessing. Randy Clark had reportedly given this blessing to the Toronto Airport Christian Fellowship by the laying on of hands. People came from all over the world to John Arnott's church to be prayed for by John and his prayer ministry team, all of whom had been blessed by the ministry of laying on of hands. The Toronto Blessing, then, was trans-mitted by "carriers," namely those who had been prayed for by one who had also been prayed for, and so on. But Randy Clark, the carrier to Toronto, had been blessed and prayed for by a South African evangelist, now residing in America, whose name was Rodney Howard-Browne.

In December of that year, 1994, Colin Dye of Kensington Temple asked me if I would like to meet Rodney Howard-Browne. Now the only thing I knew for sure about Rodney Howard-Browne was what I'd seen of him on a famous video. Gerald Coates had invited Louise and me to his home back in July 1994. Elie Mumford was there that evening; she was responsible for bringing the Toronto Blessing to HTB through the laying on of hands. Her husband, John, is the pastor of a Vineyard church in London. So Louise; Gerald and his wife, Anona; Elie; and I watched this video of Rodney Howard-Browne that showed Rodney speaking in tongues and laying hands on people.

The people would start laughing, sometimes falling down. Things went on that were absolutely unusual, to say the least! This video later became "Exhibit A" for why the Toronto Blessing must be of the devil—because everybody said it was traced back to Rodney. But for some reason, I was not offended by it. As a matter of fact, I was even touched and edified by it and felt there was something in this that was very powerful and indeed of God, because God loves to offend our sophistication.

I never thought I would meet Rodney Howard-Browne, but when Colin Dye asked if I would like to meet him I said, "Yes, I'd love to." In the early morning of December 17, 1994, Lyndon Bowring and I headed for the hotel near the Wembley Conference Center—two years and two months from the time Paul Cain and I had our first Word and Spirit Conference together there. As it happened, we were in the same restaurant, only ten feet away from where I sat with Paul, Reed Grafke, and Lyndon when I went over my "Ishmael–Isaac" sermon in detail.

I ordered a full breakfast, and Rodney sat across from me

eating corn flakes. I noticed he kept staring at me while eating. Every time I looked up from my bacon and eggs, he was looking at me. But as the conversation continued, I was beginning to have what may have been an "epiphany" experience. The more he talked, the more I felt he was not just a man of God but one with an extraordinary anointing. I began thinking of several things. *I wish this man would pray for Louise; I wish I could get him to stand behind my pulpit and pray.* And for some reason, "Baby Isaac" kept coming into my mind. I couldn't shake it off. I also kept thinking about Paul Cain's word—if not a warning—that Isaac would be an "ugly baby."

I asked Rodney whether he could come to my church on the following Saturday morning and told him that I would be there to go out street witnessing. Colin turned to him and said, "You could take your children to see the changing of the guard at Buckingham Palace," giving Rodney further motivation to come. Rodney said that he would be there on Saturday morning and seemed to brush aside the opportunity to see the palace.

After that breakfast with Rodney, I asked him to pray for me. Nothing happened that I could feel. We then went into the auditorium to hear him preach. It seemed a bit strange to be sitting on the same platform where I delivered my "prophetic" statement about Ishmael and Isaac. Rodney asked me to address the crowd that morning, and I referred briefly to my talk in the same place, noting that *Isaac* meant "laughter." What I didn't realize then was that Rodney had seen his own ministry as largely unstopping old wells—the very thing that Isaac did almost more than anything else. (See Genesis 26:17–32.) As I spoke that morning, I briefly mentioned my prophecy about Isaac. I then returned to my seat on the platform. The place was filled with a most gentle, but continuous laughter. It was wonderful. I had never witnessed anything like it in my life. Rodney himself had done nothing to bring it about, as far as I could tell. All he did was lead worship and sing fairly well-known choruses such as, "Father, We Love You, We Worship and Adore You." While sitting on the platform, someone tried to pull me away to be interviewed. I replied that I would not leave that atmosphere for anything in the world. I have the videotape of the entire morning. Lyndon sat next to me on the platform. I saw power as I'd never seen. Lyndon whispered to me, "I have been a Pentecostal all my life, and I have never seen anything like this." I had a deep-seated feeling that I really was seeing the birth of Isaac or, at least, the embryonic phase of a powerful work of the Holy Spirit.

~

Louise's depression had not lifted since the day Paul Cain had told me how serious it really was. Parallel with this came a bad cough. It was horrible. It was an extension of the asthma I mentioned earlier. It had been going on as an acute cough for at least three years. On one occasion, she went to the casualty department at St. Thomas' Hospital for her eyes. The ophthalmologist who looked at her warned her that if she didn't stop coughing she could suffer a detached retina and that she was clearly close to it. She had been sent by our local general practitioner to the Brompton Hospital for tests, even at one stage staying in overnight. She had the top "cough expert." He said that 15 percent of coughs have no sure explanation and don't seem to be cured. Our summer trips to the Florida Keys, where the air is pure, did not stop her from coughing. At least four nights out of seven she would be up in the night coughing and would sit in our family room lest I too got no sleep.

On the morning of Saturday, December 17, 1994, there was a note from Louise on our kitchen table: "It is four o'clock, and I have just taken a sleeping pill." I was so disappointed. I was not going to wake her, as she didn't seem all that excited to be prayed for by a man she did not know. But to my surprise she was up at 9:30. "I want to be prayed for by that man," she said. She drank lots of coffee, and I managed to get her to the vestry by 10:40.

When we walked into the vestry, there sat Rodney Howard-Browne and his wife, Adonica; their three children; their babysitter; and Grant Gill, who was in charge of Rodney's European ministries.

"You didn't think I'd come, did you, Doc?"

I admitted I wasn't sure.

Rodney and Adonica stood up and gathered alongside Louise, who was still feeling as if she were in a comatose state. She was a very sick woman. There was no hype, no singing, not even worship that could cause a "hydrological cycle." Rodney and Adonica simply began praying. Adonica put her hands on Louise's chest; Rodney put his hands on her head. They prayed and they prayed—also in tongues. Approximately five minutes later they stopped praying.

Louise took a deep breath. No cough. She took another deep breath. No cough. "I haven't been able to do this for five years," she said. She took another breath. No cough. She was amazed. So was I. Rodney told her to stay in the vestry—alone—after the rest of us left.

I later took Rodney into the church and asked him to pray in the pulpit to an empty auditorium. He had brought a prayer—and read it! It was a prayer that came out of the Welsh Revival, and it is included in Louise's book *Great Christian Prayers*.

Before Rodney and Adonica departed he said to me, "Doc, I want your wife to spend some time with us in the States. I will pay for her to come. She needs three weeks vacation. I want her to be in our meeting for one week, then she can decide where she wants to spend the other two weeks. Will you let her?" We agreed to think about it. I said good-bye to my new friends Rodney and Adonica and went back into the vestry.

"Have you coughed yet?"

"No," she replied.

I went to my friend's home to work on my Sunday sermon but phoned her immediately. "Have you coughed?"

"No," she replied.

I waited another hour. "Have you coughed yet?"

No.

I phoned her every hour that afternoon. No cough. The next morning she woke up after uninterrupted sleep—the first time in at least three years. The same thing followed the next morning. The cough was gone. Gone!

Louise had been instantly healed, but not of the depression, though the absence of the cough was no small relief. We decided she should take up Rodney's offer to take three weeks vacation in the United States. She chose to spend the first week at Rodney's camp meeting in Lakeland, Florida. The second week would be with our son, TR, then living in the Florida Keys, and the third week would be with her mother in Idaho.

On the second night of being at one of Rodney's meetings, Louise phoned. She was so happy. "It is the greatest thing that has ever happened to me," she said. (I vowed not to take that comment too personally.) "It is the nearest you get to heaven without dying." The next night she phoned to ask me to pray that TR would come a day early before driving back to the Florida Keys. "I just want TR to get in this meeting," she said. So we prayed hard for this. Paul Cain had always said that TR needs to see "life after life," meaning that he is saved and needs to experience the supernatural. He has been spoon-fed fairly strong doctrine, but he must see how real God is, Paul thought.

Our prayer was answered. TR came a day early. But when he walked in and heard laughter all over the building and saw one lady standing as if she were the Statue of Liberty, ("The flakes you have with you always," Rodney says— "flakes" being an American expression that refers to people who are gullible and perhaps superficial), TR wanted to get out of that place. He agreed to stay until nine o'clock. But at eleven o'clock TR was on his feet, with hands in the air, worshiping. He was flabbergasted by the time the meeting was over—at one o'clock in the morning. He and his mother drove to the Keys in the middle of the night, arriving the next morning at daylight. Two lives were now changed.

Louise flew to Idaho, as planned. Her mother met her at the airport. "What happened to you?" her mother asked. "You look so happy and peaceful." It was the best testimony one could give to anybody who had not been brought up in an atmosphere of supernatural happenings.

Louise returned to London three weeks later and gave her testimony at the Chapel on the Sunday evening. I would have to say that Louise's testimony of being healed—and now set free of depression—did more than any other thing to prepare Westminster Chapel for the Toronto Blessing. All knew of her cough; some knew of her depression. But her obvious transformation softened some of the more traditional people in the Chapel. It shows the truth of Romans 8:28. Had Louise not been sick and then touched as she was, it is possible that the Toronto Blessing issue would have seriously split the Chapel in two, but it never did.

THE TRANSFER OF THE ANOINTING

On March 17, Benjamin Chan asked whether TR might want to return to England to work with him. Yes. On April 19, TR returned to England after four years in Florida. In a matter of days, he began calling old friends to come to his room in our apartment and watch videos of Rodney Howard-Browne. Eight to ten young people began coming every Thursday night. What a sound in the next room, hearing them singing and praying, the worship being led by Kieran Grogan. I almost had to pinch myself every Thursday that our son would be interested in things like this. In a word: these young people were hungry for more of God and developed an appetite to be more and more filled by the Spirit. I wondered, *What will this lead to?*

During the summer of 1995, Rodney, Adonica, and their children planned to spend some vacation time with us. I had casually mentioned this to Mike Bickle a few weeks before when he happened to come through London. "You," he said incredulously, "are spending time with Rodney Howard-Browne?" I explained how Louise had been powerfully touched. He thought that strange things indeed were happening if I would be linking up in any shape or form with someone like Rodney. All I knew was I wanted to be near anointed people.

Louise and I flew from Miami to New Orleans on August 15 to be with Bob and Diane Ferguson and to attend Rodney's meetings that were going on there. It was that evening that I told what I initially felt when I first met Rodney—about "Baby Isaac." Rodney had not known of this until then.

For the next two days Louise and I attended Rodney's meetings in New Orleans. I kept wishing for just one thing: if only I could bring one hundred of my people from Westminster Chapel and have them sit in those meetings. There is no way to describe it. Like that morning when I first heard Rodney at Wembley (I have watched the video of that service several times, and it does not do justice to the actual moment of being there), so too is the utter inability to explain what it was like: the laughter, the tears, the testimonies, the sweet presence of God, the absence of rushing to get the service over quickly, and Rodney's throwaway comments, some of which I jotted down:

- When you hook up with your heart, a lot comes out you hadn't planned to say.
- If you haven't struck oil after twenty minutes, do you stop drilling?
- If you object to people laughing while the world is going to hell, why don't you go out and save them?
- The price Jesus paid on the cross covers every area of my life; He wouldn't save me from hell and make me pay for it by living in hell all the way to heaven.
- The New Testament laying on of hands is not symbolic; it is the transfer of the anointing.
- Hard rain after a long drought causes holes, a shift of

earth. Blame the rain, blame the revival.

- You don't grab anointing with the mind but with the heart.
- Follow what you feel in your heart.
- The cleaner the reflector, the clearer the light.
- Once you have the power of God flowing in you, there is nothing else like it.
- Arrogance is being afraid you'll make a fool out of yourself—as when you pray and nothing happens.
- This generation will not be reached apart from the power of God.
- Do you think Moses would have had the same kind of results if all he had was a message?
- And, yes, the flakes you have with you always.

Rodney and the family did in fact visit us in Key Largo. I took him fishing to my favorite spots. While out on the water, I invited him to preach at Westminster Chapel when he would be in London the following December. I was anxious about it. We lost nobody as a result of Paul Cain's many visits, but I didn't have the same assurance about having Rodney. Never mind. I wanted him to come. His son, Kenneth, later joined us on the boat, and he caught a lot of little fish. I introduced Rodney to John Sutter and Harry Spear, the best two bonefish guides in the Keys, each of whom took Rodney fishing. Rodney is a natural sportsman and loves fishing.

But the high-water marks of his visit to us in Key Largo came unexpectedly. Rodney, Adonica, and their three children came to our house—that is, where we were staying (the home of Randy and Nancy Wall). Randy had prepared hamburgers on the grill, and while eating, I suggested to Rodney that he give his testimony. Randy is an architect and builder, an elder in his church but one brought up as a "cessationist" (the belief that miracles ceased after the closing of the canon of Scripture). I wasn't entirely sure how Randy and Nancy would respond to someone like Rodney.

But, as Rodney spoke, I could see a look of hunger on

Randy's face. I suggested that Rodney pray for Randy. He walked over to Randy, laid his hands on Randy's head. Randy bowed his head, and then his head lowered while his forehead touched the table. As Rodney continued to pray, Randy said, "My head is stuck. My head is stuck. It won't move. It is glued to this table. My head is stuck." He began laughing and laughing. All the children rushed from their rooms where they were playing to see whatever was going on. When Randy's head became unstuck, he threw his head back and laughed like a man set free from a long midnight of depression. I never saw anything like it. Rodney and his family went back to their hotel room, and Randy continued laughing nonstop for over an hour. Nancy and I literally had to help him to bed—he was too drunk (in the Spirit) to walk.

On October 15, 1995, Rodney preached for Gerald Coates in Leatherhead. A group of our young people, led by our son, TR, chose to hear Rodney that Sunday evening instead of me! But Louise and I rushed to Leatherhead as soon as our evening service was over. Arriving there about ten o'clock, we found Rodney preaching away. He saw me come in as I went to the front row and sat next to Gerald. Rodney soon called me to the platform and then suggested that all from Westminster Chapel come forward for prayer. There were fifteen of them. Over half of them fell to the floor, some laughing and rolling. Gerald whispered to me, "Why don't you have them give their testimony next Sunday night in Westminster Chapel?" I knew that was the right thing to do. Little did I know that Gerald's suggestion would be so pivotal for the direction of the Chapel. I am almost ashamed to admit that I would never have thought of doing this, but I am *so* glad Gerald suggested it.

The following Sunday evening, October 22, 1995, after I preached I asked those who were blessed by Rodney's ministry to come to the platform and give their testimonies. While some said, "Nothing happened to me," others were definitely touched. I then turned to the congregation and asked, "How many of you would like to be prayed for by these young people?" Many hands were raised. I suggested we use the church lounge for those who would come for prayer. I asked the deacons to join these young people in praying for people. It seemed that the entire church came back! It was the evening that truly broke the ice—call it Toronto Blessing or whatever, but it began in Westminster Chapel that evening. Not that there were a lot of manifestations of people falling or laughing (although there was some of this); the thing that mattered was that it began our ministry of praying for people with the laying on of hands. We never looked back.

In December 1995, Rodney paid his first visit to the Chapel. He came about four o'clock in the afternoon and spent about two hours with the deacons, answering their questions. After Janny Grein sang "Stronger Than Before" in the main service, I introduced Rodney as "Baby Isaac." He preached brilliantly for slightly over half an hour on why we need the Holy Spirit, from John 14. He then walked down from the pulpit to lay hands on people, and asked that those who wanted to be prayed for by him should come forward. Many did, meaning two hundred or more. The crowd was much the same as usual since I did not announce his visit in advance. What amazed me most was that those who fell to the floor laughing were people I would never have dreamed would do so. One was a banker. He was a quiet man, who had a very conservative and biblical background. But when Rodney prayed for him, just behind the pulpit, he fell to the floor and laughed uproariously for several minutes. He literally rolled back and forth on the floor behind the pulpit, laughing his head off. I could see for the first time how the name *holy roller* could be applied to some Pentecostals!

Another member, Tom Banks, a man in his late seventies, was not greatly impressed with the evening. And when his wife said she wanted to go forward for prayer, he was a little irked. But he then said, "Well, if you go up, I'll go, too."

When Rodney came to Tom, he prayed for him and then

asked, "What do you see?"

Tom replied in a most exhilarating voice and with considerable volume, "I see Him! Jesus! I see Him!" Tom did not fall down, but continued to stand and worship. The event turned him right around, and he was never the same again.

Sadly, not all felt as those people who were blessed. Paul Cain turned up a few days later. I asked, "Will we lose any?"

He replied, "You will lose a few, but they will be replaced with pure gold." We did lose a few; about twenty members resigned.

Rodney conducted services the following week in Olympia. The place was only half filled, and it was not Rodney's best week. I stood by him to the hilt and was seen as doing such. Not all took to Rodney as I did. And yet, this was another case in which I was privileged to meet him personally and privately before hearing him publicly. It always helps to know the person himself, and God graciously let me get to know both Paul Cain and Rodney Howard-Browne before I witnessed their public ministry. Those who have (understandably) reacted to such men in a less than positive manner did not have the privilege I had. It did indeed help me to understand those, especially journalists, who based all their comments on what they saw from afar.

I probably became Rodney's number one apologist. I felt I understood him and, in part, why God chooses people like him. He is guileless, unsophisticated, and a Pentecostal to his fingertips. I have had more than one quarrel with him—sometimes intense, largely over the issue of "prosperity" and "health-and-wealth" teaching. But when I consider how much excess baggage there is in me and how God uses me in spite of myself, I cannot be too surprised that God uses the Rodney Howard-Brownes of this world to awaken the church. It is just like Him to do it that way; God is, after all, the God of surprises.

~

PART THREE

A Preacher's Dream

*Be shepherds of
God's flock that is under
your care, serving as overseers—not
because you must, but because you are
willing, as God wants you to be; not
greedy for money, but eager to serve;
not lording it over those entrusted to
you, but being examples to the flock.
And when the Chief Shepherd
appears, you will receive the
crown of glory that will
never fade away.*
—1 PETER 5:2–4

7

Preaching
and Preparation

*If I knew I would have twenty-five
years left to live, I would spend twenty
of them in preparation.*
—C. H. SPURGEON

DR. LLOYD-JONES USED to say it was impossible for anyone to preach a bad sermon at Westminster Chapel. I only wish that this statement was true. It may have been true for him and all those he heard there. But I know what it is to feel such a struggle as I preached. I would look at the clock and think to myself, *Oh no, I've got another thirty minutes*—and prayed for the sermon to end. Perhaps the people were praying harder!

There are four possibilities in preaching when it comes to a feeling as to how you did:

1. To think you preached well, but nobody else thought so
2. To think you preached poorly, and everyone thought it was great
3. To preach poorly, and everyone agreed
4. To preach well, and everyone agreed

The fourth possibility is a most wonderful feeling. If only it happened all the time!

Our youth director, Paul Rogers, once asked me what was my favorite sermon that I preached at the Chapel. I knew the answer immediately; it was on Philippians 1:12, "Now I want you to know, brothers, that what has happened to me has really served to advance the gospel." The date was March 24, 1985. It was a time when I experienced possibly the greatest level of power and anointing in my twenty-five years at the Chapel. It was one of those times when I preached well, and I knew that all felt the same way. I even said it to myself when I sat down in the chair by the pulpit after the sermon: *This time I had unction.* The place was electric, and all were talking about it.

An hour later Graham Paddon had to tell me that the sermon was not recorded. The man responsible for taping neglected to tell anybody that he couldn't be present, and it, therefore, wasn't recorded. I was amazed that God let that happen! But He did, for some reason. David Jermyn suggested that I preach this sermon two weeks later when I would be preaching in Bromley, so I did. But it wasn't even close to the anointing I had in the Chapel.

One problem I have always faced when I preach at the Chapel is the unexcited look on most of the faces that make up a typical congregation. Sometimes it is awful! I think that in a smaller building one might get people to smile more easily or look more pleasant. The faces are so often expressionless—even with the regulars in the congregation, including my best supporters! There was one exception, years ago—Harold Wiles, a man who became a deacon in my era before God took him suddenly to heaven. His face was always radiant. I think if people knew how much their facial expressions affected the preacher they would try harder! The truth is, Dr. Lloyd-Jones said he faced the same thing at the Chapel but attributed it to the English. He said it was altogether different in Wales!

What was even harder for me was how each Sunday was almost like preaching for the first time. If we had an unusually good day, I would go home on Sunday night thinking, *I can't wait until next Sunday.* But when the following Sunday finally arrived, I would have an almost entirely different congregation—tourists, new students, and the ever-changing population and transience of central London. One hardly gets used to it, people moving into and leaving London all the time. It is painful having to say good-bye to people you become attached to.

The architecture of the Chapel, especially the high pulpit that Campbell Morgan designed, certainly makes one want to preach well. But the temptation to take myself too seriously is somewhat diminished when I see over a thousand empty seats as I stand up to lead worship.

American churches often have worship leaders, but I have kept up the British tradition in that generally I conduct the entire service, especially in the mornings. We sing at least two old hymns each Sunday morning and bring in some modern songs as well. Our evening services used to be like the morning ones, but have become more informal in recent years. Our worship leader, Kieran Grogan, uses mostly modern songs but occasionally (to the delight of many) throws in an older hymn.

One problem the minister at the Chapel faces, if he goes back to the vestry after the service and waits for the people to come to him, is that he gets virtually no feedback as to how the sermon went down. For those ministers who go to the door and shake hands with the worshipers as they leave, there is frequently positive feedback: "Thank you for your word," "That was wonderful," "You were speaking straight to me," and the like. This way the minister can go home and put his feet up and feel fairly well in himself.

But not at the Chapel. The "law of the Medes and Persians" says the minister must go back to the vestry. I certainly did this for well over twenty years. Once our prayer ministry took off after the evening preaching, I began to stay in the church and be available there. But I stayed in the vestry after the morning services. The result was people would come in with their personal problems, and they usually beared no connection to what I had just preached. It can be hard for an insecure preacher who would love, say, just a little compliment or two after preaching his heart out. But don't count on it if you preach at the Chapel!

John Calvin said he would as soon go to the pulpit undressed as unprepared. Perhaps what Dr. Lloyd-Jones meant by it being impossible to preach a bad sermon at Westminster Chapel was that one certainly dare not enter the pulpit unprepared. I never did—ever. I was always prepared. Only twice that I know of did I repeat an old sermon and, yes, I was found out! The congregations come there largely for the expository preaching, and those who do so regularly want it fresh and nicely served. It puts a good deal of pressure on a man who comes from the hills of Kentucky, where a good sermon was often seen as when the preacher neither used notes nor did any preparation but only let his preaching rip!

One day Alex Buchanan came to see me at our house. He reckoned I'd have more power if I threw away my notes and just spoke as the Holy Spirit guided me. I was in pursuit of a greater anointing, so I knew I had to take Alex seriously. I thought I'd try it on Sunday nights. We were working our way through the Gospel of John, as it happened, and my first attempt to preach without any notes was on October 6, 1991. It went OK, so I tried it the following week. I kept it up for a whole year. But when I admitted to the deacons that the pressure was enormous when I stepped up to the pulpit without any notes, Mr. Paul Cowan, our Chapel patriarch as I called him, said, "Why do you put yourself under this strain? Surely this isn't right." I was set free. The following Sunday— October 11, 1992—I went to the pulpit with notes. Three people came forward that evening, which I took as a sign of God's approval that I should use notes as before.

But I have never been sorry that I tried it for a year. I probably preached as well; most people didn't know I had no notes, nor could they tell any difference when I returned to using them. And yet I know exactly what Alex meant. I knew I should lean on the Lord wholly and trust the Spirit. My Kentucky background also made me more open to Alex's suggestion. But there is one thing Alex said to me that I value more than a thousand words from many people: "We need to communicate God as well as His Word." This shook me to my fingertips, and I have prayed daily since then that I would do precisely that when I preach. When I wrote *The Sensitivity of the Spirit,* I felt there was perhaps only one person in Britain who would really understand that book. But I turned to Lyndon Bowring to see whom I should invite to write the foreword. We both agreed: Alex Buchanan.

Dr. Lloyd-Jones used to say to me that he could "hardly remember ever preaching there [at the Chapel]" though he was there for thirty years. And yet I can say the same thing after twenty-five years at the Chapel. It is like a dream that seems too awesome to be true. Who am I that I should be in a place like that? I used to say between Sundays that "next Sunday I will try to enjoy the pulpit experience," but that was not possible. That does not mean that I was unhappy, because it was the happiest experience imaginable—for me at least. I never had the presence of mind to focus on *where* I was preaching, but rather my focus was on *what* I was preaching. Before I knew it—usually—my time was up, and I would bring the sermon to a close.

My Sunday morning sermon normally lasted forty minutes. The evening sermon was somewhat over thirty. Dr. Lloyd-Jones preached for nearly an hour on Sunday nights. I tried this at first but came to the realization that I am not Dr. Lloyd-Jones. It hurt my pride to cut down to forty minutes on Sunday nights, even more so to thirty-five—and finally to nearly thirty! But I knew in my heart of hearts what I had to do. Not all would agree, and it may also be said that the amount of time I would take had virtually no connection as to how many people came. So I might have stuck to my guns and preached for an hour on Sunday nights. But my motive would have been to show I am doing what the Doctor did—which would be the wrong way to look at things.

Our Thursday lunchtime services by and large have been repeat sermons, and they would last about twenty minutes. The School of Theology lectures on Fridays were in two parts: forty minutes for the first half and about thirty for the second. The people kept coming despite the rather long evening. I would always quit in time for ten minutes of questions on Friday nights. For some this was the best part of the evening.

I have been conscious of many people praying for me over those twenty-five years. One gets a sense of being borne "on eagle's wings." All over Britain, I had total strangers say to me, "I pray for you every day," or "I pray for you every Saturday evening—or Sunday morning." This was almost overwhelming. I sensed a sovereign overruling of grace and prayer more times than I can count, which enabled me to prepare and preach sermons. I attribute this to the prayers of God's people. I miss this, but I can tell my successor that he will have this prayer support too, I am sure.

My weakest preaching has been at Easter and Christmas. I am fairly at home when working through a book. But when I am forced to preach on the resurrection or the birth of Jesus I am in difficulty, especially when I don't want to say what I've already said at least once. I once chose one School of Theology lesson to explain the meaning of Palm Sunday and decided to use the contents of no fewer than twenty-two sermons based on Christ's entry into Jerusalem. There is a lot left that I haven't touched on in this marvelous event, but if I had to preach one more fresh sermon on Palm Sunday I think I would be in trouble! The same is largely true with Easter and Christmas. I reckon I have preached fifty sermons on the resurrection of Jesus and a hundred that pertain to Christmas.

To my chagrin, there is one series I never finished: the Gospel of John. I always intended to return to it before I left. What happened was this. I was halfway through the seventh chapter of John and noted that, in a few weeks, I would shortly be at John 7:38, which says, "Whoever believes in me, as the Scripture has said, streams of living water will flow from within him." I felt ill-prepared to preach on that verse—and still feel the same way. When we reached John 7:24, I felt it was a good place to stop for a while. I had hoped that the Holy Spirit would enable me to more fully to understand and experience John 7:38 for myself, and then (but only then) would I continue preaching through the Gospel of John. The truth is, I never made it back to John.

I may have made a mistake by not pressing on. In all other cases, as in the Book of James, God always came to my rescue when I reached a particular verse I feared. This may well have happened yet again, but there were two reasons for not proceeding. The first was that I wanted to experience a fresh refilling of the Holy Spirit myself before preaching on that verse. Not that I didn't understand it or had not personally experienced this years before. It is only that I wanted an absolutely fresh renewal of the Spirit in my own heart. I didn't want to preach this verse based on my knowledge of an old experience. The second reason was that I had struggled with the Gospel of John almost from the beginning. I take comfort from one evangelical scholar's observation that "every preacher who preaches through John has an uneasy feeling when it is over that he didn't really understand it." That certainly was my continuous feeling, and I hoped for a breakthrough that I never got. But at the same time, we had some wonderful times in John.

I always wanted to preach on Job—that is, the whole book. I thought I understood it, but feared I would take too long and make the mistake Joseph Caryl made in the mid-seventeenth century. He preached for fifty years on this book, beginning with a congregation of several thousand and ending with a congregation of fifty! My weakness would have been to do that too, so I never began it. Since I preached on the life of Joseph, then Jacob, I used to think I would keep working backwards and deal with Isaac and finally with Abraham! But that was also an aspiration I was not to realize.

It is impossible to know for sure, but I have thought that my best preaching was near the end of my ministry at the Chapel, especially on those mornings when I preached for two years on the Sermon on the Mount and in my final year on the parables of Jesus. I can only go by how exciting it was for me personally. To me, my best preaching was mainly on Sunday mornings. For reasons I cannot fully understand, I never felt I did well on Sunday evenings, although my books on Joseph, Jacob, and David were based on Sunday evening sermons. I only know that I never felt as comfortable with my Sunday evening preaching.

I miss preparing sermons most of all. Before retiring, I would wonder what it would be like in my retirement years when I did not have the challenge of preparing new sermons. I feared I would resort to old ones when I traveled around the United States, since these sermons would be new to the people there. I hope and pray that God would prohibit me from resorting entirely to old stuff but challenge me to keep digging.

One great mistake I made after being at the Chapel a while was to write a book rather than preach a sermon. What happened was that I began to notice that so much of what I preached would likely go eventually into print. So I said to myself, *If I get it right the first time I preach, I won't have to take so long editing the material.* This was bad to do. I learned that I had to put the people and the preaching event first and utterly forget about books being published. And yet I have to say that my sermons, when first typed unedited from a tape recorder, would not win many Nobel prizes for literature. Reading them unedited is very embarrassing.

I decided to put the anointing first, not the content of good style or grammar. I have wished for the manifestation of God's glory on my very preaching more than anything else. I have hoped that the glory would come down in the middle of a sermon, and that either I would completely forget my prepared notes or that the Holy Spirit would utterly take over and keep me from preaching, as when the priests in the Old Testament could not perform their service "because of the cloud" (1 Kings 8:11). But it just didn't happen. My preaching has been only a pursuit of that glory. For what I wanted could not be "worked up." I wanted the real thing or nothing.

It was a privilege to preach in Westminster Chapel. I preached in that awesome place over twenty-five hundred times. As I would sit in the vestry with the portraits of G. Campbell Morgan and Martyn Lloyd-Jones looking down at me, I would pinch myself just to make sure I was still there. My survival, given my temperament and ability, is a miracle to me. I say candidly and with transparent honesty that I am so unworthy to have been given this privilege.

Sunday evening services were always more simple and quite evangelistic. That was a major adjustment for me to make because in America, Sunday-night congregations are usually smaller, and many churches have no evening service at all. In America, those people who do attend Sunday night services are perhaps the most dedicated Christians. Dr. Lloyd-Jones made Sunday evenings at the Chapel evangelistic, and I did my best to continue it during my twenty-five years at the Chapel.

But I cannot say we had a lot of success insofar as seeing many lost people saved. A few, yes, but not a lot. I have racked my brain and searched my heart to understand why we have not had more conversions. When I was seventeen, I was asked to sit in the chair at the desk of the vice president of the United States. "Make a wish," they said to me. Others may have prayed for high political office, but I remember bowing my head and saying, "Lord, make me a great soulwinner." I have hoped God heard that prayer, but there is not much evidence of it as far as I can see. I have seen more people come to the Lord from personal one-on-one ministry than from my pulpit ministry.

I often wondered what it would be like to preach to a filled church. I thought (perhaps wrongly) that I would preach better if there were more people in the congregation.

It is very hard to preach to three hundred people in an auditorium that seats at least five times that many. Dave Pope used to caution me, "Preach to those who are there and stop worrying about who isn't there." I am sure he was absolutely right. When I preached in other parts of the United Kingdom whether at Spring Harvest, Easter People, or individual churches, the places were usually filled. But then I would come back to my own church and face the hard reality that I could not have everything!

Speaking in other places was easier than speaking in the Chapel because I was speaking to a different crowd of people who had not heard my old stories or jokes. My deacons would joke about all my stories, which they heard again and again. But speaking four times every week—year in and year out—in the same place to the same people, I couldn't repeat those anecdotes too often.

~

Toward the end of 1985, it became apparent that we would be staying in London for a fairly long while. We began to realize London was now truly home.

Graham Paddon, one of our deacons and chairman of the building committee, asked Louise and me if we still had a desire to live in central London, which we did. We had moved to Ealing to be near Dr. Lloyd-Jones, but we always fantasized about how wonderful it would be to live in the heart of London. "He who is tired of London is tired of life," as Dr. Johnson would say. Graham knew that it would take a lot of money to remodel our house in Ealing and that by selling it, the church could purchase a house in town for us. We were thrilled at the idea. We looked at many properties and settled on some, only to be "gazumped" time after time.

When we saw the house in Ashley Gardens it seemed too good to be true. The owner recognized me. She had attended Westminster Chapel during Arthur Blessitt's visit. She was a member of All Souls, Langham Place. She saw how much we loved the place and gave us her word that we could have it at the agreed price—and would allow *no one* to gazump us. We moved in on December 15, 1986. Lyndon Bowring was at our door only minutes after our arrival and was the first to sign our guest book. We had met Lyndon and Celia Bowring a couple of years before and got to know them better at Spring Harvest.

HIRAM CYRUS

One evening there was a message on our answering machine. The voice had a hick Kentucky accent if I ever heard one: "This is Hiram Cyrus of Cincinnati, Ohio…" I kept playing the tape. Our phone number was unlisted, and we couldn't figure out who in the United States got this number, and whoever was Hiram Cyrus? We listened to the tape again. Suddenly I twigged. "That's Lyndon," I said. We kept the tape as a thing to be remembered for a long time.

Lyndon knew I liked to study away from home and away from the vestry. He showed me a place near the former CARE office in Mayfair. He called it a "bolt hole," and we saw each other almost daily in those days. That place became known as Hiram Cyrus—a code name that only a handful of friends understood. It is a fifteen-minute walk from the Chapel through Green Park. It was perfect for what I needed, away from phones and interruptions. I needed to find a place where nobody could reach me or disturb me. I reckon I have prepared—by conservative estimate—no fewer than a thousand sermons at Hiram Cyrus. I had a special place, barely out of sight of other people who frequented there, but nobody, as far as I know, had a clue who I was or exactly what I was doing (preparing sermons).

SERMON PREPARATION

When I told Richard Bewes I was writing this book, he kindly suggested that I take space to share how I prepare my sermons. The truth is, the way I prepare is so unspectacular that I am reluctant to go into it. Every preacher has his own way of preparing a sermon, and my own style has developed little over the years. The only major change is that I have reverted to my original manner of using alliteration. When I first began preaching while a student at Trevecca Nazarene College, Dr. T. M. Anderson, a teacher and preacher from Asbury College in Wilmore, Kentucky, profoundly influenced me. He used alliteration all the time. For some reason this caught on with me, and I kept it up to a great extent until I arrived at Westminster in 1977. When Dr. Lloyd-Jones so graciously made himself available to me, I listened carefully to him and accepted his wisdom. He loathed alliteration, almost scoffed at it, so I gave it up. But I found myself using it again in the mid-1980s.

The purpose of alliteration is, supposedly, to help the listener to focus on the main points, each of which begins with the same letter. Sometimes I use double alliteration. The trouble is, one can get into bondage and make too much of the "wisdom of words" that Paul warned against. (See 1 Corinthians 1:17, KJV.) I therefore have made it a practice to make them not too contrived so that it does not divert the listener from the impact of the Holy Spirit's message. But when the alliteration comes naturally and easily and without much work, I have taken it to mean that God would use it for His glory.

The first thing I do, however, once I have determined from which verse I will preach is to translate it in the Greek. Once I do that, I do some research on the more difficult or interesting words. I would not be without Kittel's *Theological Dictionary of the New Testament*, for here one can see not only the meaning of a word but trace its usage in the Old Testament and in ancient Hellenistic literature. When I know I am going to work at Hiram Cyrus, I photocopy the relevant material and also certain commentaries. Seldom do I turn to a commentary before I have compiled thoughts of my own. If you read a commentary before doing any original thinking for yourself, you will almost certainly use that commentary and, thus, repeat what has already been said. It seems to me that there ought to be pulpits in the land where people can receive fresh insight from the preacher rather than second-hand information that is already available to all.

Having translated the verse, then, I devote myself to writing down whatever comes into my mind as I meditate on it. I come to the verse with the total conviction that this word is infallibly inspired by the Holy Spirit. Not necessarily the translation, of course, but the original. If I did not believe that the Scriptures were fully and infallibly inspired by the Holy Spirit, I would *never* have sufficient motivation to get to the bottom of the meaning of a verse, especially if it is difficult. But because I *do* believe I am examining God's inerrant Word, I know that the Holy Spirit will help me to find the meaning—if I am on good terms with the Spirit.

I can never forget one day when I had a quarrel with my wife and then turned to my preparation. On that particular day I got nowhere—I mean *nowhere*—until I apologized to Louise. When I returned to the Bible with pen and paper in hand, the thoughts poured out faster than I could write them down. Had I been dependent on other people's sermons or commentaries, I may have managed to prepare the sermon that day, but my method is to experience the anointing as much in my preparation as I do in my actual preaching. For this reason, I am "dead" if there is anger or bitterness in my heart when I expect to get any insights.

After I have written a page or two of thoughts, I try to discern whether there is a coherent theme, and from this I will come up with a sermon title. Then I look for at least three main ideas from the text. As I write down these thoughts, what usually happens is that two or three words beginning with the same letter naturally stand out. If there are two words that begin with the same letter, I take it to mean that I should expect to find the third word. The sub-headings follow, and they too are frequently alliterated. This technique has come easily for me. No doubt I have made a lot of mistakes and caused the audience to listen to an alliterated outline at times somewhat cynically. Hopefully not too often, since the anointing is what matters. Obtrusive alliteration could easily quench the Spirit for some people.

I tend to turn to commentaries, then, for two reasons: when I am stumped and am getting nowhere, and to be sure my insights are not too far off the mark. When I find that the commentator has already made much the same observation, it makes me feel fairly safe. But if I am persuaded that the Spirit has shown me something, even if no commentator has said it, I follow what I believe to be the Holy Spirit. John F. Kennedy is quoted as saying that it is immoral to abandon your own judgment. "To thine own self be true," said Polonius to Laertes in Shakespeare's *Hamlet,* and I have sought to follow these principles, even if they were not given by theologians!

Sometimes I read commentaries from my favorite commentators: Don Carson, F. F. Bruce, Michael Eaton, Wayne Grudem, Gordon Fee, and, of course, the commentaries of John Calvin. It is sometimes hard to find a commentary where the meaning is made clear immediately. It can be painful to read a sermon or commentary that takes too long to interpret its meaning. I don't always agree with the commentaries I use, but I always feel blessed if I can have a commentary by Don Carson or Michael Eaton at my side. I would photocopy the comments on a few pages so that I could carry them and my Bible in my briefcase to Hiram Cyrus.

I have followed Dr. Lloyd-Jones's practice of working through a book in the Bible. If it is a New Testament book, I will treat each verse almost microscopically so that I miss nothing—if possible. For this reason a series can take a while. We took a year in Hebrews 11, a year in Jude, two years in James, two years in 1 John, two years in Philippians, five years in 1 Corinthians, four years in 2 Corinthians, two years in the Sermon on the Mount, and ten years in Hebrews (on Friday evenings). When I treat an Old Testament passage, I will deal with several verses at a time, in far less detail. Most Old Testament preaching (Jonah being an exception) has taken place on Sunday evenings, and such included the lives of Jacob, Joseph, David, Elijah, and the Book of Malachi.

Some of my sermon series have become books. Most of these were originally prepared at Hiram Cyrus or in a special friend's house overlooking the Thames River. I have not spent so much time at home or in the vestry to prepare sermons because of too many interruptions. When Lyndon first introduced me to Hiram Cyrus, I could not have known what a blessing it would be to me.

A lot of unexpected fun happened there as well. A few famous people have discovered my "bolt-hole." There I met Alexander Solzhenitsyn, Lauren Bacall, Bea Arthur (of *The Golden Girls*), and other well-known people. Usually I leave these people alone—as I myself would want—but occasionally I have spoken to a few of them.

One afternoon—November 26, 1996—Lyndon and I stopped by Hiram Cyrus for a cup of tea. As we waited for Clive Calver to join us I said, "Lyndon, look!" Ten feet away from us was a familiar face.

"That's not who you think it is," Lyndon replied.

I said, "It is."

"No, it can't be," Lyndon insisted.

I could take it no longer. Being an American does have some advantages, so I walked over, very respectfully, and asked, "Are...you...who...I think you are?"

He stood and flashed a big smile. "Yes. I'm Hussein." It was King Hussein of Jordan.

I looked at him and said, "Your Majesty, you and I are the exact same age. All my life I've grown up being aware of you. I've always thought that I would meet you one day, and now I can't believe I'm standing here talking to you." He seemed pleased that I came over to him and agreed to give me his autograph.

I hurried over to where Lyndon and I were sitting. "Boy, were you ever wrong!" I rubbed it in. "But I can't find any paper. All I have is my Bible. I can't let him sign my Bible—he's a Muslim."

"Go on," said Lyndon.

So I took my Bible to the king. I explained that I am a Christian minister and that Billy Graham had signed my Bible. After he signed his name in English and Arabic and wrote the date, I said, "Sir, you are the only man in the world who is loved in the West and loved in the East. Remember that Jesus said, 'Woe unto you when all men speak well of you!'" He threw his head back in laughter, showing he had a good sense of humor. Then Clive came, and I had the privilege of introducing him to both Clive and Lyndon.

This special hideaway in the center of London became a meeting point for some of my friends. Robert Amess, whom I met in Ipswich in 1983, became the pastor of the Duke Street Baptist Church in Richmond in 1986. Harry Kilbride predicted that Robert would replace himself as my best friend. (A true friend is someone who knows all about you but still likes you!) My amazement about Robert, however, is that he bears with me at all, because he is so English. He calls himself "the complete loner" because he loves his solitude. But he has shared many hours with me over the past fifteen years, some of them at Hiram Cyrus.

A true friend is also one who will speak the truth to you. I used to search high and low for an answer to a question that had puzzled me: Why did I feel a bit of coolness from some of the reformed evangelical ministers? They used to invite me to preach in their churches, but no more. Why? I assumed it was my theology or the kind of people I would invite to preach at the Chapel. But I knew it had to be more than that. So Robert carefully and lovingly explained it to me, since he comes from their "stable," as he puts it. In his opinion, I was perceived as having taken the Chapel away from them. Had I been anywhere else and held to the exact same views or even invited controversial people, I would very possibly not have been treated like this. But to invite controversy and hold on to my views at Westminster Chapel was seen as somewhat offensive. They felt the Chapel was sacrosanct and in a very real sense theirs, and I had to understand their point of view. It helped me to grasp what was most painful to me, and I could see myself feeling exactly as they did had I been in their situation. I continue to love and admire these men and thank God for them, especially when they stay in touch, such as Dr. Ken Brownell has done.

Lyndon Bowring, too, was just as candid with me on matters he alone would have the wisdom and courage to address. My preaching at Spring Harvest has been acceptable over the years largely because Lyndon knew the kind of people to whom I would be preaching. He has spent many hours at Hiram Cyrus listening to my proposed sermons, only to help me to be simpler, more relevant, and to throw in illustrations.

I will never forget sharing with Lyndon my notes that I prepared for Keswick. I decided to preach on the life of Jacob. As I read my notes, I began to weep, and he too began to be moved. We both knew that God was going to use me in that lovely place, and Lyndon's suggestions made my notes much better than they would have been without his input. He is also good at coming up with great sermon titles such as: "Fatal Attraction" (2 Sam. 13); "Going for the Gold" (Phil. 4:14); and "Overcoming Impossible Odds" (Phil. 4:13)—all sermons I preached at the Chapel.

No one will ever know how Lyndon has wept with me and rejoiced with me over the years at Hiram Cyrus. I have come into that place at times so low that, had he not shown up, I could not have coped, humanly speaking. He is one of the most unusual people I've ever known. He has extraordinary shrewdness and an amazing ability to listen. When it comes to chairing a public meeting, as Robert Amess says, he never puts a foot wrong.

It is because of Lyndon that I met Rob Parsons. I was coming out of Hiram one afternoon, and there were Lyndon and Rob, walking on Down Street. Lyndon introduced me to Rob, who had just been reading *Once Saved, Always Saved*. I was almost overwhelmed. But that was only the beginning of a relationship that would eventually be more valuable than gold. He became a friend beyond my wildest dreams. What Lyndon would do with my sermons, Rob did with my writing. Rob is one of Britain's top authors and has graced me with a lot of time in reading my manuscripts. His influence and ingenious comments and criticisms have been incalculable. Books like *The Anointing, Thorn in the Flesh, Sensitivity of the Spirit,* and *Total Forgiveness* have his "fingerprints" all over them. I find it painful to think how impoverished my writing ministry would be apart from Rob's input. Somerset Maugham once said that when people ask for criticism they really want praise. True. But Rob has given me *exactly* what I needed countless times.

"A friend loves at all times" (Prov. 17:17). God was singularly good to me while in London by giving me most unusual friends. When doors were being closed, He sent Clive Calver, also a frequent visitor at Hiram Cyrus. When I needed someone to weep or rejoice with me, He gave me Robert Amess, Lyndon Bowring, and Rob Parsons. Paul said, "Rejoice with those who rejoice; mourn with those who mourn" (Rom. 12:15). It is easier to find people who will weep with you than people who will rejoice with you, but Clive, Robert, Lyndon, and Rob have done both—many, many times. We have prayed together, laughed together, wept together, and held one another accountable. Only God knows what these four men have meant to me and my ministry. Westminster Chapel could not know what a debt they owe to these men. I can only thank God that He sent them to me when I was so very, very lonely.

One day Rob turned up at Hiram when I was feeling lonely and hurt. He shared a wonderful story with me out of his own experience. He recalled that one morning he was feeling lonely and hurt when his friend David Pawson knocked on his door. David told him that criticism was indeed hurtful. He recalled a time when he himself had cried out to God, "Lord, these rumors are hurtful." He then felt God say to him, "Well, David, they are not as bad as the truth. And I know the truth, and I still love you." What a powerful word.

Earlier I referred to 1984 as a year that will live in infamy. But 1993 was even worse on us emotionally in some ways. Like Louise, I too was battling depression. Prior to Louise's healing touch from God through Rodney Howard-Browne, Louise's depression was worsening, and I could do little to help her. In 1993, she decided to visit her mother in Idaho. A week or so later after she left, I too became very depressed—February 26 to be exact. I wrote in my journal, "I do believe I am the most depressed of any time in my whole life."

I cried out to God in desperation. I remembered how Jackie Pullinger told me she prayed in tongues for fifteen minutes every day "by the clock" but felt nothing at the time. She also insisted that I could surely speak in tongues again since I had done so once before—although only once—in 1956. My own rationale was that if God wanted me to speak in tongues, He could do it again as He had done it before. So I always resisted the urge to do anything that would appear as if I were trying to make it happen.

But that day I was so dejected that I decided I would try to speak in tongues after all. Had I not been at a rock bottom point in my life, I would never have entertained such a thought. Dave Pope once pointed out that when we hit "rock bottom" we touch the "Rock." I began praying in tongues. It was hard. I wasn't enjoying it. It seemed utterly and totally of the flesh, but I was so low I kept it up.

Suddenly a verse in Isaiah—the chapter and verse—came to my mind. I turned to it to see what it said. I was floored. The verse was truly from God, for it described all that was wrong with me. God had reached out to me when I thought He was nowhere near me. It was a major turning point for me. Things did not dramatically improve overnight, but I was soon to witness the sweetest sense of God I had known since October 31, 1955. The joy was indescribable. I have been speaking in tongues ever since. It began with my making an effort, and it led me to effortless peace and joy. I never looked back. Had it not been for Louise's depression, I would not have been open to doing what—in fact—I had to do.

One day Robert Amess came to see me and boldly pronounced, "I have a word from the Lord for you." Now Robert isn't the type to say that sort of thing very often, so he definitely had my attention. He said, "I know what your next preaching series should be."

I replied, "Go on. Tell me."

He said, "The Psalms of Ascents" (Psalms 120–134). The truth is, I did indeed need to know what to do next as I was just finishing the current series on Acts. He made me laugh when he added that anybody who preaches on the seven churches in Revelation (which it had crossed my mind to do) is in truly bad shape and desperate for a series! The more we talked, the more I was convinced that this word from God was indeed for me. The Psalms of Assent was a good series that I began a week or two later. When these sermons became a book called *Higher Ground,* I dedicated them to Robert and his lovely wife, Beth.

Robert, Beth, Louise, and I make frequent visits to a very special fish-and-chip restaurant called Geale's, near Notting Hill. We have spent countless hours there. It is said to be the top fish and chips place in Britain. It is quaint, clean, and not too far away, and the fish are always freshly caught.

Lyndon brought two other friends of his to Hiram who have now become my friends as well: Charles Colchester, whom I mentioned earlier, and Geoff Ridsdale. I had heard of Geoff first when Edward England told me that Geoff was writing an article in *Renewal* to challenge my views on tithing! I was given the right to reply to Geoff's piece, and I did. Who would have thought we would become friends, but we are indeed. A perfect way to end a day is to meet with Lyndon, Charlie, and Geoff for a cup of tea. Only God knows how these men make me laugh and keep me from taking myself too seriously. That is what friends are for.

When I took Paul Cain and his aide Reed Grafke into my bolt-hole, I was keen to point out my "corner." Paul has been there several times and said he always thinks of Jonathan Edwards and Charles Spurgeon when he comes there. Maybe he says that because he knows that these men are my theological heroes. I have wondered if men like Edwards and Spurgeon too needed a bolt-hole. I do know that their doctrinal emphases and concern for the glory of God have been my own and that most of the sermons I've preached—whether at the Chapel, Spring Harvest, or Keswick—have been written at this place I will always refer to as Hiram Cyrus.

Westminster Chapel, built in 1865 to seat 2,500.

Age eight, with my parents in the garden of our home in Ashland, Kentucky.

Louise and me in 1974 near our church in Lower Heyford. I later shaved off the beard, but the moustache stayed until the summer of 1985.

TR (age eleven) and Missy (age seven).

My father (left) and me with Dr. Lloyd Jones, pictured after an evening meal at 49 Creffield Road.

My father and me with Josif Tson.

Some of the deacons from the early years of my ministry at Westminster Chapel. Jon Bush, my first assistant, is seated on the right.

Most of the deacons at the time of my retirement. Back row (from left): Victor Brittain-Wong, Stephen Sloan, David Jermyn, Benjamin Chan, Graham Paddon. Front row (from left): Naomal Soysa, Derek Temple, Bill Reynolds, me, Mick Fallows, Paul Gardner, Ernest Paddon. Our first African deacon, MacDonald Mopho (not pictured), was elected after this photo was taken.

Arthur Blessitt in full flow at a street rally
held just outside Victoria Station.

Louise with Arthur Blessitt.

His Excellency President Daniel arap Moi of Kenya (to my right) introducing me to members of the faculty of his school in Kabark, Kenya.

Billy Graham left his hospital bed to preach at the Chapel and forgot to remove the identity bracelet from his wrist.

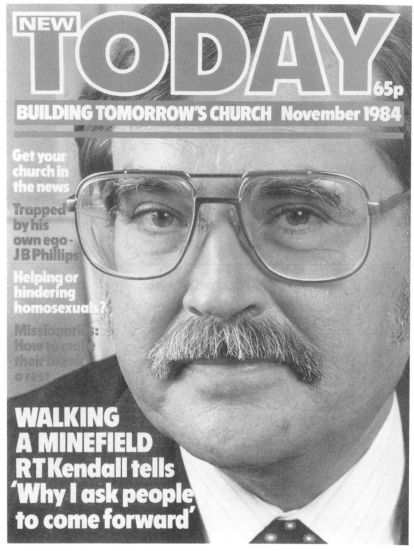

NEW TODAY

65p

BUILDING TOMORROW'S CHURCH   November 1984

Get your church in the news

Trapped by his own ego - J B Phillips

Helping or hindering homosexuals?

Missionaries: How to give their brains a rest

WALKING A MINEFIELD
RT Kendall tells 'Why I ask people to come forward'

I hit the front pages in November 1984 with my introduction of an altar call!

Louise and me with Paul Cain (second from left) and John Wimber.

Louise and me with Rodney Howard-Browne.

Robed and ready for action! I preached in a Geneva gown for my first five years at the Chapel.

At a March for Jesus rally.

Louise and I move into our new home in Ashley Gardens with Missy's dog, Sugar, in December 1986.

"Paws" for thought. Relaxing with TR's cat, Gizmo.

With O. S. Hawkins at a banquet in 1983.

On the platform with (left to right) T. W. Wilson, George Hamilton IV, and
George Beverly Shea.

With Lyndon Bowring.

With Robert Amess.

With Rob Parson and Steve Chalke (right) at my sixtieth birthday party.

With Margaret Thatcher, the former British prime minister, in 1985.

A bonefish on the line!

An eight-pound bonefish caught on camera before it was released back into the sea.

The ones that didn't get away! With TR, Don Gurgiolo, and Bruce Porter (far right) at the end of a successful day of deep-sea fishing.

Relaxing with Louise at "Hiram Cyrus."

TR and Annette's wedding.

TR, Louise, Melissa, and me at my sixtieth birthday celebration.

8

A Glimpse
of a Happy Church

Then the church... enjoyed a time of peace.
—ACTS 9:31

IN THE SPRING of 1985, we introduced our first Prayer Covenant. Graham Lacey gave me the idea. The urgent need at the time was the Chapel's unity. As I said earlier, Arthur Blessitt's visit to us in the spring of 1982 resulted in big upheaval. But by early 1985 we had made the turn, and it seemed that my ministry would continue. Yet there was an unsettledness that existed, so the Prayer Covenant was created to strengthen our unity.

The idea of such a covenant is based largely on two verses. The first scripture is found in Matthew 18:19:

> Again, I tell you that if two of you on earth agree about anything you ask for, it will be done for you by my Father in heaven.

Those who would agree to pray twice a day for the petitions on the Prayer Covenant were to do the following: sign their names to the card that they accepted, get another person to pray the same petitions, and to sign his name on the same card. The two would then agree to pray twice a day for:

1. True revival in Westminster Chapel
2. Unction on Dr. Kendall
3. The unity of the body of Christ in Westminster Chapel
4. Our evangelistic outreach and the discipleship of new Christians
5. That we would be more like Jesus

Over three hundred people signed up.
The second verse was Luke 18:1:

> Then Jesus told his disciples a parable to show them that they should always pray and not give up.

The example of the persistent widow in the parable that followed became our impetus to keep praying twice daily. We kept it up for exactly five years, and then I publicly released everybody from having to keep it up, although many continued to pray through these petitions anyway.

In the spring of 1994, there was a growing desire that we should go back to praying our old Prayer Covenant. (See chapter six.) We all agreed to renew this covenant with some changes in the petitions:

1. *"We thank God for the continued unity of the body of Christ in Westminster Chapel."*

The one undoubted thing the first Prayer Covenant did was to ensure unity. This time we had unity, so we simply began the new Prayer Covenant with a word of thanks, thanking God for our unity. This is partly based upon Philippians 4:6: "Do not be anxious about anything, but in everything, by prayer and petition, with *thanksgiving*, present your requests to God" (emphasis added).

2. *"We pray for an ever-increasing anointing on the minister and his family as well as all those*

*who have entered into this prayer covenant—
and all their families as well."*

Therefore, everyone involved in the new Prayer Covenant is covered in prayer.

3.   *"We pray for the manifestation of God's glory
in our midst along with an ever-increasing
openness in us to the way God chooses to manifest that glory."*

As I said earlier, this third petition sprang out of our knowledge of church history, namely that God does not necessarily manifest His glory in every generation the same way as He did before. Note also that, instead of praying for revival, this time we prayed for the manifestation of God's glory—however He may be pleased to show up. But because church history has shown that we may be required to move outside our comfort zone in the light of such a manifestation, we felt the need to make ourselves pray to be open to the way God may choose to work; otherwise, we might miss what he is doing.

4.   *"We pray to speak only blessings into people's
lives and to speak evil of no one."*

This is a thought I got from Randy Wall of Key Largo, Florida. It is based largely on Colossians 4:6: "Let your conversation be always full of grace, seasoned with salt, so that you may know how to answer everyone." I can tell you that this petition, possibly more than any of the others, has done much to change all of us!

The fifth petition we left blank. We encouraged each person to fill in their own personal request, encouraging everyone to be "a little bit selfish" if it meant praying daily for what they really would like to happen. In our own case, Louise and I prayed for our children's spirituality. The pursuit of the manifestation of God's glory continues. Our own personal requests for our children have been largely answered—to the praise of God!

The one thing of which I am equally in awe was our unity. Prior to starting our first Prayer Covenant, things were bad. When we launched the new Prayer Covenant ten years later, we were exceedingly grateful for this unity. I believe it can be traced to both of our Prayer Covenants.

PILOT LIGHTS MINISTRY

One Saturday morning—January 4, 1986—I was seriously thinking of closing down the Pilot Lights. We had not seen a conversion in weeks, and the numbers that Saturday were so low that I began rehearsing a speech I would give on Sunday as to why we were bringing this ministry to an end. The fact that it was the coldest day I could remember in years did not help. As I walked through the Chapel yard to begin two hours of witnessing on the Chapel steps, rehearsing my little speech for the next day, someone said, "There is a man who wants to talk to you." That man's name was Charlie Stride, a taxi driver.

"I'm looking for the man who wrote this tract," he said to me.

"I wrote that tract," I replied.

"Are you really the same Dr. Kendall who wrote this?" showing me his copy of *What Is Christianity?*

I assured him I was.

He was in tears. "This pamphlet shook me rigid, and I need to talk to someone as soon as possible."

When I saw his cab a few feet away, taking note of the cold day, I suggested we sit in the back seat of his taxi! In forty-five minutes, I led him to the Lord. Not only was a man saved, but so was the Pilot Lights ministry. Charlie is now one of the most loved members of the Chapel. It all began when Tony Gaylor had given him a tract the week before.

On Saturday February 19, 1994, a lady passed by the steps of the Chapel, and I walked over to her. I have often been so glad that I did not have my head turned or was not preoccupied with someone else; otherwise I would have missed the opportunity to witness to her. We did, however, pray weekly: "Send us those whom You want us to talk to and keep all others away." As I asked her if she knew she would go to heaven if she died that day, tears welled up in her eyes. I detected a slight accent, but her English was impeccable. We stepped inside the Chapel, and I presented the gospel to her. She was converted soundly and gloriously. Her name is Luba. She lives in Moscow. She is also Jewish but knew next to nothing about Jesus and the Bible. Two years later she turned up on a Saturday with fifteen Russians. "Do for them what you did for me," she asked. She translated as I presented the gospel. Seven of them repeated the sinner's prayer. I cannot be sure they were all converted, but Luba found a church in Moscow where she attends regularly. So far as I know, she led her mother to Christ but not her husband.

The first Saturday in June marks a birthday for the Pilot Lights. We have tried to have a little party each year and, when possible, to have a speaker. On June 1, 1991, which was our ninth birthday, I was unable to get a speaker. But who would be walking down Buckingham Gate that Saturday but Tony Campolo! I explained to him what we were doing and that we had hoped to have a speaker an hour later for this our ninth birthday, and would he be willing to speak. He said yes. It was so wonderful. About forty people turned up that day, and little did they know that they would be addressed by a world-class preacher. Tony was at his best. He treated us with the same dignity as if he was speaking to ten thousand people. It moved us to tears.

Benjamin Chan, one of our deacons, asked if he could begin a prayer meeting at the Chapel on Saturday mornings. This would serve to pray for the Pilot Lights while we were on the streets. At first only two or three older ladies turned up to pray with him. On one such morning, the late George Thomas (also known as Lord Tonypandy), former Speaker of the House of Commons, appeared. He had briefly addressed the Chapel on a Sunday evening some months before, but this particular Saturday morning he happened to be passing by and stopped in. I told him that three people were conducting a prayer meeting inside and asked him if he would come in to greet them. He was delighted to do so. Imagine the look on the faces of those three discouraged prayer warriors when I interrupted them to be greeted by the former Speaker of the House of Commons! After that encounter, the numbers quickly went up.

LOYAL ASSISTANCE

It is important to have total loyalty among one's staff. I was blessed with loyal men as my assistants during my time at Westminster Chapel. I can never thank God enough for my first assistant, Jon Bush. He and Kim (who typed many of my sermons for the *Westminster Record*) were gifts of God. Peter Mockett, who had the makings of a very good preacher, became my assistant in 1989. He worked efficiently and faithfully alongside me until he went to study for the Baptist ministry at Spurgeon's in 1991. Jon Bush recommended Colin Webster as a man who could be both an able assistant and a worship leader. He had been working with Saltmine. Colin succeeded Peter and became my assistant in 1991. He functioned as my assistant, youth leader, and worship leader. He was, and is, pure gold. His loyalty and devotion did so much to encourage me when I needed someone to uplift me in prayer. Colin left us in 1993 to attend Moorlands Bible College. I had the privilege of performing the marriage ceremonies of two of my assistants: that of Colin who married Vicky, a doctor in the Chapel, and that of Peter Mockett who married Julia.

Brian Reed came to our staff as my assistant on April 1, 1994. Brian and his wife, Kathy, excel in the area of Christian counseling. I simply do not have the time to counsel people, and Brian was a blessing in this area. Brian also did the hard work in preparing the biographical details for our book *Great Christian Prayers*. He, like all my assistants before, was at my side each week on the steps of the Chapel on Saturday mornings. Being my assistant is a thankless task and is not glamorous. It is hard work being a gofer, but this frees me to prepare sermons and preach.

The Chapel has always had a verger who lives on the premises. Fred and Marta Jinks were with us in this capacity for thirty-one years. They were succeeded by Ken and Rosina Heagren, and then Rob and Irene Mandry as well as a verger's assistant, Kevin Fitzpatrick. Patience Adamah worked alongside Rob and Kevin. Although the Chapel staff was never very large, we hired our first Chapel manager, Rick Hillard, in September 2000. How did we ever manage without Rick and his wife, Helen, who often assisted at leading worship, I'll never know. Pam Harris was my secretary for fourteen years. Sheila Penton was my secretary for over nine years, and my third secretary is Beryl Grogan, who is like a member of the family. Beryl and Melissa have been best friends since we arrived in 1977. Beryl's husband, Kieran, was our worship leader. Our organist, Ray Knight, has a Pentecostal background that comes through beautifully in his playing, which was exactly what we needed.

Our youth director, Paul Rogers, oversaw the entire youth ministry, including those in their twenties, but had a hands-on responsibility especially for our Junior Church (ages five to fourteen) and teenagers. Paul and his wife, Alison, had been members in the early 1990s but moved to Newcastle where he was a school teacher. As we looked high and low over Britain, we all felt led to ask Paul, in 1998, if he would come on our staff. He was what we needed, and his openness to the Spirit was a thrilling ingredient in Chapel life.

MEMORIES OF THE CHAPEL

On January 3, 1989, we began what turned out to be a new tradition: a day of prayer and fasting. We not only wanted to thank God for our unity, but also to pray for His blessing on us in the coming year. This became an annual event, and we often extended it to other days. We hoped all members would fast unless they were ill and asked as many as could to join us for two hours of prayer that evening. Those evening prayer meetings invariably turned out to be the shortest and most wonderful times of all!

We have sought a number of ways to make the Chapel more of a church than just a preaching center. We had varying degrees of success with area prayer groups that meet midweek, usually once a month. Newcomers' suppers were considerably successful over the years. We would invite new members of the congregation to a meeting in the small hall of the Chapel for food and fellowship, a chance to get to know Louise and me better, and to explain the primary purpose of Westminster Chapel.

While our main goal was to reach those in the areas surrounding the Chapel, we also touched the lives of many people who are not near by. One couple, Mick and Hazel Fallows, decided to visit one Sunday in order to attend Westminster Central Hall. Journeying from Bury St. Edmunds to London they got lost as they looked for a parking place and found themselves next to Westminster Chapel, which was unknown to them. As it was already eleven o'clock, they decided to come inside the Chapel. They eventually came every Sunday, and Mick became a deacon and chairman of our building committee.

One of the highlights of the year, though not strictly a Chapel affair, is to celebrate Chinese New Year, which occurs in January or February. Our Chinese constituency was made up of people mostly from Malaysia, Singapore, Brunei, or Hong Kong and grew steadily. The highlight of a Chinese New Year celebration is the food! Sometimes we would go to a restaurant in central London or meet in a home, and people would bring homemade Chinese food. After eating, we would have a time of worship and a brief word.

Parallel with fellowship with the Chinese was our time with one of our larger Indian families, made up of the Philips and Jesudasens. Indian food has become our favorite, and this unusual family entertained us with the finest Indian cuisine imaginable. Best of all, they love the Lord, and I was honored to be their pastor.

It was quite hard to get all the members together at one time, especially between Sundays. We continually made attempts to have area prayer groups with varying degrees of success. Even those who meet in a particular area often found they were still so far from each other. I sympathize with people who believe that a local church is a church near where you live. Some people understandably do not admire a church to which people must drive or use public transport from miles and miles away. Central London needs churches that uphold the infallibility of Scripture and the consistent preaching of the gospel, if not also the practice of expository preaching. I only know that Westminster Chapel has stood for this for a long time.

On November 22, 1989, I invited Clive Calver, former General Secretary of the Evangelical Alliance, to address a church meeting. In 1966, Dr. Lloyd-Jones had withdrawn the Chapel from EA affiliation, so inviting him was controversial at the time. But things had vastly changed over the years, and Clive endeared himself to all who were present, answering every single question with adroitness. On January 17, 1990, the members of Westminster Chapel voted unanimously to return to the EA. We remained affiliated to the British Evangelical Council, the Fellowship of Independent Evangelical Churches, and the Evangelical Fellowship of Congregational Churches.

On November 19, 1990, I went to see Mrs. Lloyd-Jones. We spent most of the time talking about Paul Cain, whom I had met the previous month. She was fascinated and expressed warmth toward what I told her about him. I have always believed that the Doctor would have fully accepted Paul. I had no idea that it would be my last time to visit her. Several weeks later Elizabeth Catherwood phoned to say that her mother had just passed away. "She died in my arms," Elizabeth replied. On a Sunday afternoon, February 10, it was my privilege to conduct her memorial service at the Chapel. Next to my wife, Louise, Mrs. Lloyd-Jones was the most extraordinary woman I ever knew.

While on summer vacation in 1991, Louise had an accident and punctured her eardrum. She temporarily lost her hearing because of the resulting tinnitus. On the first Sunday back at the Chapel in September, she sat near Judith Brittain, a deaf lady who was visiting the Chapel for the first time. Louise instantly somehow knew she should learn sign language. She felt she understood what it was like not to be able to hear. She soon began her first sign language course and started signing to deaf people who came to the Chapel. The word began to spread in the deaf community, and the deaf ministry at the Chapel flourished. Several deaf people were converted, and some even became members. Other Chapel members who learned signing included Darshika Roe, Marta Jinks, and Victor Wong Yewweng, a deacon who married Judith—the very woman who began it all!

We were blessed in the Chapel with some unusual people. One of them was Dr. Anita Davies, who is both a medical doctor and a homeopathic physician. She attended Her Majesty the Queen Mother and other members of the royal family. What is more, she looked after our family!

Dr. Davies began calling at our home in Ealing in 1984 to check my blood pressure. The stress from church troubles could make my blood pressure soar to 160 over 105, which is not good. But Anita monitored it regularly. A year later my high blood pressure began to subside. How blessed we were to have physicians in the Chapel. Dr. Naomal Soysa, one of our deacons, showed the same loving care, looking after me for all the other ailments I've developed in my old age! God is so good to our family.

In 1993, during the time Louise was already beset with physical and emotional problems, the registrar of a local hospital recommended she have a lumpectomy. Dr. Davies always felt the operation was unwarranted. The night before Louise was scheduled to go into the hospital for the operation, Dr. Davies unexpectedly called on her to persuade Louise not to have the operation. Louise, having psychologically prepared for the surgery, felt that she must go through with it. But Anita insisted that Louise not have the operation.

"You don't have cancer," Dr. Davies insisted.

"But how do you know?" Louise replied.

Anita pleaded with Louise to see the very top expert at the Brompton Hospital first, and *then* have the operation if necessary. Louise agreed, canceled the operation, and went the next day with Anita to see the consultant. It turned out that Dr. Davies was right after all; Louise didn't need surgery. Dr. Davies stopped an unnecessary operation. We are so very thankful to God that Louise was spared any unnecessary pain.

Louise's spectacular healing as a result of Rodney and Adonica Howard-Browne praying for her on December 17, 1994, was pivotal for her but also for the Chapel. All knew about her cough, and several knew of her deep depression. The depression left while she attended the camp meeting in Lakeland, Florida, in January 1995. As I said above, Louise's testimony upon her return was very moving and almost certainly did much to make the Chapel more open to the Holy Spirit. As her eardrum puncture led to our deaf ministry, so her illness led to our being a "Spirit" church, not just a "Word" church. Truly:

> God moves in a mysterious way
> His wonders to perform;
> He plants his footsteps in the sea
> And rides upon the storm!
>
> —WILLIAM COWPER

During these years, especially after our first Prayer Covenant, my relationship with the twelve deacons became more and more precious. I tried to keep them informed on all my wishes for the Chapel and to make sure they personally met the strategic people I began inviting to the Chapel. For instance, Paul Cain spent nearly three hours with the deacons and their wives one evening in March 1991. When the afore-mentioned video of Rodney Howard-Browne was being passed around the country in 1994 by those who were anti-Toronto—as "Exhibit A" against the movement of the Spirit—I asked the deacons to watch it with me. The night Rodney was scheduled to preach at the Chapel—the evening of December 3, 1995—he came two hours early just to be with the deacons and to answer their questions.

Likewise, the deacons had the privilege of meeting people like John Arnott, who first came to us on Sunday, November 10, 1996, and Randy Clark, who visited the Chapel on the weekend of November 13, 1998. I sometimes speculate that had I developed this kind of relationship with the deacons before 1982, we might have avoided an upheaval. I didn't ask the deacons about Arthur Blessitt—I just brought him to us. I was never sorry that he came, but I did, nonetheless, try to keep a solid, closer relationship with these beloved men. It was, in my opinion, the greatest factor of all in keeping a united Chapel. My heart goes out to min-isters, vicars, and church leaders who don't have people around them to love and support them as I had in the latter part of my ministry at the Chapel.

In early 1997, I decided that our Sunday evening wor-ship had been so well received that we should do the same in the morning service. I knew it was time for me to move out of my own comfort zone and be *willing* to further our repu-tation as being "charismatic," precisely the sort of reputation I didn't want. I have always resisted this label because I felt uncomfortable around some charismatics who, it seemed to me, largely neglected the Word. But I decided I would not worry about our church's reputation and let people call us anything they like. So we began a worship style using guitars and the electric keyboard in the morning service. I had hoped that God would honor this pursuit of not worrying about our reputation.

Dale Gentry, from Texas, came to see me. He had been in the previous Sunday morning's service and noted our freedom and charismatic style of worship. To my great surprise—because Dale is a card-carrying charismatic if there ever was one—he warned me that I was making a grave mistake.

"You are going to lose or scare away people who want and need your expository ministry," he cautioned. "Keep your Sunday morning service more traditional, and do what you want on Sunday nights."

His words rang true. They brought to mind something similar that Dr. Lloyd-Jones had said to me in 1980. We immediately reverted to the more traditional service for the mornings, but our evenings were as lively as any charismatic or Pentecostal church.

"You are a clandestine Pentecostal, aren't you?" Joel Edwards, the director general of the Evangelical Alliance, once said to me. I pleaded guilty.

Yet, it was not until December 7, 1997, that drums were used in our worship! Some had resisted drums on the premise that you can't find them in the Bible. I pointed out that percussion instruments are the equivalent. (See Psalm 150.) But I prayed that a set of drums would come to us, as if handed on a platter, so that it would be obvious to all that this was right. In no time a young man asked for church membership and happened to say, as he walked out of the vestry, that he had his own set of drums! He brought them in, and we never looked back. There is no doubt that the drums enhance lively singing as much as the keyboard, flute, oboe, saxophone, and guitars.

One of the things I struggled with most in the Chapel services was getting members of the congregation to raise their hands in worship. To me this has nothing to do with whether or not you are a charismatic; it is a God-honoring and soul-emancipating thing to do. One member objected to doing this on the basis that the only reference to it in the New Testament is with reference to prayer. (See 1 Timothy 2:8.)

As if God wants us to do this when we pray but not in worship!

To me there is no more beautiful sight than a congregation filled with hands in the air. I believe with all my heart that God loves it! What I am sure He doesn't like is people singing with one hand in their pockets and their eyes glued to a hymnal (though one should know the words by heart) with no feeling. But Westminster Chapel seems to attract people who are traditional, and I had but modest success in persuading people to raise their hands in worship. One member was fairly regular to caution me nearly every time I pushed the people in this direction a little bit; he said I would lose some valuable supporters.

Moving outside of our comfort zone—for us at least—possibly pertained to two things in particular: beginning to raise hands in worship and the willingness to speak in tongues. All I know is I did not make an issue of these things but stated repeatedly that we honored God by moving in this direction. It wasn't easy being the minister of a church like this, but I am sure there are many ministers who have suffered more than I. The people loved me and stayed with me despite reluctance in some areas.

I have to remember, too, that my own background made it easier for me than for some of them—at least in a good number of cases. Because of my Nazarene background, especially in Kentucky, freedom in worship was common. In Ashland, Kentucky, the neighbors called us "Noisyrenes." Therefore, for me to encourage this practice to people whose background was Brethren, Strict and Particular Baptist, or Church of England was to ask people to do what was extremely difficult for them. I tried to be patient.

Thus to take the congregation one step further and ask people to pray out loud all together was even more risky! I might never have had the courage to do this in the Chapel had I not been with the people of Holy Trinity Brompton for one evening on the Thames. Jeremy Jennings (the best I have come across to lead a prayer meeting) led several hundred people to pray on a boat they hired—aloud, all at once—and I am sure that the people on either shore must have thought we were mad! But it was marvelous. From that moment on I longed to see this in my own church. To be honest, we have come a long way. But is it not true that nearly all revivals have one ingredient in common: people praying aloud at the same time. (See Acts 4:24.)

STATUS QUO

"Bonefish Sam," the legendary fishing guide from Bimini in the Bahamas, told me a story that served me extremely well in the pastorate. He said that there was a spot in Bimini where he could *always* find bonefish. But you could seldom catch them there, because there were mangrove shoots everywhere in that area. Once you succeeded in getting the fish to take the bait, you would bust the fishing line nearly every time because of the mangroves, so that it was hardly worth the effort to go there. One day Sam spent an hour pulling up every single mangrove shoot in order to make it easy to catch a fish. The problem was, however, that the fish deserted that area entirely, and it was no use to go there. When the mangrove shoots grew back within a year or two, the fish returned. He learned this lesson: leave the mangrove shoots alone no matter how much of a nuisance they are, for it is far better to have a splendid supply of fish around.

Problem people in the church are like those mangrove shoots, whether they be the abrasive type, critical, flakes, always complaining, unspiritual, or superspiritual. If you want the presence of the Lord, you leave things alone and accept people as they are. If you try to weed out people you don't particularly like, you also grieve the Holy Spirit. The Lord never chased problem people away but loved and accepted them. I am sure that I myself have been like a problem mangrove shoot to a number of people in times past. They may well have wished for my demise, but God accepted me. We are all strange to some degree and make up the body of Christ that includes *all* kinds of people. John Calvin said that in every saint there is something reprehensible.

During my twenty-five years at Westminster Chapel, I had the great privilege of baptizing believers. It is still an adjustment for me to accept that not all who joined the Chapel were baptized, and not all who were baptized joined the Chapel. What was even more difficult for me to come to terms with was how people took years to decide to be baptized at all. In the Book of Acts, new believers did it on the same day they were converted! I have baptized just under four hundred people. The baptistry is under the floor in the Main Hall.

We had seventy-four baby dedications. These were among the most precious times and took place after the morning service. I performed ninety weddings. Following Dr. Lloyd-Jones's practice of wearing his academic gown, I wore my Oxford gown for weddings. All my wedding sermons were much the same, but one couple, Paul and Clare Gardner, followed the words "until death us do part" with one delightful line: "or until Jesus comes again." When I inserted this in Jim and Lori Bakker's wedding in Burbank, California, the people cheered! It is indeed a thrilling addition to the wedding ceremony. Every wedding has been different and with a character of its own. But I will never forget the day I married Matt and Rachel Round just a few yards away from the scintillating waters of the River Dee. Another unforgettable moment was not only walking down the aisle with Darshika Inbaraj to give her away to Richard Roe, but also performing the marriage ceremony!

On December 19, 1998, Louise and I had supper with Sandy and Annette Millar of Holy Trinity Brompton. Sandy had insisted that we come over, and it was obvious something was on his heart.

"I'm wondering if in some way we can work together," he said.

He proposed that a number of his own people from Holy Trinity Brompton would come along with some of their clergy and worship group. He knew that our congregations were not large. He never forgot that we stood by them when the Toronto Blessing came through Holy Trinity Brompton while so many Anglican churches ostracized them. He wanted to help us in some way.

"What do you think?" he then asked.

"It can't be wrong," I said. "Because if the Chapel began to grow and the place filled, I could get no credit. That must mean it is right."

The following May 25, some of their worship group, along with Jeremy Jennings, came to the Chapel. I asked all present from HTB to stand, there being between forty and fifty. Jeremy read the lesson and led in prayers. It was a fantastic evening. The next six months represented one of the sweetest eras of my twenty-five years. They always had some of their staff with them, sometimes Sandy himself, sometimes Nicky Gumbel or Nicky Lee. They loosened us up—especially me! I began to "dress down," as Sandy put it, and we started using the lower platform in these evening services. Their input was invaluable, and I thank God for Sandy and HTB for their love and wisdom. What an honor it was for us.

Saturday, October 14, 2000, will live on as one of the happiest days of our lives. That day our son, TR, married Annette Reiche, a member of the Chapel. I always prayed for TR and Melissa as my dad prayed for me: "Don't let our children fall in love with the wrong person." TR waited a good while for the perfect bride—and he got her! I never knew the exhilaration of a father's joy as I felt it on that day.

9

Sweet Moments

God is never too late, never too early;
he is always just on time.
C. B. FUGETT

I HAD NOT realized that one of the fringe benefits of being the minister of Westminster Chapel meant I would get to meet a lot of interesting people. Over the years, I met people I never dreamed I would see face-to-face. Some of these people remain my friends, and we stay in touch.

PAUL REES

One day in 1983, an elderly and distinguished-looking man came into the vestry. "My name is Paul Rees," he said. I was thrilled to bits.

"Do you know me?" he asked.

"I know exactly who you are. Your father was Seth Rees, founder of the Pilgrim Holiness Church." He was surprised. I began quoting things I knew about him, and he could see how much I really knew. It began a friendship that meant a lot to me. He had preached in the Chapel years before, when he followed Billy Graham's crusades and addressed local ministers. Dr. Lloyd-Jones once told me that a friend he knew well regarded Seth Rees as the greatest preacher he'd ever heard. I told this to Paul Rees, who was very pleased.

A year later he wrote me a letter out of the blue. "I can bear it no longer," he said. "Why this heaviness on my heart when I pray for you?"

It was 1984. I wrote back to tell him I was in the middle of one of the worst times of my ministry. I was so moved that he wrote to me at all, but even more so to think that he lived so close to God that he could sense such a burden for me.

JONI EARECKSON TADA

I will never forget the day I met Joni Eareckson Tada. I was almost completely overwhelmed by her cheerful spirit, theological mind, and robust faith in the sovereignty of God. When she and her husband, Ken, came into the vestry I began to cry. My reaction seemed to upset her, and she asked why I was weeping, as if to say, "Have you never seen a quadriplegic in a wheelchair before?" I tried to make her understand that it was not her physical condition but her radiant spirit in that condition that touched me. I was so privileged to meet her, but I was not prepared to see her with such a staunch faith in the sovereignty of God. What also thrilled me was the apparent reciprocity of our theological views when it came to soteriology—the doctrine of salvation. What is more, her husband is a great fisherman!

DR. KENNETH TAYLOR

In 1972, I began reading *The Living Bible*. A few years later— March 6, 1988 to be exact—I had the privilege of interviewing Dr. Kenneth Taylor, the translator of *The Living Bible*, at the Chapel. He explained how his children had difficulty in understanding some of the archaic language of the King James Version and how, as a family, they would come up with paraphrases that explained the verses without changing the meaning. The eventual result was *The Living Bible*, a version that has been translated into countless languages. What an honor to meet the man himself.

MARGARET THATCHER

One day in the spring of 1985, Harvey Thomas phoned me to see if I would like to meet Prime Minister Margaret Thatcher. Yes! It seemed that she had agreed to give a speech at the Royal Albert Hall to six thousand lawyers from the United States, and there was a request that a prayer be given at the beginning of the occasion. He asked if I would give the prayer; if so, I could spend fifteen minutes with Mrs. Thatcher in advance of the meeting. On July 15, two days after my fiftieth birthday, Harvey introduced me to her. I looked at her and said, "Prime Minister, no priest, minister, or rabbi in London admires you more or likes you more than I do."

"Let's sit down and talk," she replied, and we had several minutes together.

BILLY GRAHAM TEAM

When Billy Graham ministered in different venues around London in 1989, I invited his close friend T. W. Wilson— now in heaven—to preach at the Chapel on June 18. Billy teased TW (who also goes by his initials) that he should frame the invitation. So we presented TW with a framed copy of the advertisements we gave out in the Victoria area. What also made the night particularly memorable was not only TW's wonderful sermon (several were converted), but also having George Beverly Shea sing the chorus "I'd Rather Have Jesus." I had managed to persuade him to come for the occasion and almost needed to pinch myself that I was listening to America's beloved gospel singer in my own pulpit. George Hamilton IV, the American country and western singer, sang for us as well on the same evening. Two weeks later, I persuaded Cliff Barrows to preach for us. Cliff was Billy's song leader, but he is also a wonderful preacher. I did ask him to lead the congregation in singing "Blessed Assurance." I now look back and try to grasp that almost the entire team—Billy Graham, T. W. Wilson, George Beverly Shea, and Cliff Barrows—was in my pulpit!

The greatest compliment I received in my twenty-five years at Westminster Chapel came in connection with T. W. Wilson's book, *The Secret to Everlasting Joy*. Billy Graham wrote the foreword to the American edition, but the publisher actually asked me to write the foreword for the British edition. I said to them, "Surely you don't want me when you have got Billy Graham?" They replied that they would use part of Billy's statement on the dust jacket, but they wanted a British person to write the foreword. I pointed out to them that I am not British, but they replied, "Yes, you are." That warmed my heart.

THE GREATEST MOMENTS

But there was a moment that was more moving to me than any of the above. It was hearing Janny Grein sing "Stronger Than Before." When Louise had been touched by Rodney Howard-Browne's ministry in January 1995, she kept saying that a lot of her transformation came as a result of hearing Janny sing when in Lakeland. Louise brought home a tape of the song that particularly ministered to her:

> Broken wings take time to mend
> Before they learn to fly again.
> On the breath of God they'll soar,
> They'll be stronger than before.
> Don't look back into the past,
> What was fire now is ash.
> Let it all be dead and gone,
> The time is now for moving on.[1]

Louise and I would play that tape again and again for months. When Rodney came to preach for us, he surprised us by bringing Janny with him. I immediately invited her to sing, and she had brought the accompaniment tape for that song. As she sang, she turned back and looked at me. I was trying to take it all in. It was perhaps the most emotional moment in an evening service of my twenty-five years.

Yet when Darlene Zschech sang "Shout to the Lord" in June 1998, I almost thought I had died and gone to heaven! That hymn had gone around the world within three weeks of the time Darlene wrote it. Now here she was leading worship and singing it in Westminster Chapel. Many had come to hear her, and as I look back, I now am somewhat embarrassed that I bothered to preach that evening. I should have let her take the whole service.

~

It was awesome to see the top gallery filled at our second Word and Spirit Conference at the Chapel in 1996. I had seen the Chapel *completely* filled only three times: at Dr. Lloyd-Jones's memorial service in April 1981; when Arthur Blessitt addressed the FIEC meeting in April 1982; and when Billy Graham preached for us in May 1984. Knowing I was dreading having to preach to a much emptier Chapel the Sunday morning after the second Word and Spirit Conference, the deacons had taken a plaque from my desk in the vestry and placed it next to the pulpit. A sweet lady from Cornwall, Mrs. Evelyn Harvey, had made it and sent it to me. It reads: "Maybe today." I always took it to mean that, maybe revival would break out any time. I kept it next to the pulpit ever since.

Our twentieth anniversary at the Chapel, in 1997, was blessed by having two men who may well be the people most responsible for our ever coming to Westminster: Dr. Barrie White, who had been my supervisor at Oxford, and the Rev. Terence Aldridge, the man who first recommended that I preach at the Chapel. It was a special moment. Terence Aldridge led in prayer. Barrie White read the Scripture. Barrie was seriously ill for several years. We were not certain if he would be able to do the reading, but he did. Our people caught the significance of this unusual moment, and I myself was full of gratitude for the men whose influence on us had been most profound. My sermon that day was entitled, "If Revival Doesn't Come," based on Habakkuk 3:17–18:

> Though the fig tree does not bud
>> and there are no grapes on the vines,
> though the olive crop fails
>> and the fields produce no food,
> though there are no sheep in the pen
>> and no cattle in the stalls,
> yet I will rejoice in the LORD,
>> I will be joyful in God my Savior.

The following Saturday, I was utterly taken aback by a surprise party at the Chapel to commemorate our twenty years. Greetings were sent in by a number of friends. Robert Amess sat with Louise and me. It was an occasion that let us know that we were loved.

The best thing to happen to me in Britain, in many ways, was Spring Harvest. As I wrote these lines, I was sitting in my chalet at Skegness, that time being my last Spring Harvest. I was so honored to be asked to give the Bible readings for sixteen years. Clive Calver's invitation to speak first at Leadership '84 and at Spring Harvest in Minehead in 1986 began a new era and did more to widen my ministry than any other single factor. I'll be honest, a Butlin's chalet was not my idea of a perfect vacation, but it was a small thing to endure for the privilege of preaching to three or four thousand people each morning. Some of my sermons appeared in my book *The God of the Bible*, which I dedicated to Lyndon and Celia Bowring. Lyndon did more than anyone to help me preach in a manner that relates to Spring Harvest people.

In April 1989, Eldin Corsie, then general superintendent of the Elim Pentecostal Church, invited me to preach at their annual conference in Bognor Regis. I will never forget the feeling I had within seconds of walking into the premises there. It was a feeling of being at home. I don't know why, but there was an atmosphere that took me right back to my

Nazarene days in Kentucky. Then when I stood up to speak, I realized why. The people were just like the old Nazarenes I had been used to! And when Eldin stepped up to continue the worship, singing "Oh, the Blood of Jesus," I was almost overwhelmed. Eldin Corsie is one of the finest and most godly men I have ever known. To see his face when preaching is heavenly. His face shines and would inspire any preacher. I was later invited to the Elim Conference, held in Prestatyn by my friend Wyn Lewis, Eldin's successor. John Glass, another general superintendent, is another friend of mine. My relationships with Elim generally and Kensington Temple particularly were the most precious gifts of God during our twenty-five years. It was through Wyn that I met Paul Cain; it was through Colin Dye, minister of Kensington Temple, that I met Rodney Howard-Browne.

Maurice Rowlandson, who was secretary to the Billy Graham Evangelistic Association in Britain for many years, has been a special friend. We made three trips to Israel together. One of them was a part of a Mediterranean cruise where I gave daily Bible readings on the ship, and Dave Pope led the worship. On the occasions we did trips to Israel, I would supplement the Israeli tour guide's lectures with biblical observations.

On Easter morning in 1994, I preached at the Garden Tomb in Jerusalem. The occasion was the one hundredth anniversary of the tomb's discovery in 1894 by General Gordon. It is one of my greatest honors in twenty-five years. The Garden Tomb has been in British hands for over a century, and it is possibly the most popular spot for Christian tourists who go to the Holy Land. Louise and I were privileged to stay for ten days as guests in the general premises of the Garden Tomb, only a few feet away from the tomb itself. When leaving Israel and going through security, we were asked where we had stayed for the previous ten days. "In the tomb," I replied, not realizing at first how ridiculous this sounded to the Israeli security person. My answer delayed our departure for a while.

CHURCH OF THE NAZARENE

On a Sunday morning, October 10, 1988, I was thrilled to introduce as the guest speaker Dr. William M. Greathouse, former general superintendent of the Church of the Nazarene. Rarely did I invite a preacher when I wasn't on vacation, but Dr. Greathouse was very special. I was his assistant when I was a student at Trevecca Nazarene College. Much to his chagrin I became a Calvinist. He later became president of Trevecca and eventually general superintendent of the Church of the Nazarene. He was extremely well received at Westminster Chapel. He explained how the college was named after Trevecca in Wales, and how Lady Huntingdon, a great supporter of George Whitefield, founded the college. Trevecca had been raised up as a place where Arminians and Calvinists could work, study, and pray together. Dr. Greathouse recalled how I became a Calvinist when I was his assistant in 1956, but we remained close friends.

~

During the Gulf War of 1991, travel restrictions changed many people's schedules. One day I received a phone call from Dr. Herbert McGonigle, former principal of the Nazarene College, explaining to me that the General Superintendent of the Church of the Nazarene had to cancel his plans to come to their annual district assembly in Britain. He called to ask me to preach the sermon on the night Dr. McGonigle was scheduled. I was thrilled to do so. I told him how thrilled my father would be to know that I was taking the place of a Nazarene general superintendent! Having been named after his favorite preacher, Dr. R. T. Williams, a general superintendent, I knew full well my father always hoped I'd become one some day as well. (But the nearest I came to becoming a general superintendent was to take place of one!) I will always cherish my relationship with the Church of the Nazarene in Britain.

WEEPING AND "WHALING"

In the early years of our Pilot Lights ministry, a Danish man named Jesper Christiensen was given a tract in Victoria. He eventually came to the Chapel and made it his church while he was in London as a research student. He also became a regular Pilot Light. He returned to Denmark and became a professor at the University of Aalborg. In 1989, a group of Danish Christians invited me to Denmark to preach at their annual camp. About a thousand Danish people attended who were a part of the established church but very open to the immediate and direct power of the Holy Spirit. A most hilarious thing happened one evening as I was preaching on Luke 16 about the rich man and Lazarus. Explaining the awfulness of hell, I quoted Matthew 13:42, which says "there shall be *wailing* and gnashing of teeth," (KJV, emphasis added). I then said, "Did you ever hear the sound of a wail?" I remembered a childhood experience when I heard a mother wailing over the loss of her son in the Korean War. As I proceeded to demonstrate the sound of that mother's lament, the congregation started laughing. I couldn't figure out what was so funny because this was the most serious part of the sermon. I suddenly twigged. I realized that the translator thought I meant *W-H-A-L-E*, and that meaning coupled with my lamenting sound was hilarious. When I spelled out the correct term—*W-A-I-L*—for him and he proceeded to translate, the crowd roared with laughter even more. It was an embarrassing experience for me, but I was invited back twice after that time. It all began with Pilot Lights.

JOHN WIMBER

I came in from street witnessing one Saturday in September 1994 to spend some time with John Wimber, who kindly came to see me. He wanted to assure me that great revival—really and truly extraordinary—was going to break out in our area. He had stayed at St. Ermin's Hotel (a five-minute walk from the Chapel) a few years before, when he was awakened in the middle of the night with one of the most powerful witnesses of the Spirit he had ever known. "Very near here," he felt, "a most extraordinary revival will break out." He hinted strongly that it must have meant Westminster Chapel.

I had hoped so. As we were discussing revival, I then heard Bill Reynolds' voice outside the vestry and called him to look inside and meet John Wimber. Before they exchanged greetings John said to Bill, "You are a Cornelius—your prayers have ascended as a memorial to God." Then John began to prophesy about Bill's two sons—saying virtually the same thing Paul Cain said years before about them. Bill was flabbergasted.

I said, "Bet you weren't expecting that!"

"I can't turn it on, and I can't turn it off," John said.

By this John apparently meant he couldn't work it up. All I know is, John could not possibly have known that Bill had two sons or that Paul Cain also prophesied about them.

"MISSION '86"

In February 1986, we put on a series of services called "Mission '86." It was Jon Bush's idea, and it coincided with O. S. Hawkins' offer to bring fifty of his members from First Baptist Church of Fort Lauderdale, Florida, and help us. It was wonderful. The group came to England at their own expense and stayed in the nearby Reuben's Hotel. We all went out every day between Wednesday and Saturday, knocking on doors in the area. OS spoke the first night, Graham Lacey the second. On Saturday night Arthur Blessitt spoke, and Cliff Richard joined us. The one thing Arthur could never get the people at Westminster Chapel to do was to follow him in a "Jesus cheer"—that is, "Give me a J, give me an E..." It seemed too unsophisticated for Westminster Chapel. But I urged him to do it, and on the Saturday Cliff Richard came to sing—with the place filled with more young people—it happened! It was fantastic.

Britain's best-known singer, Cliff—now Sir Cliff—Richard, opened the service with the song "When I Survey" without any accompaniment. You could hear a pin drop. Mission '86 saw a good number of people professing faith in Christ and did more to draw the Chapel members closer together than any previous event.

DR. JAMES DOBSON

Lyndon Bowring asked me one day if I had heard of Dr. James Dobson. Certainly. Next to Billy Graham, I reckon more Christians in America respect him than any other person. Lyndon introduced me to Dr. Dobson shortly after that, and we became friends. Jim and Shirley Dobson, though Nazarenes, attended Westminster Chapel whenever they could. During one visit on a Sunday morning before the service, Jim and Shirley came into the vestry. Jim said he wanted to write a book on the subject "When God Doesn't Make Sense" and wondered if I had any ideas. I shared some of my thoughts with him and then forgot all about it.

On July 22, 1993, when I was in the middle of the darkest year insofar as personal family problems were concerned—near the height of Louise's illness—there came a Federal Express package from Focus on the Family. In the package was an autographed copy of James Dobson's book *When God Doesn't Make Sense*. Then I turned over a couple of pages, and lo and behold he had actually dedicated the book to *me*. I was speechless with joy. It was one of the loveliest things that had ever happened to me. I could never have known that some of the ideas I shared with Jim would be what I myself would need to read. Jim had no idea how God would use that book dedication to minister to me, and how it came at a time when I needed it most.

GOD MEANT IT FOR GOOD

My book *God Meant It for Good* apparently had some impact on two men in particular. One of those two men was

Professor Washington Okumu, the man whose influence in South Africa led to Nelson Mandela's rise to power. A friend of mine, Ken Costa, had been talking to Professor Washington, and Ken called me on June 22, 1997, to say that Professor Washington actually wanted to meet me! I was thrilled at this prospect, and two days later Professor Washington came to see Louise and me. He said that *God Meant It for Good* had changed his life. He went further than that. The book had impacted him so much that he insisted that it led him, a Kenyan, to go to South Africa in order to make a contribution in the unsettled political situation there. Dr. Henry Kissinger had mentored Professor Okumu at Harvard. His visit to South Africa resulted in bringing together former President De Klerk, Chief Mangosuthu Buthelezi, and Nelson Mandela. Washington insists that he would never have made such an effort had he not read *God Meant It for Good*.

The other person touched by this book was former TV evangelist Jim Bakker. While in prison he wrote to me to say that the book *God Meant It for Good* had changed his life. After he was released, he spent one week with me fishing during the summer of 1997. A year later, he asked me to officiate his and Lori Beth's wedding ceremony. During their honeymoon in London they stayed in a humble place, certainly not a five-star hotel! He preached for us on Sunday evening, September 13, 1998. All this occurred because some person sent him *God Meant It for Good* during the darkest hour in his life. He has subsequently been totally vindicated of the charges that led to his imprisonment.

PRAYER PARTNERS

Apart from my closest friends Robert Amess and Lyndon Bowring, I have met with at least five different sets of friends who have been like prayer partners. Flowing from my relationship with Spring Harvest, I began to meet with Dave Pope, Colin Saunders, and Steve Gaukroger three or four times a year. The pattern would be to spend time in prayer, and then, sometimes our wives joined us at a restaurant or to attend a play in the West End or even in Stratford.

David Coffey and David Cohen joined Lyndon and me as a prayer partnership for a number of years. David Coffey was the brilliant general secretary of the Baptist Union. David Cohen was the head of Scripture Union but later returned to his native Australia. Paul Cain was able to meet with us on occasions and spoke into all our lives. When David Cohen left Britain, we invited Doug Balfour, the general director of Tear Fund, to meet with us. This formed a bond I will miss.

THE "LONDON SEVEN"

I valued being considered part of the "London Seven," a sweet fellowship of Christian leaders that included Sandy Millar, Gerald Coates, Colin Dye, Lynn Green, Roger Forster, Lyndon Bowring, and myself. We met for prayer and fellowship, either at breakfast or lunch. Our common theological denominator was our openness to the Holy Spirit. I cannot say we all saw eye to eye on the details of soteriology, but our love for the Lord and the Spirit transcended the issues of Calvinism and Arminianism.

PRECIOUS FRIENDS

Richard Bewes and John Stott graciously met with me quite regularly. It was an honor to have such highly esteemed and able friends. Dr. Stott was a guest lecturer at our School of Theology in my final year and thrilled the crowd with his reflections of over eighty years! Richard and I are almost exactly the same age, and no one has been kinder to me than he.

My friendships with Colin Dye and Lyndon Bowring are the most precious to me. It was Colin's predecessor, Wyn Lewis, who enabled me to meet Paul Cain, and it was Colin who introduced me to Rodney Howard-Browne. The three of us would meet for two to three hours at breakfast three or four times a year. We would pray for each other's families every day. Colin invited me regularly to lecture at his Bible School, which is attended by hundreds of international students and powerfully serves churches all over Britain.

The purpose of all these friendships is to keep in touch, demonstrate Christian unity that crosses denomination and theological lines, and to listen to each other. I have profited immensely from my brothers, but also I have been encouraged by simply feeling needed and wanted. Robert Amess introduced me to Richard Lake, who has frequently brought together many of the people named in this book for food and fellowship, sometimes at the Savoy!

Many Christians, namely church leaders, wish they could cross such ecclesiastical and theological lines in order to have fellowship on earth. We will certainly meet in heaven! Why wait until then to show a love and interest in one another? I have been blessed to experience such unity now with these men who are unashamed to call me their friend.

Another friendship I cherish deeply is that of Desmond Burrows, a professor and one of the world's top dermatologists. During some of my visits to Northern Ireland, I was often a guest in the home of Professor and Mrs. Burrows. During one of our visits to their London home, Louise asked him to look at a small mole on her upper arm. He assured her not to worry about it and invited us to their home near Richmond shortly thereafter. During that visit—in the Burrows' kitchen—he removed the mole within a couple of minutes. He had sent it to a laboratory for testing, where it was found to be malignant, but he had managed to get all of it out! This is just another example of God's kindness to us.

KENYA, AFRICA

In early October 2001, Sir Fred Catherwood called on me at the vestry and asked me, "What is the most fun you have had in twenty-five years?"

I answered, "Preaching at Keswick."

But had he asked that question only two weeks later I

would have given a different answer. On Sunday morning, October 21, I flew to Nairobi, Kenya, with the High Commissioner of Kenya, Nancy Kirui. Upon our arrival, a small plane was ready to fly us to Kabarak, a remote spot in the Rift Valley of Kenya. His Excellency, President Daniel arap Moi, welcomed me. President Moi kindly invited me to spend a week in Kenya as his personal guest. He had asked me to preach at the school he had founded in Kabarak. The same Sunday morning that I arrived, I preached to over a thousand students, and the sermon was even televised to the whole of Kenya. Immediately after my address, the president stood up to speak and endorsed my speech, which was quite amazing. I had preached a sermon on total forgiveness, based on Genesis 45.

President Moi joined me on two safari trips, during which we saw lions, buffalos, baboons, zebras, giraffes, and many other wild animals. President Moi treated me as if I were a head of state. During the week, Dr. Michael Eaton was invited to join us at breakfast, and then Michael and I were flown to a remote spot on the Indian Ocean, on the East Coast of Africa, where I introduced Michael to fishing. He had never fished a day in his life but caught more than I did on our first trip. We ate the fish we caught for supper that night. Michael and I later had lunch with the president at the State House in Nairobi before my return to London. The six days in Kenya provided a lovely touch from God just before Louise's and my return to America.

THE KENDALL FAMILY

Every marriage has its times of severe stress, and ours is no exception. Any person in ministry knows that it is difficult to find people in whom you can confide. We used to suffer in silence and often wished for help. Lyndon Bowring introduced us to Alan and Julia Bell, who graciously listened to both of us in an impartial manner and who helped us tremendously in our time of need. Church leaders need this kind of help. We are all human. I am grateful that we found a highly gifted couple who were God's angels to us.

~

In the early 1990s, our daughter, Melissa, wandered away from the church. Certain people had deeply hurt her—including myself. We made her go to church—even on Fridays—and the forced obedience eventually backfired on us. She moved away from central London and did not darken the door of the Chapel for six or seven years. Rick Joyner prophesied to Louise about Melissa and assured us that Melissa was not rebellious but only hurt by people, some of whom were peers. Jackie Pullinger introduced Derek Brant to me, and we began praying for Missy in those days. He said the exact same thing: she is not rebellious, only hurt.

On another occasion, Paul Cain stood at our kitchen door and spontaneously gave Louise a word. He said that God had Melissa in a safety box, but that we must let her go. Melissa began to look in the world for friends. Louise questioned Paul, "How long will this be?"

"It will be a while," Paul said. Then Paul gave this word to Louise: "Something will happen to you that will change your life. This will have a deep effect on TR. Something good is going to happen to TR that will bring Melissa back."

Louise and I hung on to those words and prayed day and night.

In 1993, I became well acquainted with J John, a colorful and gifted Anglican evangelist. As soon as I mentioned Melissa's name to him, he felt the Holy Spirit quicken him to pray for her regularly. Immediately he and his wife, Killy, began to pray for our daughter, Missy, every night before they retired for bed. In the meantime our relationship with J John grew. He became a close friend. He has an amazing anointing—both publicly and privately. If only I could communicate like him! But in private he has a way of encouraging a person that is unexcelled. He would *always* leave us feeling good—*always*. Not many people are like that.

In 1995, as stated earlier, Louise was powerfully touched by the ministry of Rodney Howard-Browne. TR was powerfully blessed only days later and soon returned to London. But Louise would keep saying to TR, "Paul Cain said that it would be through you that Missy would come back."

"Mom, I don't know what more I can do," he replied. Nothing worked.

On October 14, 2000, TR and Annette's wedding day, Melissa, who was one of the bridesmaids, would have to come back. She dreaded having to step inside the Chapel, especially to the reception in the back hall. But when the people welcomed her so warmly—especially the new people—she was almost overwhelmed. A couple of weeks later Charles Carrin ministered to the people at the Chapel, and someone persuaded Melissa to come that Sunday evening. When she saw the move of the Spirit (which we feared might make her say "yuck"), she was deeply impressed and asked to be prayed for. The Chapel was utterly different to her. "Only the building is the same," she said. She was gloriously restored and continued to go to the Chapel every week after that, becoming actively involved.

Three months later we invited Killy and J John to our home so Melissa could meet them. We had finally told Missy about J John and how he and Killy prayed for her. It was an evening of an incalculable sense of thanksgiving to God. Our daughter was now home. It was one of the sweetest moments.

---

1. "Stronger Than Before," words and music by Janny Grein. Copyright © 1988 SpiritQuest Music, Mighty Wind Music. All rights reserved. Used by permission. 50% publishing by Gaither Copyright Management o/b/o SpiritQuest Music.

~

PART FOUR

What
I Have Taught

*You, however, know all about my
teaching, my way of life.*
—2 TIMOTHY 3:10

10

Theological Principles

Every Christian is called to be a theologian.
—KARL BARTH

IF YOU ARE a parent, you do not want your own children to doubt whether they are secure in the family. I want my children to know they are loved unconditionally and are secure with us. Are we better than God? Certainly not! As sons and daughters of God, He does not want us to doubt our salvation. God, the perfect Parent, does not want us to doubt His love.

ASSURANCE OF SALVATION

God's plan is not only that we become Christians, but also that we live with the assurance that we belong to Him. We become Christians by faith and repentance. Faith is directed to Christ alone—His blood and righteousness. *Faith* is the persuasion that Christ has died for us and we, therefore, rely on Him *alone* for our salvation. The word *repentance* comes from the Greek *metanoia*, which means "change of mind." When we come to the realization that we have been wrong, that we have sinned against God and that we are sorry, then we have repented.

The issue of *ordo salutis*—order of salvation—is not unimportant. Although it is in a sense like the old question "Which comes first, the chicken or the egg?", it is vital to know who does the saving. In a word: God. Regeneration begins as an unconscious work. And in the same way that conception precedes birth since life is in the womb before the child is born, so it is with the work of the Spirit. Some say they know the day and the hour and the place they were saved, and I know what they mean by that. But the truth is probably better stated that they know precisely when they were assured. For God was at work prior to that moment. On the one hand, there are many Christians (probably most) who cannot tell you precisely when they were saved. But Augustus Toplady's observation will do nicely: "You may know the sun is up although you were not awake the moment it arose."

There are basically two ways, or levels, of coming to assurance of salvation: by the "practical syllogism," as the Puritans called it, and by the "immediate and direct" witness of the Holy Spirit, to use Dr. Lloyd-Jones's phrase. The first level of assurance is by simple reasoning: All who believe on Christ are saved. I believe on Christ; therefore, I am saved. There is nothing wrong with that. It is the way most people grasp assurance. They are trusting Christ alone, not their works, and refuse to be defeated by the absence of good works to prove that they are saved. This is why John Calvin put faith before repentance in the *ordo salutis*, for people who are highly conscientious will always fear they have not repented enough. As long as repentance is defined as I have done above, it does not really matter which you put first. But if repentance is defined (as some want) as turning from every known sin and that this repentance must precede faith, whoever can be absolutely sure they have repented?

There are two hymns I quote to help people come to assurance.

The Solid Rock

My hope is built on nothing less
Than Jesus' blood and righteousness;
I dare not trust the sweetest frame,
But wholly lean on Jesus' name.

—EDWARD MOTE

Just As I Am

Just as I am, without one plea
But that Thy blood was shed for me,
And that Thou bidd'st me come to Thee,
O Lamb of God, I come.

—CHARLOTTE ELLIOTT AND A. H. BROWN

The second level of assurance is that work of the Spirit that by-passes any need to reason one's way through. It is the Spirit's own witness. Some call it the baptism of the Spirit (which may have nothing to do with tongues). Dr. Lloyd-Jones calls it the sealing of the Spirit, the "highest form of assurance." It is usually, but not always, subsequent to one's conversion. You should pray for this wonderful rest of faith if you have not experienced it. But it doesn't make you more of a Christian, for the first level is sufficient for this. It does, however, almost certainly, make you a better and more effective Christian.

In any case, no Christian should have to tarry for the first level of assurance of salvation. This is purchased by the death of Christ and is the first thing any Christian should be able to know for sure. I regard it as sad that some Christians wait long and hard for what should have been their joy from the first time they received the gospel.

CHRIST DIED FOR ALL

Any cursory reading of the New Testament would lead the reader to accept this without any further questions. But because reformed theology has posited otherwise, I have had to make this an issue at times. Yet, no one was more surprised than I was to discover that John Calvin himself, though regarded as the father of reformed theology, rejected the teaching of limited atonement—the view that Christ died only for the elect. Because I have no desire to turn this book into an academic debate, I will have to refer those who care to explore this matter to my book *Calvin and English Calvinism to 1648*.

If Christ did not die for everybody, however, then you can understand why some people lack assurance of salvation. The view that Christ did not die for all leads to the question, "However, can I believe He died for *me*?" For this reason the poor seeker of assurance cannot look directly to Christ, for he may be trusting in one who never died for him in the first place. In such a case, the only place to look is toward his own good works or sanctification. The problem here is, how can you be sure you have amassed a sufficient number of good works to be sure? Or how can you know that your sanctification is now adequate? People who seek assurance of salvation in this manner tend to be in perpetual doubt. But to the question, "How do we know Christ has *interceded* for us?", the reply is simple: Christ ever lives to make intercession for those who come unto God through Him (Heb. 7:25). If you come to God through Jesus it is because He has *interceded* for you!

Martin Luther is often quoted as saying, "I'm so glad that John 3:16 says that God so loved the *world* that He gave His only begotten Son that whoever believes in Him shall not perish but have eternal life. Because if it said that God so loved Martin Luther that if Martin Luther believes, Martin Luther will not perish but have eternal life, I would be afraid it referred to another Martin Luther."

Christ died for all. Therefore anybody can avoid the endless pain of doubt if he takes the free offer of the gospel on board. Assurance of salvation for all believers and the premise that Christ died for everybody are bound together.

ONCE SAVED, ALWAYS SAVED

I did not always believe this. I was brought up in a Christian denomination that taught you could be genuinely converted but could, nonetheless, forfeit the promise of going to heaven when you die by sinning. As to what sin could disqualify you from heaven ranged from wearing make-up and smoking to committing adultery.

Once we are saved, we are assured that we will go to heaven. My own assurance of eternal salvation came after my conversion. Until I was blessed with that immediate and direct witness of the Spirit, I simply tried to live the best Christian life I knew how to live and walked as close to the Lord as you could imagine. I was not looking to Christ for my salvation, but rather was depending on my good works to save me. However, when I was given assurance of my own salvation by grace, for a while I believed that this was true in my own case but not necessarily anybody else's, until I read Romans 4. I then knew that what was true of me is true of anybody to whom the righteousness of Christ has been imputed. I then realized that all who embrace the promise are as saved as I was!

One of my earliest thoughts after my experience of October 31, 1955, was the blissful knowledge that I would not be going to hell. I believe in hell today as much as I believed it then, and the thought in those days that I would certainly go to heaven, not hell, gave me indescribable joy.

Ever since then, I have sought to spread this joy to anybody who would listen to me, and I taught it for a quarter of a century in Westminster Chapel. It is, to my mind, foundational. For those who can't believe that they are saved—apart from works—invariably and ultimately are trusting in their own works to some extent. They may not realize it, but they do. It is works, not the knowledge that Christ has paid their debt, that probably keeps some people on the straight and narrow. They cannot, at the end of the day, sing with total confidence, "My hope is built on nothing less than Jesus' blood and righteousness," if they equally believe they could be lost—somehow.

FULFILLING THE LAW BY LOVE

When I began the Friday Bible studies, I chose the Book of Galatians. This series lasted four years. Until we got to Galatians 5:16, I had Dr. Lloyd-Jones tutoring me week by week. All I have taught regarding the Mosaic Law is summed up in Romans 13:8–10:

> Let no debt remain outstanding, except the continuing debt to love one another, for he who loves his fellowman has fulfilled the law. The commandments, "Do not commit adultery," "Do not murder," "Do not steal," "Do not covet," and whatever other commandment there may be, are summed up in this one rule: "Love your neighbor as yourself." Love does no harm to its neighbor. Therefore love is the fulfilment of the law.

This shows that the standard of righteousness God requires for His people is unchanging. The difference is that under the Mosaic Law God used force; fear of punishment motivated people. Under the New Covenant, we are to be led by the Holy Spirit, and when we walk in the Spirit, we will keep every single one of the Ten Commandments. It is impossible to walk in the Spirit and break any of the commands.

The mistake many good Christians make, in my opinion, is to allow the keeping of the Law to be the basis of assurance of salvation. This is a precarious thing to do. First, you would be leaning on a temporary measure. The Law was actually a parenthesis, or interlude, between the promise to Abraham and its fulfillment in Christ. The Law came in aside—"added" (Gal. 3:19)—but was only a temporary measure to enforce righteousness through fear of punishment because of the transgressions of the ancient people of God. The Law was fulfilled when Jesus died on the cross and said, "It is finished" (John 19:30). This is why our Lord said that Abraham saw Jesus' day and was "glad" (John 8:56). We get our assurance from Christ because we are under His blood. The moment one looks to the Law and not Christ for assurance, that assurance will be very shaky.

But when we walk in the Spirit, showing all the fruits of righteousness (Gal. 5:22f), we manifest the godliness that truly glorifies God—and keep the Law without effort. Yet none of us are without sin (1 John 1:8), and we are frail children of dust who don't always walk in the Spirit as we should. But the motive to please God and obey His commands comes not from fear but love (2 Tim. 1:7). This results in an unself-righteous and nonlegalistic morality that honors God and the gospel.

CHASTENING OR BEING DISCIPLINED

"Because the Lord disciplines those he loves, and he punishes everyone he accepts as a son" (Heb. 12:6). The Greek word for *disciplining* means "enforced learning." God has many ways of teaching us a lesson. It can be very painful. No Christian is without it.

Why does God chasten us? To keep us on the straight and narrow. We all need it from time to time and to some degree. "If you are not disciplined (and everyone undergoes discipline), then you are illegitimate children and not true sons" (Heb. 12:8).

There are three levels of chastening: internal, external, and terminal. *Internal chastening* comes through the Word—preaching and good teaching. It is God working from *within* us. This is the best way to deal with our problems. This is God's Plan A. It is when His two-edged sword operates on our hearts and we say, "Yes, Lord." It is listening to the Holy Spirit who says, "Do not harden your hearts" (Heb. 3:8).

External chastening is God's Plan B. It is God working on us using external sources and situations. It is when we did not heed God's Word, and now He must work from without, as it were. He may use sickness. He may put us flat on our backs. It could be a financial hardship. It could be being found out like Jonah (Jonah 1). It may be the withholding of vindication. In other words, whatever it takes for God to get our attention, Plan B usually works.

But there is a third stage, *terminal chastening,* and this normally takes shape one of two ways. It may be a case of spiritual stone deafness setting in, when the child of God can no longer hear God speak, is no longer being changed from glory to glory (2 Cor. 3:18), and therefore cannot be renewed again to repentance (Heb. 6:4–6). It is terminal chastening because we choose to ignore His Word and the external signs, so God no longer uses His Word (Plan A) or situations (Plan B) to get our attention. But in some cases God may say, "Your time is up." This is the death some Corinthians experienced (1 Cor. 11:30). John calls it the sin that leads to death, namely, premature physical death (1 John 5:16). This is also why I call it terminal.

God initiates chastening upon all of His children, but not necessarily in the same manner. It is because we can abuse the gospel. Once saved, always saved is a wonderful thing; God puts us on our honor. But if we dishonor Him, He is forced to deal with us. I thank God for His chastening. Chastening is not God "getting even" with us; God is satisfied with the cross (Ps. 103:10–12). Chastening is preparation; it is proof that we are saved and that He has more to show us.

ELECTION AND PREDESTINATION

At the bottom of all, I believe, is the sovereignty of God. Not all who believe in God's sovereignty believe as I do about election and predestination. But these principles have been absolutely foundational to me. I could not have coped over the years had I not believed as I do regarding the sovereignty of God.

I have made this consistently clear at Westminster Chapel, but not always outside the Chapel. I have not wanted to stir up people in the various churches and places where I have preached over this particular issue. But at the place where I have been at home for twenty-five years all discover, sooner or later, that I believe that God has predestined the elect He chose—not on the basis of foreseen faith or good works but according to His own purpose and grace from the foundation of the world (2 Tim. 1:9). The only way we can know for sure that God will triumph in the end is because He has predestined it.

Predestination is the *a posteriori* explanation why some believe and others do not. Why God chose to do it this way is a mystery to me, but I accept it. Why He does not choose all but only some, I do not know. I only know that "those he predestined, he also called; those he called, he also justified; those he justified, he also glorified" (Rom. 8:30). God said a long time ago to Moses, "I will have mercy on whom I have mercy, and I will have compassion on whom I have compassion" (Rom. 9:15). I live with this because God does nothing wrong and everything right.

After our first Word and Spirit Conference in 1992, Hugh Osgood wrote to me asking whether it was necessary to accept reformed theology to qualify for believing in the Word as well as the Spirit. Probably not. John Wesley was an example of one who combined the Word and the Spirit in his preaching and teaching, and he did not believe in predestination as I do. I do believe, however, that Wesley was a greater proponent of the sovereignty of God than many today who claim to follow in his steps. It seems to me that a robust theology of the sovereignty of God—providing one is open to the Holy Spirit—is a very good corrective to the man-centered gospel that we all know about so well. I do pray that those who are open to the Spirit will be open to the sovereignty of God as well.

THE REMARRIAGE OF
THE WORD AND SPIRIT

There has been a silent divorce in the church, figuratively speaking, between the Word and the Spirit. When there is a divorce sometimes the children stay with the mother, sometimes with the father. In this divorce it is often a case of either "Word" churches or "Spirit" churches. What is the difference? Those on the Word side emphasize expository preaching and sound teaching. They say, "We must get back to the theology of the Reformation and to the God of Jonathan Edwards and Charles Spurgeon." What is wrong with that emphasis? Well, very little—it is *almost* right.

Those on the Spirit side emphasize the gifts of the Spirit—signs, wonders, and miracles. They say, "We must get back to the Book of Acts and see a demonstration of the Spirit's power as they experienced it." What is wrong with that emphasis? Well, very little—it is *almost* right.

Jesus replied to the Sadducees, "You are in error because you do not know the Scriptures or the power of God" (Matt. 22:29). While the Sadducees were ignorant of both, it seems to me that we today are at home with one or the other. What is needed is *both*—simultaneously.

The problem is, you cannot get many in a Word church to admit they don't have much openness to the Spirit. "Of course we are open to the Holy Spirit," they will say in all honesty. And you can't get very many in a Spirit church to admit they don't emphasize the Word and teaching enough. "What do you mean that we don't teach the Word? That is all we believe." Thus the great gulf is fixed and neither will become vulnerable, be willing to learn, and to cross over into the area of their neglect.

THE INFALLIBILITY OF SCRIPTURE

Behind all I have preached and taught for twenty-five years in Westminster Chapel is my firm conviction in the total inspiration, utter reliability, and truthfulness of the Bible.

> All Scripture is God-breathed and is useful for teaching, rebuking, correcting and training in righteousness.
>
> —2 TIMOTHY 3:16

> For prophecy never had its origin in the will of
> man, but men spoke from God as they were
> carried along by the Holy Spirit.
>
> —2 PETER 1:21

There are two ways we come to believe in the full inspiration of the Bible: the external witness and the internal witness. The former lies within the realm of apologetics, whereby various "proofs" of Scripture are given that uphold the reliability of the Bible. I do not dismiss this at all, but as the old saying goes, "A man convinced against his will is of the same opinion still." The external witness of Scripture will convince no one unless there is an effectual application of the Spirit.

For this reason, I have emphasized the internal witness of the Spirit. This is one of Calvin's chief contributions to the Reformation. It is by the "internal testimony" of the Spirit that we come to believe the Bible is the inspired Word of God. Calvin based all he believed on what he called the "analogy of faith," based largely on Romans 12:6: "We have different gifts, according to the grace given us. If a man's gift is prophesying, let him use it in proportion to his faith." In this verse the word *proportion* comes from the Greek word *analogia*. It comes to this: comparing scripture with scripture.

My old seminary in Louisville, Kentucky, was dominated when I was there by professors who assumed that the critical approach to Scripture was the only valid option. Had I not been a mature student (I entered at the age of thirty-five) at that time, I might have abandoned my belief in infallibility. I heard all the arguments, but I came through them stronger than ever.

And, yet, what has possibly convinced me the most is having to preach through a book of the Bible at a time, as I have consistently done. When I came upon the most difficult verses and was tempted to move on to the next one, what held me and caused me to stay with such a verse was my persuasion that the Holy Spirit actually wrote those words. The result was rewarding beyond my wildest expectations. I came up with the most refreshing and illuminating insights as a consequence of this conviction. There are a lot of verses I still don't understand, but I have yet to preach through a book in which the Holy Spirit did not rescue me regarding what I needed to know at the time.

THE PERSON AND WORK OF JESUS CHRIST

In a word: the gospel. I have followed Dr. Lloyd-Jones's practice of preaching the gospel every Sunday evening—without exception. Not that there is not something for the Christians, for, after all, *God Meant It for Good* (the life of Joseph), *A Man After God's Own Heart* (the life of David), and *All's Well That Ends Well* (the life of Jacob) were based entirely on Sunday evening sermons. But I have tried to preach the gospel to the lost in such a way that even if the person was not only lost, but totally ignorant of Christianity, he would understand me.

Jesus was and is the God-man. He was God as though He were not man and man as though He were not God. The same writers who stress His deity (as in John and Hebrews) equally emphasize His humanity to such a degree that it sometimes seems incredible that the same author is still writing about the same Jesus. The second person of the Trinity is the Creator (John 1:3; Heb. 1:1–3) but very much a man who could be physically tired (John 4:6), could be thirsty (John 19:28), and was even made perfect by the things He suffered (Heb. 2:10; 5:8).

Some Christians, even though they don't realize it, have a docetic doctrine of Christ. Docetism, one of the early heresies of the Christian church, held that Jesus was truly God but not really man; He only "appeared" (from the Greek *dokeo*, "to appear") to be a man. There are those Christians who believe in His deity but are sometimes shocked when they hear preaching that demonstrates how human Jesus really was. And yet the Apostles' Creed was designed to show Jesus' humanity!

This same Jesus died on the cross to pay our debt. Charles Spurgeon used to say that there is no true gospel without *substitution* and *satisfaction*. Jesus died as our substitute—taking our place and suffering God's wrath:

> God made him who had no sin to be sin for us, so that in him we might become the righteousness of God.
>
> —2 Corinthians 5:21

Not only was He our substitute, but He also satisfied the divine justice by His blood. When we trust Christ's blood and not our good works (however sincere or commendable they may be) we are, therefore, promised a full pardon of all our sins. When we confess that Jesus is Lord and believe in our hearts (not head knowledge) that God raised Him from the dead, then we are saved (Rom. 10:9).

After Jesus rose from the dead, He ascended to God's right hand (Heb. 1:4) where He intercedes for us as our great High Priest (Heb. 4:14–15) and remains capable of sympathizing with our temptations because He never forgot what it was like. He is coming again (Heb. 9:28) and will judge the living and the dead.

I cannot say I have emphasized eschatology (doctrine of last things) very much. When I was a young minister in Tennessee, I knew all about last things! My dad warned me, quoting Dr. R. T. Williams: "You young men should stay away from preaching on prophecy (meaning the signs of the times and the events that precede the Second Coming), and let the older men preach on such because they won't be around to see their mistakes."

THE FAITH OF CHRIST

I touched on this doctrine earlier in the book, but must mention it again, because it is vital to understanding Paul's doctrine of justification by faith. I fervently wish that the New International Version translated the literal Greek as the King James Version does in key passages such as Romans 1:17; 3:22; and Galatians 2:16, 20.

When Paul said that the righteousness of God is revealed "from faith to faith" (Rom. 1:17, KJV) he tells exactly what he meant by that when he mentions the righteousness of God in Romans 3:22. *Faith to faith* means "Christ's faith and our faith." Paul said that we have believed *in* Christ in order that we might be justified *by* the faith *of* Christ. It is our faith in Christ's faith that justifies. (See my book *He Saves.*)

As a man, Jesus had perfect faith (Heb. 2:13). He was given the Spirit without measure (John 3:34), which is why He had a perfect faith. You and I have a measure, or limit, to our faith (Rom. 12:3), but not Jesus. His faith is what lay behind His perfect obedience. Hence Jesus was our substitute as a man throughout the whole of His life. He believed perfectly on our behalf, which is why He is the only person who could fulfill the Law (Matt. 5:17). Therefore we are not only saved by His death but also by His life! Our imperfect faith is covered because His righteousness—which He produced by a perfect faith—is put to our credit (Rom. 4:5). You and I are not required to produce a perfect faith to be saved, only faith in a perfect Savior.

When Paul says, "I live by the faith of the Son of God" (Gal. 2:20, KJV)—the translation in the Greek literally means "I live by faith, viz. that of the Son of God." Paul is showing how he continues to trust not his own faith but that of Jesus. This perfect faith continues because Jesus intercedes for us in no degree of unbelief or doubt whatsoever. That is why we can trust His intercessory work at God's right hand. No wonder, then, that Paul could testify that he lives by the faith of the Son of God. No one should rely on his own faith, but a person can certainly rely on His—both that by which Jesus lived before He died and by His intercessory faith in heaven now.

THE JUDGMENT SEAT OF CHRIST

Of all the doctrines I taught during my twenty-five years at Westminster Chapel, whether theological or practical, this is possibly the one that has affected my personal life the most. Once I saw how real and true this is, my life was to be governed by a different kind of motivation deeper than anything else I hold dear. In a word: I shall face the Lord Himself, probably with everybody watching, and give an account of my life on earth. It will be then, and only then, that all who have known me will know for sure whether I walked in integrity or was a phony.

"Just as man is destined to die once, and after that to face judgment" (Heb. 9:27). This judgment will be comprised of two phases: the judgment of the wicked, and the judgment of the righteous. Concerning the former, the wicked will be judged accordingly and experience total separation from God (or hell). The judgment of the righteous, or saved, will take place at the judgment seat, where they will either receive eternal rewards or not based on their faithfulness and service to God.

The same man who had the most to say about justification by faith alone also said:

> For we must all appear before the judgment seat of Christ, that each one may receive what is due him for the things done while in the body, whether good or bad.
>
> —2 CORINTHIANS 5:10

In other words, the imputed righteousness of Christ fits us for heaven, but not necessarily for a reward at the judgment seat of Christ. Some will receive a reward, others will be saved only by fire (1 Cor. 3:15), and the fire will reveal whether we have built a superstructure of wood, hay, and straw or one of gold, silver, and precious stones (1 Cor. 3:12ff).

Some Christians say, "I don't care about a reward. I just want to make it to heaven." I can understand this, but it is not a very spiritual outlook. The truth is, receiving a reward, prize, or crown (these words are used interchangeably) was very important to Paul. "I beat my body and make it my slave so that after I have preached to others, I myself will not be disqualified for the prize" (1 Cor. 9:27).

The effect of this teaching on me has been profound. The thought of it all shakes me rigid. While my teaching of total forgiveness has been perhaps my greatest impetus for a greater anointing, the teaching of the judgment seat of Christ has shaped *every* aspect of my life. I want a rich welcome into the heavenly kingdom (2 Pet. 1:11); I do not want to be saved by fire.

Every Christian may receive such a prize. I do not say that it means "stars in my crown" or a greater mansion; hearing from the lips of Jesus Himself "Well done" is good enough for me. When I know that nothing will be concealed (except sin under the blood of Christ) and all will be revealed, it is enough to keep me walking faithfully in all the light God gives. Or it will mean unconfessed sin that will be out in the open.

Our profile here below does not affect our eternal reward—unless, of course, it serves to make us all the more conscious that our friends and followers will witness the whole matter. It is highly possible that the higher profile given here below, the less the reward above. For example, if someone manages to be famous, God may say to them, "You wanted to be known, and you got it. That's it; no reward for you at the judgment." I have thought a lot about Absalom, who wanted to be sure he would be remembered so he made a monument to himself. (See 2 Samuel 18:18.) The thought of leaving behind any kind of monument to oneself, building an empire, or ensuring that people will remember us is to forfeit what God Himself would have done for us. The glory that will come from God alone (John 5:44) is worth the wait.

THE GLORY OF GOD

"From the sixth hour until the ninth hour darkness came over all the land" (Matt. 27:45). Some people regard the reference to darkness as an eclipse of the sun or just a dark cloud that hid the sun, although some would say that it was a darkness that must have been greater than that which would normally appear from dark clouds. I believe the darkness was not only supernatural but the very glory of God.

In Leviticus 16, we have the instructions from God

regarding the Day of Atonement. The chapter is introduced with words that show that the glory of God would be manifested by a *cloud* over the "atonement cover"—meaning the mercy seat. "The LORD said to Moses: 'Tell your brother Aaron not to come whenever he chooses into the Most Holy Place behind the curtain in front of the atonement cover on the ark, or else he will die, because *I appear in the cloud* over the atonement cover,'" (Lev. 16:2, emphasis added).

There is no indication at this juncture that the cloud—which came to be called the "Shekinah glory"—would be dark. But Solomon somehow knew it was dark. This became obvious when Solomon had finished building the temple and brought the ark into it. The ark of the covenant was an oblong chest that had a lid on the top called the mercy seat. When the ark was brought into the temple, the priests could not do their work "because of the cloud, for the glory of the LORD filled his temple" (1 Kings 8:11). At this stage one could readily conclude that this was a seal of God on what was happening, for the glory filled the temple as if to honor the ark and the mercy seat—the place of atonement.

"Then Solomon said, 'The LORD has said that he would dwell in a dark cloud'" (1 Kings 8:12). I used to wonder with surprise that the cloud was a "dark cloud," for I had always taken the Shekinah to be described as a golden haze, if not brightness. Perhaps it sometimes is. All I know is that Solomon said it was "dark."

On Good Friday, God manifested His glory in the land by putting His undoubted seal on Jesus' work. Jesus' crucifixion was *atonement*. The blood of the cross was about to be sprinkled on the *real* mercy seat. What was brought into the temple was but a copy of the real thing (Exod. 25:40; Heb. 8:5). What Solomon witnessed was but a taste of things to come. The darkness, therefore, was the Shekinah glory, showing God's redemptive work. The Gospels of Matthew and Mark don't say what specific things *meant*, whether it be why Jesus cried out as He did in a loud voice, "*Eloi, Eloi, lama sabachthani?*," which means, "My God, my God, why have you forsaken me?" (Matt. 27:46) or why the veil of the temple was torn from top to bottom (Matt. 27:51). But these events indicated that God was in Christ reconciling the world to Himself (2 Cor. 5:19). The smoke that filled the temple—the "dark cloud"—was probably far greater on Good Friday, when Jesus atoned for our sins, than ever it was when Solomon saw it a thousand years before.

HEBREWS 6:18—
THE PROMISE AND THE OATH

For many years, I was puzzled by the reference in Hebrews 6:18 to "two unchangeable things." Fortunately *The Living Bible* makes it clear: these two things in which it is impossible for God to lie are the *promise* and the *oath*. But what is the difference? They are both equally truthful and reliable, but why the two?

The oath was not sworn by God to Abraham until he became totally willing to sacrifice Isaac. But what kind of communication had existed between God and Abraham for all those years prior to that event? The answer: God gave Abraham a series of *promises*. The first was in Genesis 12:2–3. Then came the historic moment that God counted Abraham's faith as righteousness because he believed the promise: "He took him outside and said, 'Look up at the heavens and count the stars—if indeed you can count them.' Then he said to him, 'So shall your offspring be.' Abram believed the LORD, and he credited it to him as righteousness" (Gen. 15:5–6). These were promises, not oaths.

First came the promise, and then, years later, came the oath. In the meantime, however, it was as though Abraham would become a little discouraged and God would communicate again—but by the same promises. Between Genesis 12 and Genesis 22 there were several promises given to Abraham, all much the same. But one day God swore an *oath* to Abraham. What was the difference? What Abraham had believed by faith was now confirmed by the oath—which, as Hebrews 6:16 says, put an end to all the argument. The oath was much more powerful.

What, then, is the difference between the promise and the oath if both are equally true and infallible? The answer is that the promise, generally speaking, is given with conditions. The oath, however, is almost always unconditional. When you are given a promise there is usually a condition attached, but once the oath comes you know beyond any doubt that what God promised *will indeed happen*—no matter what. Before the oath came, Abraham believed, yes, but he often struggled. Once the oath came, Abraham knew without any doubt that his seed would be as the sand on the seashore and the stars of heaven. Abraham never doubted again as he used to do.

God wants to do that for each of us. What we have believed but still struggle with can be transcended by God's oath—with little room for doubting left. The writer of Hebrews wanted to assure his readers that God's oath is worth waiting for. It will put an end to all argument! God will become so real that we can hardly believe we ever doubted. It is carried out by the immediate and direct witness of the Spirit, and that is what happened to Abraham in Genesis 22:12. It is what God wants to do for each of us—if we don't give up.

STONE DEAFNESS TO THE SPIRIT

It is impossible for those who have once been enlightened, who have tasted the heavenly gift, who have shared in the Holy Spirit, who have tasted the goodness of the word of God and the powers of the coming age, if they fall away, to be brought back to repentance, because to their loss they are crucifying the Son of God all over again and subjecting him to public disgrace.

—HEBREWS 6:4–6

This difficult passage has threatened both Calvinists and Arminians. Calvinists struggle with it since they teach that Christians can't fall away, but this passage says you can. Arminians are embarrassed by it because they teach that the backslider—the one who falls from grace—can be restored, but this passage says you can't! Here is my explanation of this passage.

The key to the passage is found in the context that began with the warning of Hebrews 3:7: "So, as the Holy Spirit says: 'Today, if you hear his voice.'" Then Hebrews 5:11 introduced: "We have much to say about this, but it is hard to explain because you are slow to learn." "Slow to learn" is not a good translation. We must get to the original Greek, which the King James Version correctly translates "dull of hearing." It means being "hard of hearing." In other words, these Jewish Christians were already, spiritually speaking, barely able to hear the Holy Spirit's voice. The warning of Hebrews 6:4, therefore, means that, if this hardness of hearing continues, there is the possibility that they will eventually become permanently deaf—spiritually speaking—and will therefore be unable to be renewed again to repentance.

Are these people genuine Christians? Yes. In my opinion, they do not lose their salvation. They lose the spiritual acumen to hear God speak again. It is so sad. It had already happened at that time, for the Greek literally reads that they have fallen away, as the Revised Standard Version translates it. These people were not only converted but had developed to considerable spiritual maturity. The writer stresses this in verses 4 and 5. To say they are not Christians is to approach the passage with a theological axe to grind. I once held that these people were not Christians; they only 'tasted' of the heavenly gift. But then I read that Christ tasted death for every person (Heb. 2:9). Does this mean that Jesus didn't really die? I once held that these Christians were illuminated but not regenerated. But the Greek word for *illumination* is the same word used to describe Christians in

Ephesians 1:18: "I pray also that the eyes of your heart may be enlightened in order that you may know the hope to which he has called you, the riches of his glorious inheritance in the saints." I realize there will be those who have a different point of view, but this is what I believe.

I do not believe one falls away (the same thought is in Hebrews 10:26–31 where it is said the Lord will judge "his people") by the sins of the flesh, as in the case of King David, because David was restored (Ps. 51).

The sin described in Hebrews 6:4–6 refers to repeatedly rejecting the warnings of the Holy Spirit. The sins of the flesh may certainly come alongside, but the immediate danger is the Christian not taking the call to intimacy with God seriously enough, so that he or she ceases to hear God speak at all. It is a form of the terminal chastening to which I referred to earlier.

The proof that it has not happened to you or me is that we are still gripped by God's Word, that we can still hear Him speak, and that we want more of the Holy Spirit than we want anything on earth.

ETERNAL PUNISHMENT

It should not give anyone one bit of pleasure to preach on hell. Hell is not our idea. Ludwig Feuerbach said that God is nothing more than man's projection upon the backdrop of the universe. In other words, people want to believe there is a God out there who will give them heaven when they die, so they construct the idea of God in their minds. But what man would ever have thought of hell? It is unthinkable and unspeakably horrible. I have thought of writing a book on this, but others have done a better job than I. I only know it is what I am required to believe—if I accept all the teachings of Jesus—and what I must preach. I have done this from day one at the Chapel.

I didn't say it at every service, but I mentioned it on a consistent basis at the services in Westminster Chapel. Many of my friends and some of the most valued servants of Christ

I know have opted for the teaching of annihilation—the view that hell ultimately and completely annihilates the individual so that they are given nonexistence. I could defend this position intelligently and probably convincingly. Those who accept annihilation are not God-haters or people who deny the Word of God. They believe this is what the Bible actually teaches. I believe they are wrong.

Dr. Lloyd-Jones's admonition to me, "Don't forget your Nazarene background," probably referred mainly to openness to the Spirit. But this teaching on hell was also what I heard from childhood. I can recall how the Holy Spirit convicted congregations with this preaching. When God delivered me from what I take to be a false view of salvation and sanctification, He could just as easily have shown me that immortality is not inherent in man but is given solely to believers. (This is at the bottom of what most annihilationists believe.) But He never did. To teach annihilation is to present a theological rationale to the unbelievers on a silver platter of precisely what they hope is true anyway. The motivation to evangelize is considerably diminished, and I doubt many preach annihilation in an evangelistic meeting; it would cut across a solid motivation to flee from the wrath of God. John the Baptist's message to flee from such wrath would have had little impact had his hearers perceived that annihilation was meant.

If pushed to summarize briefly why I believe there is a hell and that it is conscious and never-ending punishment, I would say:

1. It is a natural reading of the texts that refer to hell that would lead the unbiased reader to believe that it is conscious and eternal. (See Matthew 13:49; Mark 9:43–48; Revelation 14:11.)

2. The same God who alone has immortality also chose to bestow immortality on human beings when He created man and woman in

His own image (Gen. 1:28), and this forms part of the basis for conscious existence beyond the grave for the lost.

3.   Jesus said it would be better if Judas Iscariot had never been born (Matt. 26:24), so annihilation must not have awaited Judas (since he was lost—John 17:12) because the very point of annihilation is to render someone without existence as if they'd never been born in the first place.

4.   Revelation 20:10 could not be clearer that the devil will not be annihilated; therefore, those who are punished must expect not to be annihilated (Matt. 25:41).

Mrs. Lloyd Jones said that the verse that had held her over the years was the word of Abraham, "Shall not the judge of all the earth do right?" (Gen. 18:25). I can live with that verse when I must preach what I don't fully understand.

11

Practical Principles

You must totally forgive them.
—JOSIF TSON

WHILE AT WESTMINSTER Chapel, I urged the members to spend a minimum of thirty minutes a day in private prayer time before the Lord. At first, many thought this was a bit unreasonable. Someone once said to me very candidly, "I don't actually know what to pray for after five minutes." I said to him, "Start a prayer list, and you will be surprised how much longer and more intimate your prayer times become."

PERSONAL PRAYER LIFE

I had a head start in this matter. One of my earlier memories of my father was seeing him on his knees for thirty minutes every morning before he went to work at eight o'clock. Before his Alzheimer's totally set in, I asked him, "Dad, why did you—a layman—pray so much?" He replied that his old pastor, Gene Phillips, urged every member of the Church of the Nazarene in Ashland, Kentucky, to pray thirty minutes a day. He simply followed his pastor's leadership and never looked back. What an example he set for me!

There will be no praying in heaven. Worship, praise, and joy—yes, but no praying. When we stand before the Lord at His judgment seat, we may have many regrets regarding our use of time and money. But I doubt very much that we will have regrets over how much time we set aside to be alone with God. Rob Parsons has commented that no person on his deathbed says, "I wish I had spent more time in the office."

If a layman is to be asked to spend at least thirty minutes a day in private prayer, is it unreasonable for those of us in church leadership to spend an hour? I think not. A poll taken years ago revealed that the average church leader (pastor, vicar, and the like)—on both sides of the Atlantic—spent an average of *four* minutes a day in quiet time! Read these words carefully from Martin Luther's journal: "I have a very busy day today. I must spend not two, but three, hours in prayer." Isn't this kind of relationship with God rare nowadays? Then we wonder why the church is powerless. John Wesley arose each day at four o'clock to pray for two hours. But there aren't many Wesleys or Luthers around today.

I have no way of knowing how many of my members took on board my suggestion of praying thirty minutes a day. I think some of them did. Compiling a prayer list helps a lot. With each new request added to the list, it becomes so long that there is no way one could cover all the items in thirty minutes.

Should we pray through the same list every single day? Yes. The persistent widow went back to the unjust judge every day with her plea, and the Lord said we should be like that (Luke 18:1–8). Those who have consistently done this sort of thing will never be sorry.

FLOWING IN THE
UNGRIEVED SPIRIT

All Christians have the Holy Spirit (Rom. 8:9), but not all Christians experience the flow of the *ungrieved* Spirit. This is because the Holy Spirit is a very sensitive person. He can be grieved (Eph. 4:30), and He can be quenched (1 Thess. 5:19,

KJV). This may seem strange given the fact of the Holy Spirit's omnipotence and irresistible ability to carry out the Father's will, but it is true. The word that translates "grieve" in Ephesians 4:30 comes from a word that shows the Holy Spirit can get His feelings hurt easily.

Normally, we tend to say that a hypersensitive person has a personality defect; it is not a very attractive quality. But like it or not, that is the way the Holy Spirit is. When we grieve the Spirit, it does not mean He totally departs from us, for the Spirit comes to abide in us forever (John 14:16). But when He is grieved, His power in us diminishes, and we cannot function as we should. It means we lose presence of mind, clear thinking, and the ability to know what to do next—which is what wisdom is. Therefore, for us to be at our best it is required that we learn what grieves the Spirit and avoid doing so.

The scary thing is, we usually feel nothing at the time when we grieve the Spirit. The Dove quietly flies away, and we realize later—sometimes much later—that we grieved the Spirit. Samson did not realize that he had done this—"he did not know that the LORD had left him" (Judg. 16:20), one of the most sobering verses in the Bible—but found out when he tried to function as he had always done before. I find that grieving the Spirit is the easiest thing in the world to do, and not doing this presents a tremendous challenge to the person who aspires to walk in intimacy with God.

Any sin grieves the Spirit, but bitterness is the chief way we tend to grieve Him. Bitterness heads the list when Paul admonishes us to not grieve the Spirit:

> And do not grieve the Holy Spirit of God, with whom you were sealed for the day of redemption. Get rid of all bitterness, rage and anger, brawling and slander, along with every form of malice. Be kind and compassionate to one another, forgiving each other, just as in Christ God forgave you.
>
> —EPHESIANS 4:30–32

Grieving the Spirit, then, does not forfeit our salvation, since we are "sealed" until the day of redemption. Nothing could be clearer than that. But any grudge we hold, any loss of temper, or even speaking unkindly about another person grieves the Spirit. (I have covered this in considerable detail in my book *The Sensitivity of the Spirit.*) The truth is, the bitterness that we feel and that grieves the Spirit always seems justified at the time. Sooner or later we tend to learn that God is not likely to bend the rules for any of us and, therefore, requires us to discover precisely what we do that chases the Dove away.

Years ago a British couple, Sandy and Bernice, accepted a call from their denomination to be missionaries in Israel. A house was provided for them near Jerusalem. After they moved into their new home, they noticed that a dove had come to live in the eaves of the house. They were honored to be living near Jerusalem and were particularly thrilled to have the dove come and live there. They considered it to be something of a seal of approval from the Lord, a confirmation that they were in the right place.

Sandy noticed an unsettling pattern in the dove's behavior, however. Every time a door slammed shut, or if there was a lot of noise in the house or they raised their voices, the dove would be disturbed and flutter off, and sometimes it would not return for a good while. This worried Sandy as he felt they were in danger of frightening the dove off permanently. With this in mind, he brought up the matter with his wife.

"Have you noticed that every time there is a lot of noise, or if we slam the door, the dove flies away?" he asked.

"Yes, and it makes me feel sad, and I am afraid the dove will fly away and never come back."

"Well," said Sandy, "either the dove will adjust his behavior to us or, if we really want to make sure we never lose him, we will have to adjust our behavior to the dove."

Watching that dove was a daily reminder to that

precious couple of how sensitive the Spirit is. It changed their lives forever.

Flowing in the "ungrieved Spirit" has possibly become theological jargon for Westminster Chapel people. I only hope it has made a difference in their lives. I know that it has made a difference in me, although I fear that I continue to grieve the Spirit too often. But the challenge is always pre-sented again by a loving Father who remembers that we are dust (Ps. 103:14).

TOTAL FORGIVENESS

Those who know much about my ministry will have heard the following story more often than they probably care to remember, but I must tell it again.

I was in one of the greatest trials of my life at the time I was bitter and filled to overflowing with self-justifying, self-pity. I thank God that one man—Josif Tson—dared to look me in the eye and say, "RT, you must *totally forgive* them. Until you *totally forgive* them, you will be in chains. Release them, and you will be released." It was the greatest single word anybody ever said to me. I would never be the same again.

I will not go over the material covered fully in *Total Forgiveness*, but for a few observations. I was given to see how often and how deeply I had grieved the Holy Spirit over the years. I marvel that God ever used me. I can only attribute it to His gracious overwhelming mercy. Books like *Jonah* and *Believing God* were written when—underneath—I was full of bitterness but didn't know it. So let no one think that an unforgiving spirit necessarily renders you useless or that holding a grudge forfeits all blessings. But I must say, nonetheless, how deprived I was over the years for not seeing the truth of total forgiveness. The insights into God's Word I have received since the day Josif spoke to me as he did have been multiplied wonderfully. Holding a grudge is simply not worth it.

It wasn't until reading Genesis 45 in my series on the life

of Joseph that I was able to articulate what it means to forgive totally. The way Joseph forgave his brothers is the way God forgives us and the way we must forgive those who have hurt us. The proof that Joseph had totally forgiven—and the proof we too have totally forgiven—is: (1) we do not tell what they did; (2) we will not allow them to be afraid of us; (3) we will not make them feel guilty; (4) we let them save face; (5) we protect them so that their greatest fear will not be realized; (6) we make forgiveness a lifetime commitment (Gen. 45:1–15; 50:15–21); and (7) we will pray for them to be blessed.

Little did I know that my greatest trial yet was in the future at the time. Two things prepared me for that crisis: learning to dignify the trial and grasping total forgiveness. Had God not graciously taught me to dignify the trial and to forgive, the ensuing crisis would have ruined me. It may be that these words will help some reader who struggles to forgive. Forgiving is the hardest thing I ever had to do. I am not saying it will be easy.

As *In Pursuit of His Glory* comes to a close, may I urge you to forgive what has been done to you—no matter how great the injustice or how unfair that person may have been. It is an invitation from God to you to become more like Jesus and to enjoy the blessings of the ungrieved Spirit that will exceed your greatest expectation. Release them, and you will be released.

DIGNIFYING THE TRIAL

I have not written much on this subject, and I would therefore like to spend more time in explaining what I mean by this.

In the autumn of 1979, I began my series on the Book of James. I had never preached from this book and feared I would not be up to the most difficult section—James 2:14, "What good is it, my brothers, if a man claims to have faith but has no deeds? Can such faith save him?" But I felt so strongly that I was to preach on James that I simply trusted that the Holy Spirit would be present to help me once we reached that passage.

Knowing I would be dealing with James 1:2, "Consider it pure joy, my brothers, whenever you face trials of many kinds," early on, I began praying and thinking about this passage above all else.

As it happened, our family planned another trip to Disney World during the summer of 1979. We had been to Disney World the previous summer, and the kids were begging to return. I remembered the best pizza I had ever eaten in my life the year before in Kissimmee, so I made sure we stayed in a motel near that pizza parlor.

We checked into the motel and drove about half a mile to this pizza place. We all put our orders in. I even remembered what I ordered—a pizza with everything on it that I loved: mushrooms, peppers, sausages, onions, and anchovies. The pizzas should have been ready in fifteen or twenty minutes. After half an hour, I asked if our pizzas were ready. The chef had misplaced the order, and the waiter asked again what exactly we wanted on our pizzas. I'm afraid I wasn't the most gracious customer they had that day, but finally they called our name. We paid for the pizzas without smiling and headed back to our motel. It had begun raining. Hard. It was raining so hard, I could hardly see to drive. By the time we pulled up to our room, there was a foot of water when we opened the car door. The kids made a run for the room. Louise, TR, and Melissa had managed to get their pizzas inside the room *dry*. The rain, however, had soaked the brown paper bag that my own pizza was placed in, and out came the whole thing—with mushrooms, peppers, sausages, onions, and anchovies—into a foot of water. My sanctification let me down.

I headed back to the pizza parlor, very upset, to order another pizza, but something wonderful happened on the way there. I can only call it the sheer grace of God. I felt so ashamed that I got so angry over something like this. I began to repent. I immediately thought of James 1:2 and the words of Jesus in Luke 16:10, "Whoever can be trusted with very little can also be trusted with much and whoever is dishonest with very little will also be dishonest with much." In that moment a phrase came to me: *I must "dignify the trial."* I repented as deeply as I knew how. God gave His presence of mind. The same waiter did not look overjoyed when he saw me walk in—until, perhaps, he saw the expression on my face. I apologized for my behavior and explained what had happened. He took my order and wouldn't let me pay! I returned to the motel a new man.

I remember the sense of God I felt the next day as we went from one ride to another in the Disney World theme park. My spirit was light. I was careful to do nothing to grieve the Spirit, no matter how hot the weather or how long the lines. I had determined to "dignify that trial" to the hilt and any other that would come my way—ever—no matter how small or great the trial. That event, silly though it may seem, actually changed my life.

That scenario was my preparation for more to come. A few weeks after we returned to London and the series on James was under way, a policeman stopped me for speeding on my way back to Ealing on the A40. The policeman asked to see my driver's license. I confidently whipped out my Florida license.

"That's no good here," he said. I explained to him that it was indeed valid since I had my passport stamped once a year.

"Who told you that?" he asked. I couldn't remember. He allowed me to drive to our Ealing home but warned me I had no valid license.

He was right. I verified what he said with Scotland Yard the next day: "You do not have a valid license. Do not drive your car, do not even let the car roll one inch out of your driveway." That news came at 3:15 in the afternoon, moments before we had to go to Montpelier School to fetch TR and Melissa.

I called Louise into the living room, and I told her I had something important to say. "Honey," she said, "I have to go get the children."

I replied, "I'm afraid you won't be able. I've got some hard news."

"Then tell me when I get back," she insisted. "I've got to go right now."

I looked at her and said, "Either what I preach is true or it isn't. I've been preaching lately on 'dignifying the trial.' And now, my dear, God has given us a dandy."

I then explained that we couldn't drive the car—at all. She had some bad news of her own. She replied that both the washing machine and the dryer had just broken down, and we couldn't get either fixed for several days.

"I'm so homesick, I want to go home," she then said, feeling distraught.

It was not an easy time. These trials made the pizza incident look like a piece of cake. But there would be more trials down the road that would make *this* incident look like a piece of cake. God doesn't lead us from A to Z but from A to B, B to C, and so on. This was a vital part of our preparation for a fairly long ministry in Westminster Chapel. It too was a major spiritual turning point in our journey.

Johnny Catherwood kindly agreed to pick up the children that day. For the next few months we had to be chaperoned, whether it be shopping for groceries, picking up the kids, or traveling into central London. Louise and I had to also take driving lessons! We have an American friend, Dr. Lewis Drummond, who lived in London for a few years and who also had a pilot's license. He said to me, "Getting a driving license in Britain is harder than getting a pilot's license in America." After six lessons, I passed my first driving test. It seemed a greater accomplishment to me than earning my doctor of philosophy degree at Oxford!

My secretary, Pam Harris, fortunately lived very near us and kindly accompanied us in our own car in those days whenever we had to go somewhere. Miss Harris, as I called her at first (it seemed right since she is very English!), was my secretary for fourteen years. Dr. Lloyd-Jones arranged for her to work in the Chapel office after he left, and I thus inherited her as my secretary. Utterly devoted to the Doctor but also to me, Pam did her best for me. When she thought I preached exceedingly well, she would say, on a Monday morning, "You sounded like the Doctor yesterday," to encourage me.

Those were not easy days, but we learned so much. James 1:2 helped us to no end, but I wonder if we would have coped so well had I not been forced to preach on that verse.

Incidentally, it was the principle of "dignifying the trial" that reached into a prison cell and touched the heart of Jim Bakker as he read my book *God Meant It for Good*.

PERSONAL EVANGELISM

If God had not brought Arthur Blessitt to us in 1982, I wonder if the matter of my becoming a personal soulwinner to strangers would have entered my mind. As I have shown earlier in the book, the Lord used Arthur to change all that. From then on, I have almost always carried a selection of pamphlets in several languages to give to those who cross my path. Sometimes I will try to engage others in conversation and, if possible, present the gospel and lead them to Jesus Christ right on the spot. Until Arthur came, I assumed I had done my job as an evangelist (2 Tim. 4:5) by preaching the gospel from the pulpit on Sunday nights in Westminster Chapel.

Back in the days when I was pastor of Lauderdale Manors Baptist Church, however, I swallowed my pride and asked Dr. D. James Kennedy to teach me Evangelism Explosion, the best method I knew of to lead another person to Jesus Christ. He was gracious and taught me well. I began using it immediately but only in situations where I called on people in their homes who had signed a visitor's card the previous Sunday. I had the privilege of leading dozens to the

Lord in my church in Fort Lauderdale, in Salem, Indiana, and at Lower Heyford, Oxfordshire. So when I took to the streets with Arthur, I simply used the EE approach and presentation.

Not all our members were Pilot Lights. I wish we had seen more out on Saturdays than we did. Far more people can do this kind of evangelism than most imagine. After all, we are all called to be soulwinners, but I never made it a big issue except when I gave the Pilot Lights ministry a high profile in the Chapel. One of our members, Derek Temple, a very quiet, laid-back Englishman who had been a member since Dr. Lloyd-Jones's day, came out with us one Saturday. I was amazed but thrilled to see him. He returned the following week and actually led a person to Christ. He kept coming and never missed a Saturday. He led dozens of people from all over the world to pray to receive the Lord. He became a deacon.

Our emphasis on personal evangelism is what really changed the Chapel. I will believe until I die that God has honored us to the degree that we have been blessed because we made evangelism a priority. It is what led to the freedom we enjoyed and also was the main reason we began to see people of all races and class distinction feel welcome in our services.

REACHING OUT TO ALL KINDS OF PEOPLE

For the first five years of my ministry at the Chapel, I can safely say we were a very middle-class church. I am also sorry to say that this didn't bother me or worry me one bit. But what Arthur Blessitt taught me through his own example really put me to shame. For one thing, he had what seemed like endless patience with one person, no matter what he or she was like. He would keep people waiting in long lines by talking with an individual I would have given up on or dismissed because he did not seem to have more potential.

I will never forget one occasion when Arthur wanted to

have a "street meeting." We found a spot near Victoria Station. Arthur began preaching and then called different ones up to give their testimonies as a crowd gathered. In the meantime, Arthur brought a drunk to us and said, "Here is my kind of person." The man hung on to his bottle of gin and listened while Arthur spoke. Arthur always said that "if they can count their change, you can lead them to Jesus." He could produce many examples of people in an inebriated state whom he led to the Lord—and who then sobered up and went on with God. He refused to bypass anyone. It sobered me!

As I have mentioned, when Jackie Pullinger spoke for us, she took a similar line. "People think that the most important thing is to reach students," she said. "But I say we should begin with the poor." I was disappointed that we did not reach more students, but her words would set me free to reach out to all. I knew from then on that God did not want us to be a student church, an intellectual church, or a middle-class church. I have further wished that our church would mirror London: that is, reach the same proportions of Nigerians, Indians, Malaysians, and South Americans as live in London.

I have concluded that if the kind of person who was attracted to Jesus is not attracted to us, something is surely wrong with us. Jesus was approachable and accepted people as they were. If I am to be like Him, I must be approachable and accept people for who they are. Dr. Lloyd-Jones used to say to me, "Christianity in this country [England] has not touched the working class." If so, then we need to find out why.

Our efforts to reach all kinds were met with modest success. We failed to reach the middle class who lived within a few hundred feet of the Chapel's doors. During our ministry at the Chapel, we did our best to reach all people—whether those who are well off or those of lower incomes. I only know that God has called us to be a church filled with all kinds who feel welcome because they sense that Jesus is with us.

TITHING

Only once have I gone to a publisher and asked to write a book. I did so in 1981 when I asked an English publisher (Hodder & Stoughton) if they would let me do a book on the subject of tithing. Their response was not a very positive one! They came back and asked me if Westminster Chapel would buy a thousand copies in advance. Yes. So they came out with *Tithing*, which proved to be a bestseller. The publisher later renamed it *The Gift of Giving*, and it is still in print.

When it comes to money, I think many British and American Christians view it as sex was regarded in the Victorian Age: everybody thought about it, but nobody talked about it. I will not repeat all my arguments about why Christians should tithe except to make two points: one practical, the other theological.

Most Christians don't tithe simply because they have not been taught to do so. When they are taught, they are usually grateful for the "discovery," and most keep it up. My dad was a tither. He was never wealthy, to put it mildly, but he tithed even in the hardest times. When he earned eight dollars a day, he made sure that eighty cents went to his church. So I was taught it as a boy. I have learned that if people are gently taught, they will accept it with cheerfulness.

A few people, however, do not tithe for "theological" reasons. They reckon that tithing is going back to the Law. Wrong. It is going back to Abraham who, as far as we know, was the first tither. He was the Old Testament example of justification by faith (Gen. 15:6) and also the example of a tither (Gen. 14:20). The Law came in 430 years *after* Abraham. The Law was a 1,300-year parenthesis during which people were motivated by fear of punishment (Gen. 3:17–19). The Law enforced what Abraham did voluntarily. We are not under a legal mandate to tithe but nonetheless are told to give cheerfully.

> Remember this: Whoever sows sparingly will also reap sparingly, and whoever sows generously will also reap generously. Each man should give what he has decided in his heart to give, not reluctantly or under compulsion, for God loves a cheerful giver. And God is able to make all grace abound to you, so that in all things at all times, having all that you need, you will abound in every good work.
>
> —2 CORINTHIANS 9:6–8

Paul wants us to know we cannot outgive the Lord.

But giving 10 percent of our income to the "storehouse" (Mal. 3:8–10), which I take to be one's own local church, must be taught and continually encouraged. For we all could easily spend the money elsewhere. It is true that God has no needs (Ps. 50:10), and yet He invites us to join with Him in using our material possession to extend His kingdom. There is the incredible idea in Scripture of "lending to the Lord." We may well have many regrets when we stand before the Lord at the judgment seat of Christ, but not one of us will regret a single penny given to the Lord—for it is the only money we keep!

OPENNESS TO THE HOLY SPIRIT

By this I mean not merely a theoretical openness but, dare I say it, an aggressive openness. A theoretical openness may merely be a denial of cessationism—the belief of some that signs, words, miracles, and the various gifts of the Holy Spirit ceased after the canon of Scripture was formed. Therefore some would claim they are open to the Spirit because they believe signs and wonders may appear today. But to me that is not enough.

When Paul said that we should desire earnestly the best gifts (1 Cor. 12:31), he calls for an active pursuit. Hence some are passively open (if God wills to pour out His Spirit, fine), but I have taught consistently at Westminster Chapel that we must be eager. Mind you, God is sovereign, and it is just like Him to pour out His Spirit on those who have not labored for His blessing (as in Matthew 20:1–16). But I believe that it is honoring to God to seek His face and not be content with anything less than what was demonstrated in the early church as seen in the Book of Acts; to crave for such is to pursue His glory.

For those who are but passively open (although this is certainly better than being closed), there is often skepticism if not cynicism toward any movement of the Spirit that requires moving outside of their comfort zone. I think too that some good people have but a *soteriological* doctrine of the Spirit. This means that the Holy Spirit applies the gospel and leads people to Christ effectually by the Spirit. They might even call this openness to the Spirit. But opening ourselves up to the Spirit is more than being open, in the sense that one is *willing* for God to manifest His glory immediately and directly, but actively expecting God to move in power.

If it were not for Dr. Lloyd-Jones, I would never have survived Westminster Chapel. The reason is because of his own view of "the sealing of the Spirit" (Eph. 1:13), which, as I have said earlier, is exactly what I believe. Everybody in the Chapel who had been present in Dr. Lloyd-Jones's day, especially the older deacons, knew exactly the position the Doctor took. This made it easier for me.

By openness to the Spirit, I therefore mean the "immediate and direct" witness of the Spirit, a phrase Dr. Lloyd-Jones would use again and again. It means that we want to know the Holy Spirit directly—not simply through the Word. As I said, many good people only have a soteriological view of the Spirit.

I have taught that we must be open to any way God would choose to turn up, whether it has to do with the gifts of the Spirit or signs, wonders, and miracles. This is why I have been open to people like Paul Cain and Rodney Howard-Browne. Being open to the Holy Spirit in some ways means being open to ministers of the gospel who have a powerful ministry of the Spirit. Being closed, therefore, means that you will not listen to anybody unless they take your own party line! This to me is a fatal mistake, and I have tried to be open to any minister of the gospel who had an emphasis on the Spirit, providing he was sound in his basic teaching of Scripture and on the person of Jesus Christ.

The Chapel's openness to the Spirit grew over the years, especially after Paul Cain became a member. This paved the way for our accepting the Toronto Blessing and people like Rodney, John Arnott, and Randy Clark. We were open to the prophetic as well as the laying on of hands by which either healing, deliverance, or a tremendous blessing comes to the individual being prayed for.

It was a good while before I could say we had truly become a "Spirit" church. But I think we accomplished this—at last. It may well turn out to be that my chief legacy was that I helped to make, by the help of the Lord, a new wineskin into which new wine may be poured. I had hoped to see some of the new wine in my day, but if I find out later that the wineskin enabled new wine to be poured into it, I will be thrilled.

THE ANOINTING

A greater anointing, namely more power by the ungrieved Spirit, is my greatest desire. It is what I covet most regarding my preaching and what I need most in my daily personal life apart from ministry. But one of the most painful matters I have had to reckon with is having to accept the limits of my anointing. This relates to every single Christian, whether one is a church leader or not.

We are all given a "measure" of faith (Rom. 12:3). This also means we have limited anointing. This is why Paul went on to talk about various types of calling: prophesying, serving, teaching, encouraging, leadership, and so on (Rom. 12:6–8). We therefore must live within the limits of our anointing. *Anointing* also means "ability, calling, or gifting."

The trouble is, we all want more—not just more anointing on our particular gift but sometimes even another's anointing. But nobody can do everything! First Corinthians 12 not only refers to the various gifts of the Spirit (vv. 8–10, 28–31), but also to our role in the body of Christ. Regarding the latter Paul says some are the head or eye (partly meaning high profile in the church), and some are the intestines (no visibility but absolutely necessary). All of these functions make the church work (vv. 12–27). We, therefore, cannot do everything, and each person must come to terms with his particular anointing and not try to go outside it. Once we attempt to go outside the anointing God has so sovereignly ordained for each of us, we promote ourselves to the level of our incompetence, and the result is fatigue, frustration, and burnout.

This anointing applies to what we are by gifting and also temperament. A person, for example, who is naturally phlegmatic will not become choleric if they have more of the Spirit; a melancholic person does not change into a sanguine temperament because they get close to God. In the world, a Christian who has been trained and prepared for a particular vocation should see God's hand in this and live within their anointing. Godliness with contentment is great gain (1 Tim. 6:6). God may want you to be a nurse, an attorney, a physician, or a taxi driver. In the church, you may be the pastor, teacher, deacon, or the person in charge of the flowers. When God made Martin Luther, He threw away the mold, and when God made you, He threw away the mold!

I wish I had Rodney Howard-Browne's or Charles Carrin's gift to impart power via the laying on of hands. When they pray for people, God touches them so powerfully they often fall down; when I pray for people, they usually stay standing like the Statue of Liberty! We all tend to see in another a gift we think is more desirable. I have had to come to terms with myself as I am and the way God made me. But I still pray for a greater anointing on my anointing!

SHOWING GRATITUDE

The doctrine of sanctification is perhaps best called "the doctrine of gratitude." This is because sanctification is our way of saying, "Thank You, Lord, for saving my soul." Sanctification is not a condition for salvation, otherwise people would always be pursuing holiness to be sure they are saved. Sanctification is the way that true believers live to show their gratitude.

What God taught me during my twenty-five years at Westminster Chapel is that He likes it when we remember to thank Him. When Jesus healed ten lepers, only one came back to say thank you, and Jesus' only response was to inquire why the other nine did not do the same (Luke 17:15–17). That is one of the strongest hints in the Bible of how much God notices it when we thank Him and how much He notices it when we don't.

In January 1985, I began a series on Philippians. When we came to Philippians 4:6, I was struck by the phrase with thanksgiving: "Do not be anxious about anything, but in everything, by prayer and petition, *with thanksgiving*, present your requests to God" (emphasis added). I was at once so convicted and moved by my own ingratitude over the years that I made a commitment from that very day to be thankful for every single thing—big or small—I could think of. For example, as you may have gathered, I keep a journal in considerable detail. I have made it a habit to read my journal each morning and thank the Lord for every single thing He did the day before, for every insight (which is what I largely live for), every good thing that happened, every person I was privileged to meet or help, every situation He got me through. I try to miss *nothing*.

I believe God likes this. If it is true that we cannot out-give the Lord (and it *really* is), it is also true that we can't out-thank the Lord. He loves gratitude. Like it or not, that is the way He is. The degree to which we adjust to His ways will be the degree to which we get to know Him better. At the end of the day, gratitude almost becomes a selfish motivation, because when we see what it does for God and how He blesses us as a result, it becomes something in our own interest to remember to show thanks—and say it. At our deacons' meetings, we take time to thank God for everything we can think of. At our prayer meetings, we take time to do nothing but thank and praise the Lord. At our church meetings, we take time to thank Him for our financial blessings and other things that we are so aware of. Try it! It is a wonderful thing to do.

WORSHIP

This is closely akin to the previous point, but here I specifically mean corporate worship at church—singing praises to God. I regret to say that this too came belatedly in my ministry. Until Paul Cain preached a most wonderful sermon on worship in 1995, I had sadly grossly underestimated the place of worship in our services.

Until then, I suspect that many of our people felt much the same way—but not all. Although we have endeavored to make the Chapel more and more a church, not just a preaching center, I was never too bothered that worship was not a vital part of our services. Most people who come to the Chapel choose to do so largely because they assume the preaching and teaching to be central. Many have actually said to me that they endured our traditional style of worship to get to the preaching. This did not bother me at the time.

But I now know it was very wrong to feel this way. While we had brought in chorus singing after Arthur Blessitt's visit in 1982, the worship part of the service never really took off. Not only that; when we came to Philippians 3:3 in our series on Philippians, I spent about thirty weeks dealing with the subject of worship. There was nothing wrong in anything I said. In fact, it became a book, *Worshipping God*, and Darlene Zschech even wrote a foreword to it. But the truth was, worship, as an *integral* part of our services, had not yet fully set in.

After our son, TR, came back from Florida in 1995 and started prayer meetings with some of his friends, he urged me to consider Kieran Grogan to be our worship leader. Because Kieran was young and inexperienced, I was reluctant. But one day I asked Kieran to lead the worship the next Sunday night. It went very well. I asked him to do it again the following Sunday night. When the worship time was finished, I publicly gave the job to him! It was the right choice. He was marvelous, partly because of his openness and sensitivity to the Holy Spirit.

We now give almost the same amount of time to the worship as we do to the preaching in the Sunday evening service. These services have taken on a new liberty, a fresh anointing, and we now no longer "endure" this aspect of the service but love every minute of it. I have urged Kieran to include some of the older hymns as well, for they too have great relevance for today. We have a wonderful worship group, and our organist Ray Knight quietly plays the organ behind the guitars, flute, oboe, and saxophone, for those deep bass notes make the singing and praise thrilling. It was long overdue.

NOT WORRYING

I have to say at this point I feel like an utter fraud for even mentioning this. I have preached beyond my own experience. I am one of the greatest worriers that ever lived. I am haunted by John Wesley's words, "I would as soon curse as to worry." For worry is sin. It is unbelief, a failure to trust God as we should.

It has been my custom at Westminster Chapel to designate a particular verse of Scripture for the New Year. For the year 2000, I chose Isaiah 30:15 as our verse for the year: "This is what the Sovereign LORD, the Holy One of Israel, says: 'In repentance and rest is your salvation, in quietness and trust is your strength, but you would have none of it.'" For the year 2001, I chose Philippians 4:6: "Do not be anxious about anything, but in everything, by prayer and petition, with thanksgiving, present your requests to God." I have largely preached to myself when I introduced these verses. However, I can possibly say with John Newton: "I'm not what I ought to be, I'm not what I hope to be, and I'm not what I will be, but thank God I'm not what I used to be."

It is comforting to know that God does not want us to worry. Many of us are afraid not to worry. We feel it would be irresponsible not to worry. "Who will look after things if I don't show concern?" is our rationale. What helped me more than anything was the sheer knowledge that worry is not God's idea—it is our own weakness. He really does not want us to worry. Josif Tson says that the phrase "Fear not" (or its equivalent) is found 366 times in the Bible: "One for every day in the year and one for leap year."

JAMES 2:14:
THE DISILLUSIONED POOR MAN

The section of James 2:14–26 has been a puzzle for those Christians who have wanted to believe the Pauline teaching of justification by faith alone and also the infallibility of the New Testament, including James. As I mentioned in chapter one, Martin Luther sadly referred to James as an epistle of "straw" because he thought James' teaching militated against his own rediscovery of justification by faith—which turned the world upside down in the sixteenth century. He, like most Protestants ever since, assumed that James was claiming we cannot be truly justified by faith unless there are also works in the person who claims to have faith.

To understand James 2:14, you must begin with James 2:6: "But you have insulted the poor. Is it not the rich who are exploiting you? Are they not the ones who are dragging you into court?" The Greek that is translated "poor" is *protochon—literally* "poor man," as it is accusative masculine singular in the Greek. Some versions (the New English Bible, for example) translate it as "the poor man." Had all the versions translated *protochon* as "poor man" instead of "the poor" (which implies plurality), a lot of confusion could have been eliminated at once. The theme of the poor man—which James uses as an example—continues beyond James 2:14.

James 2:14 reads: "What good is it, my brothers, if a man claims to have faith but has no deeds? Can such faith save him?" People have assumed that the "him" is the same person who claims to have faith. They have concluded this because they also assumed this was a new section in the epistle and that James has now changed the subject from the "poor man" who dominates the first thirteen verses. Wrong.

James has not changed the subject at all. He still has the "poor man" in mind. He has chosen to illustrate his point that we must show love for our neighbors by our works—not mere conversation, as saying, "God bless you." The "him" of James 2:14 is therefore the same "poor man" of verse 6. In other words, James selects "the poor man" out there who sees Christians and hears them say "God bless you," but it leaves him cold.

When James says, "Can faith save *him*?" then, he was still referring to the poor man of verse 6, whom the succeeding verse continues to talk about. The "him" is also accusative masculine singular, which shows not only that James has not changed the subject, but illustrates the consequences of claiming to have faith but doing nothing for the poor. This Christian just says, "Go, I wish you well; keep warm and well fed," and does nothing about the poor man's physical needs (James 2:15). The rest of the chapter reads by itself and says nothing whatever to contradict Paul—or Luther! Sadly, Luther hastily assumed that James was teaching justification by works in the sense that we are saved by works.

The verb *to justify* also means "to vindicate" (as in 1 Timothy 3:16). That is the preferable translation in this section, although there is nothing wrong with saying we are justified by works in the sense that we are showing that we truly have faith by our obedience. But it is not what saves the person who claims to have faith; it is what may well lead to the salvation of the poor man out there who can be so quickly disillusioned by Christians who do not care for him by demonstrating love. This interpretation of James illuminates the rest of the entire chapter. James does not disagree with Paul at all.

PART FIVE

~

Some
Final Reflections

Though the fig tree does not bud
and there are no grapes on the vines,
though the olive crop fails
and the fields produce no food,
though there are no sheep in the pen
and no cattle in the stalls,
yet I will rejoice in the LORD,
I will be joyful in God my Savior.
—HABAKKUK 3:17–18

12

A Dream
Deferred

What happens to a dream deferred?
Does it dry up like a raisin in the sun?
Or does it explode?
—LANGSTON HUGHES

IT WAS A scenario I had hoped would end. The adrenaline rush from my heightened anxiety would begin to flow. After the deacons prayed for me, I would walk from the vestry, make a right turn into the Chapel, mount the eight steps onto the high platform only to see virtually the same number of people sitting in the congregation that came the previous week. And the week before that…and the month before that…and the year before that. Indeed, the many years before that.

I would try to pretend not to notice the small crowds. I would lay my Bible and sermon notes on the pulpit, take my seat just behind it and to the left, bow my head, and pray for help. I think, just maybe, I learned eventually to look pleasant and call the congregation to worship with a measure of dignity. I tried my best to sing hymns like "Join All the Glorious Names" or "Praise My Soul, the King of Heaven." When I would catch visitors or friends, in particular, looking around when they too were supposed to be worshiping, I almost knew what they were thinking as well.

Funnily enough, it was the scenario that no doubt saved me, given my personality generally and my tendency particularly to take myself too seriously. God knew exactly what He was doing in withholding from me the measure of success for which my ego cried out. It kept me on my knees and made me even more open to the Holy Spirit. "You can always tell a successful man, but you can't tell him much," or so the saying goes. I doubt not that, had God given me my dream—a church filled to capacity—I would have been the worst example of that old saying. I never imagined that one day I would actually thank God for my relatively small congregations while at Westminster Chapel. I thank Him for withholding numerical success after all.

Yet, it still hurts. It is so embarrassing, especially because the wonderful people of Westminster Chapel, not to mention the Christian testimony in London as a whole, deserved better. I only felt that God put me there and knew that He would not yet allow me to leave. When people made comments like, "He's certainly not the Doctor," all I could do was to agree with them.

I never will forget the first time I saw Dr. Martyn Lloyd-Jones. It was at Winona Lake, Indiana, in the summer of 1963. A few months before, our old friend Ernest Reisinger had given me a copy of Dr. Lloyd-Jones's *Sermon on the Mount*. It changed my life and my preaching. That day he preached on Luke 24, about Jesus on the road to Emmaus. It was the greatest sermon I had ever heard. I rushed to the platform to meet him and asked him to sign my book. He smiled and recognized my name as I had been in correspondence with him. I remember asking him, "How many are in your church?" I don't blame people for asking me that, because I can never forget I asked him that same question.

It is impossible to know exactly how many were present

when I first preached at Westminster Chapel in February 1976 and afterward in the following September. Perhaps one hundred fifty, but no more than two hundred. The congregations from February 1977 were much the same but they did increase somewhat, possibly to three or maybe four hundred. Except for the rare occasion, that is about what they are as I write this book.

As the reader will know by now, the greatest cross I bore was that I never saw my church full. However, on my final Saturday evening, January 25, 2002, before my departure, the place was not only filled with over two thousand people, but hundreds were turned away. The irony is that it took leaving to fill it!

LIGHTEN UP

There is no doubt in my mind that the Chapel not being filled has helped me not to take myself more seriously than I otherwise would have. Some friends point out that God has given me a writing ministry, but it isn't what I yearned for. I knew all too well that when my readers visited the Chapel they would see the numbers for themselves. The relatively low attendance numbers helped to save me from feeling too important.

God also used the lack of phenomenal growth to show me who were my true friends. But through it all, Chapel members continued to love me. It was during this time that some friendships were forged while others came and went like the wind. These superficial friendships drove me to my knees in prayer and forced me to practice total forgiveness. For some of these people I was tomorrow's man (read my book *The Anointing*), but regardless of strategic invitations, how well I preached, or how many bestsellers I wrote, this group of so-called friends were gone when I didn't fill the Chapel to capacity. My true friends showed that they loved me no matter what happened. I can't even fathom how I would have managed without them.

But the failure to draw great crowds consistently kept me teachable. Some observers sincerely thought I invited people like Arthur Blessitt or Paul Cain because, they said, "RT would do anything to fill his church." I understand why they would say this, and they have a point, but that is not really true. What is fair to say is that, had the Chapel been full, I might not otherwise have been open to the spiritual contribution of these men. I did not invite them to get big crowds. In fact, the opposite is true. I actually resented it when people would come from nowhere for a "show." Sometimes we even refrained from announcing who would be preaching. I only invited people who I thought would enrich the church and me personally. If these people filled the Chapel, moreover, that would do nothing for my self-esteem at all! For I had hoped *my preaching* would do it. It never did.

Dr. Lloyd-Jones often quoted G. Campbell Morgan as saying: "Westminster Chapel is not a church, it is a preaching center." I once asked him, "Doctor, was Westminster Chapel a *church* in your day?"

He paused and took what seemed like a minute to answer: "Just barely," he finally replied. He always said that the Chapel would rise or fall with the preaching, that nothing else really mattered very much. This is why it hurt so much that my own ministry was not blessed with great numbers. When I wrote *The Thorn in the Flesh*, I came very close to claiming that my own thorn in the flesh had partly consisted of this very thing.

Dr. Lloyd-Jones always said that "it is impossible to preach a bad sermon in Westminster Chapel." I'm sure that used to be true! There is certainly no pulpit like it. The grandeur of it in this beautiful vast auditorium brings out the best in a preacher—but also the worst if he tries too hard. It was humbling for me to take Sandy Millar's advice in 1999 and stop preaching from the high pulpit and use the lower one. I decided to do this for the evening services. Although our evening congregations remained much the same as the morning ones, we have never been sorry for doing this.

I used to surprise people with the comment that I did not have "unction" (an older word for anointing) on my preaching. I should probably never have said that. It was misunderstood by sincere people who were genuinely helped by my ministry and was used against me by some enemies. One man in a church meeting in 1984 actually stood up and implied that I was surely not worth supporting "since Dr. Kendall himself says he does not have unction when he preaches." I no longer said that but prayed for a "double anointing." The standard of anointing I wished for—and still do—is what came upon great men of the past on certain occasions. But I was unwise to have said I didn't have unction because I am sure that many times I did have it. In any case, the measure of anointing I have had was apparently not enough to increase the size of our congregations. Therefore one could plausibly argue that my desire for a greater anointing is as selfish as it is spiritual.

The beginning of each service was always the worst part. I noticed how many empty seats there were when I first called people to worship. I have treasured something George Hamilton IV once shared with me regarding his own experience of how he feels when he looks out at a half-full auditorium. He told me that when the crowds were down in an auditorium in which he was to perform, almost without fail that would be the day when close friends or journalists from a magazine or newspaper would be present! I loved the fact that he revealed this to me. Except, in my case, it seemed to be all the time!

During the summer of 1988, my sister Marilyn flew from Atlanta, Georgia, to London to visit us. It was her first time in England and the first time she would hear me—her brother—preach in many years. My dad, of course, told her how an invitation to be the minister of Westminster Chapel was a great honor. She had always looked up to me and was thrilled to be at the Chapel. The only thing I prayed for was ·

"Lord, please let the congregation look full—at least once—to make my sister proud of me." That day the crowds were, without doubt, the lowest I had seen since I arrived. If there were more than one hundred fifty people I would have been surprised. It was such an acute embarrassment for me. In the same congregation was the president of one of America's best-known Bible colleges. I was told that he came with an invitation in his pocket for me to speak at their college graduation ceremony, but he did not even come back to meet me after the service.

For the better part of those former years, from 1977 to 1981, virtually every word I was to utter from the pulpit of Westminster Chapel had been vetted by Dr. Lloyd-Jones. When I complained that the crowds were not increasing, he was, next to Louise, my greatest encourager. "London is slow," he would say. "I know my London." After one particular Sunday when there was a larger congregation and I had reportedly preached well, he said to me, "You are going to do what I did." But the following Sunday the crowds were down again. "London is slow," he would keep saying. He was extremely patient with me in those days.

Dr. J. I. Packer visited Louise and me at Durward House in the spring of 1977. Jim Packer had been virtually a second supervisor when I was at Oxford. While Dr. White was very economical with encouragement, Jim Packer's affirmations when I would call on him in Bristol (where he was a lecturer at Trinity College) kept me going. One of the first comments he made when he came to see us in London was, "Dr. Lloyd-Jones always said that no American could succeed in London." Jim wondered what my reaction would be. I reported this to Dr. Lloyd-Jones who retorted, "What I said was, that no American has ever succeeded in London."

In the summer of 1987, *Renewal* magazine (a Christian publication edited by Edward England) did a feature article on us, marking our tenth year of ministry at the Chapel. Louise and I were featured on the cover. The title of the article was "The American London Loves"; that really warmed my heart. The page following that title showed a large picture of my Sunday morning congregation. Any reader would wonder what that title meant! Only a handful was present when the photographer took the picture at eleven o'clock—at the beginning of the service. It would have looked a little better had the photographer waited a few minutes. I have often wished that article would never appear.

HUMBLE NUMBERS KEPT ME HUMBLED

You may wonder why a minister such as I would think so much about numbers of people present in the congregation. It is not easy to explain to someone who truly finds the entire matter perplexing. I might excuse myself somewhat if I said that there is hardly a minister, vicar, or church leader alive who has not had the same wish—to speak to or lead a church that is filled. I certainly do not say it is a spiritual aspiration. I would admit that it is possibly of the flesh. But that is the way I am. Knowing the former days of glory with previous ministers, plus hearing of the kind of success so many of my old friends and fellow ministers across the Atlantic were enjoying, I never really got the victory over numbers. I'm sorry, but that is the way it is. How could people across the Atlantic feel proud of an American in such a historic church when he did not preach to the numbers that his predecessors had? God simply guaranteed that any welcome home would one day keep me humbled in my retirement years. I admit that, possibly, if I were more spiritual and more godly I would be detached from this concern. But such an internal victory over numbers in the congregation never came. I prayed many, many times to reach the place where two or three hundred in an auditorium that seats two thousand didn't phase me, but the Lord never answered that prayer.

I remember a conversation with Terence Aldridge a couple of years after I began my ministry at Westminster

Chapel. He said to me, "I suppose you'll go back in a year or so if you don't fill the Chapel." He didn't really know me very well. In fact, it was the low attendance numbers that kept me in the Chapel during those early days. I couldn't bear to face my friends in America knowing that they knew I had not achieved very much insofar as numerical success goes. Having been the minister of this church—possibly better known in America than in England—but not having the congregations like Campbell Morgan and Martyn Lloyd-Jones was hardly a plus to them. It was God's way of keeping me humble and getting my attention. It kept me in pursuit of *His* glory.

It worked in some ways. It drove me to a greater prayer life than I had ever experienced. I began to set my clock much earlier than in former days—to spend time alone with God. I began to enjoy communion and intimacy with the Holy Spirit such as I'd not known. I have thought many times that had I preached to a full church or had I a successful ministry in the United States I would have never felt the need for such dependence on the Holy Spirit. Mind you, God never answered my prayer either for a packed church or for an internal victory over the size of the congregations, but so much more did happen that was so wonderful, namely getting to know Jesus more than I would have otherwise. It was better than anything I had prayed for. My greatest disappointment, then, was also the best thing that happened to me.

I often think of that verse, "And he gave them their request; but sent leanness to their soul" (Ps. 106:15, KJV). God graciously refused my request—one I must have put to Him a thousand times. But what He gave instead was better. I would not exchange what He in fact granted to me for anything in the world.

In researching for the book *Great Christian Prayers*, Louise came across this anonymous prayer:

> O God, I asked for strength that I might achieve; I
> was made weak that I might learn humbly to obey.
> I asked for help that I might do greater things; I

was given infirmity that I might do better things. I
asked for riches that I might be happy; I was given
poverty that I might be wise. I asked for power that
I might have the praise of men; I was given weakness that I might feel the need of God. I asked for
all things that I might enjoy life; I was given life
that I might enjoy all things. I got nothing that I
asked for but everything I hoped for. Almost
despite myself, my unspoken prayers were
answered. I am among all men most richly blessed.

—A CONFEDERATE SOLDIER

There is one big difference in this connection between
British Christians and American evangelicals—at least when it
comes to my own personal knowledge and experience. The
British loved us knowing fully what our congregations were
like. There was never the remotest hint from a deacon or
member of the Chapel that I should "pack it in" because of
small crowds. Invitations continued to come to me from all
over Britain when it is well known that we have not been
filled from top to bottom. Even publishers still ask for my
stuff. I'm sorry to say that I doubt very much that this would
be the case in America. In America, the pressure would be too
great if the minister were to stay in the same place without
greater numerical success. This may not be the case in the
smaller churches in the United States, but I suspect it would
be so in the larger ones. I cannot begin to express my love for
the British when I contemplate that low numbers are unimportant to them. It was so wonderful and peaceful. Never in
our lives did we ever feel so loved. We were at home—loved
and accepted for what was preached and taught and what we
sought to be before God, not for great success in numbers.

SEND US TRUE REVIVAL

The low numbers were, however, my keenest disappointment.
And for all I know, perhaps Westminster Chapel needed a little
humbling too! But I will now share one other disappointment.

I had hoped to see true revival in the Chapel. That is really what I had in mind when we prayed for the manifestation of His glory.

The old-fashioned, but hackneyed, term *revival* is still the best word I know to describe a sovereign outpouring of the Holy Spirit that leads to many conversions. In America, we probably use the term hastily; the British word *mission* is better if one plans in advance to use strategy to reach the unconverted. In America, the word *revival* is often used to describe a series of meetings whether or not the Spirit comes down in great power.

When I was a student at Trevecca Nazarene College in 1956, I thought that God would one day use me in international revival. I would have told you the Spirit revealed this to me, even as I thought I was shown that one day I would have an international ministry. The latter certainly materialized, but not the former, certainly not as this book goes to print. When I accepted the invitation to come to Westminster Chapel with the call of Acts 28:26–27 ("Go to this people and say, 'You will be ever hearing but never understanding; you will be ever seeing but never perceiving'"), I should have known from the beginning that it was not exactly a mandate for another Pentecost. But that did not keep me from praying for it with all my heart or from doing anything under the sun I felt was right.

Large crowds and revival are not the same thing, however. Dr. Lloyd-Jones never felt that his day was characterized by true revival. Most students of revival would not even call Spurgeon's era a time of Christian revival. And I too, along with many other church leaders, could not claim to have seen what I wanted most, namely that sovereign outpouring of the Spirit that leads to many conversions but is also accompanied with signs and wonders.

What we had in Westminster Chapel were only light touches of the Spirit from time to time. Arthur Blessitt's visit was accompanied by an undoubted touch of God. Our Pilot

Lights ministry was born in that time. It paved the way for Billy Graham's visit and, later, unusual preachers like Paul Cain, Rodney Howard-Browne, and John Arnott. The contributions of men like Jack Taylor and Charles Carrin were worth their weight in gold during my final year at the Chapel.

We saw a good number of conversions although not as many as I had wanted. The Lord gave us perhaps just enough conversions to keep us from becoming discouraged, but not so many that we might become tempted to overclaim. When I was tempted to give up altogether, just in the nick of time God would convert someone from out of the blue. He was so gracious to us. He kept us humbled over the years lest we became unteachable, and yet He gave us sufficient encouragement from time to time lest we became demoralized.

In my first year at the Chapel, I became so certain that revival was at hand that I announced we were in a pre-revival alert! I remember as I made this bold public announcement that one of my dearest supporters buried her head into her left hand. That gave me pause there and then. I knew she didn't believe it, and I feared then that she was right. She was right.

On the other hand, expectancy and anticipation are so motivating. The very thought that revival is indeed very near enabled me to prepare my sermons with more zeal and care. It was contagious enough that some really did believe revival was coming. A conversion now and then was seen as "mercy drops around us falling" in advance of the "showers of blessing."

This syndrome of anticipation, which began after a year or so of our coming, continued virtually nonstop for these twenty-five years! I could now slip into a bit of cynicism and say it was like the proverbial dangling of a carrot in front of a donkey. Perhaps I needed precisely that to function as well as I did. Had I *no* hope of revival I am sure I would not have stayed for so long.

The late Ron Dunn preached one of the best sermons I have ever heard in my life. In it he referred to King David's disappointment in not getting to build the temple. He used a brilliant personal illustration to parallel David's disappointment. During a family outing at an amusement park in Dallas, his daughter asked for a balloon at the start of the day. Exhausted from the heat and long lines, they headed home late that evening when his daughter, whimpering in the back seat, reminded him, "I didn't get my balloon." Ron reminded her how many rides they had enjoyed, how many things they had done, but the balloon that she asked for at the beginning of the day and didn't get was all she could now think about. Ron compared this illustration to David's achievements—from conquering Jerusalem and bringing the ark back to writing many psalms. David was told he couldn't build the temple—like Ron's daughter not getting the balloon.

Like David, and Ron's daughter, I enjoyed so many blessings during our time at Westminster Chapel, but after Ron preached that sermon, I looked at him and said, "I wonder if my balloon is my not seeing revival at my church." That story was told to me in 1983. When I saw Ron in 1999, the first thing he mentioned was that conversation. He asked, "Do you still think that revival at the Chapel is your balloon?" I replied that I knew exactly what he meant, but that I was still hoping. I never did see revival at Westminster Chapel, but I never lost hope!

The hope for revival kept me going during those twenty-five years. Such expectancy did me no harm. I loved entering a service with a feeling of "It's going to be today!" That small plaque saying "Maybe today" was always next to the pulpit; I looked at it every Sunday. After all, the very thought that God could come down momentarily was no small reason for wanting to worship with all my heart and preach my very best. If I ultimately conclude that my hope for revival was one of the chief motivating factors in causing me to walk closer to the Lord, prepare harder, and preach better, I have no complaints. None. It was His way of motivating me to pursue *His* glory. I can only conclude how kind God has been to keep me out of mischief by giving me something for which to live.

Mind you, we tried hard. I cannot think of anything—big or small—that came our way that I did not deal with when it came to walking in the light and pursuing revival. Whether it was temptations of the flesh; dignifying trials; going to the streets to do personal evangelism; reaching out to the poor; listening to total strangers who had their prophetic "words of knowledge"; welcoming tramps and beggars; inviting the most controversial speakers; more prayer meetings; fasting; allowing some of our people to have their own meetings on the premises; taking invitations that could in no way be "strategic"; witnessing to the drunks as I might do with a merchant banker; witnessing to people on buses, trains, and subways; totally forgiving those who had hurt me; learning what grieves or quenches the Holy Spirit and working overtime not to do so; accepting one's thorn in the flesh with utter submission; being careful not to retort when falsely accused or attacked; not speaking against anyone (or at least trying hard not to); being willing to apologize, whether to my wife or my deacons (which I had to do more often than I care to admit); losing face and appearing to be a wimp—and a lot more. But revival never came. Charles Finney, the nineteenth-century American evangelist (whom I admire), taught that if we do certain things, God will do certain things; therefore, any church can see true revival. It may have worked for him, but I have to say it didn't work for us.

It will be recalled that our first Prayer Covenant, which we introduced in 1985, allowed the Chapel members to sign up and agree to pray five petitions every day. The first on the list was to pray for true revival. Three hundred people praying daily for years and years didn't bring revival, nor did our days of prayer and fasting do it. Our second Prayer Covenant (1994) simply included the petition for the manifestation of God's glory. But, as I said, we still hoped it would mean revival.

I became so hungry for revival that I was willing to witness to the outcasts of society (and welcome them to the Chapel) to such an extent that in 1982 I asked the church to consider buying property to house such people. There was a mixed response. But I went on record that, should a sizeable inheritance turn up within twelve months, I would insist that it be used for such a project. No such money came. Ten years later we received a sizeable inheritance that was more than enough to purchase such a house, but the money went for refurbishing the Chapel instead. Had that money come within those twelve months, I can assure you that is how it would have been spent. Why? I was willing to do *anything* for true revival.

We were no worse off for such openness to the Spirit and efforts to please the Lord. We were all the better for this, in my opinion. All the things I listed earlier are the "good works" that a church ought to do in any case! In other words, this is what the Lord asks us to do, and such commands are to be obeyed without any reference whatever as to whether we receive any further benefits.

> So you also, when you have done everything you were told to do, should say, "We are unworthy servants; we have only done our duty."
> —LUKE 17:10

All I know is that it took the desire for the manifestation of God's glory to motivate me to do these things. I'm not sorry that we did our best to get God's attention, for we were no worse off for it. If you say He did not answer our prayer for revival because our motives were selfish, I could not disagree.

I used to get anonymous weekly letters from someone who supplied me with tracts saying that women should wear hats in church. These pamphlets centered on 1 Corinthians 11:5–6. The person would write to me that if I truly wanted to see revival in Westminster Chapel, I should order the women in the Chapel to wear hats. This person noted that there were quite a number who didn't do so, and this was precisely why God had not sent revival to us. I was so *desperate* for revival that I became prepared to do this—until I realized that there are many strict churches around England who have practiced this for years without any hint of revival.

Revival is a sovereign intervention of the Holy Spirit and comes as a sign of God's mercy, *not* necessarily anybody's worthiness. I held to this point of view throughout my ministry at the Chapel. I have always realized that if revival came it would not be due to one's own godliness or our church's readiness, but only because of God's graciousness. At the same time, however, I have continued to believe that we should do all we can to please God in every detail. And yet, surely, one may go too far in an effort to get things right. I hope we didn't go too far. I only know that, if bringing revival had been left to us, there was nothing more we could have done that I know of. God is sovereign and may unveil His glory to the Chapel under the leadership of my successor or to those elsewhere who turn up at the eleventh hour. (See Matthew 20:9–16.) For all I know, it may come to those who weren't even praying for revival at all!

DREAMS AND VISIONS

We had a number of prophetic words given to us that encouraged us to believe that not only was revival coming, but also a manifestation of God's glory that would seem quite extraordinary. When Jackie Pullinger spoke for us in 1991, she brought along with her some of the Chinese brothers from Hong Kong. Praying with her in the vestry just before the service, one of those brothers began to prophesy—in Chinese. Jackie translated: "With this church London I will shake, with London England I will shake, and with England the world I will shake." After that Paul Cain stood in the pulpit at the Chapel and sensed that we would see revival as in Jonathan Edwards' day. John Paul Jackson stood in the pulpit and exclaimed, "I see a balloon. It gets bigger and bigger; it fills the whole church—and bursts—and the effect is felt around the world." I have had other prophetic words by notable church leaders. I had so many prophetic words spoken to us that I said I didn't think I could bear another single prophecy to us!

In September 1985, I had a vision for the first time since 1956. (In 1955–1956, I had a series of visions, about twenty, but then they stopped.) On that evening in 1985, however, in the vision I saw Westminster filled from top to bottom with people. In 1987, I had another vision—very similar—that indicated hundreds (I would even say thousands) of people were trying to get into the Chapel. I concluded one of two things: either my vision was my own fanciful wish and not from the Holy Spirit at all, or the vision would be fulfilled after my departure. I am happy for the latter to be the case. I *think* I really mean that. Like King David, God has been good to me—"the boundary lines have fallen for me in pleasant places" (Ps. 16:6), and I cannot complain because I didn't get my "balloon." I never deserved to be where God put me in the first place, and I am thankful to have had the great privilege that was mine for twenty-five years.

In September 1987, after returning from summer vacation, my assistant Jon Bush told me there was a group in the Chapel who wanted to have a special time in which they could worship charismatic style—to speak in tongues, prophesy, and see the gifts of the Spirit manifested. I said, "Yes!" He was a little surprised but seemed relieved. Westminster Chapel has not exactly been a card-carrying charismatic church. But I had to be willing for revival to come *any way* God may want to bring it and *through whom* God may be pleased to send it. So this group began having services on Wednesday nights. They began with about sixty of our young people. One of our deacons, the late Harold Wiles, looked after the group. Within a few weeks they were down to forty, then twenty, then ten. It seemed that they were exceedingly zealous and very sincere but didn't always know when to close down for the evening. The feeling was, "If we wait before God another thirty minutes, the Spirit may come down." The Spirit never came down, as far as one could tell, and after a year I stepped in and closed down the meetings. Some never forgave me; they felt I had quenched the Spirit. It eventually led to a strong feeling that I was not taking the Chapel far or fast enough. We lost a few people, but I *know* how much I hoped God would use that group.

When Ronald Reagan became the fortieth president of the United States, he had a slogan on his desk that said, "There is no limit to how far a person may go as long as he doesn't care who gets the credit." To me this is a profound statement. I wanted revival to come so much that I was willing to let anybody else be God's sovereign vessel. This explains my willingness to have people like Rodney Howard-Browne, John Arnott, Randy Clark, Charles Carrin, and Jack Taylor.

When the Toronto Blessing began to flourish at Holy Trinity Brompton, I invited Sandy and some of his people to come to the Chapel and address our deacons. They did this graciously, and a little blessing of the Spirit came upon some of us. But it did not really "take off" at that time. And yet, it was one more effort to do anything we could possibly do to bring the Holy Spirit's blessing to the Chapel. I was open to Sandy Millar's proposal in 1999 to bring a number of his people to us on Sunday nights. I knew that, if it had worked, I would not get any credit, and that was fine with me. I thought it would certainly increase our numbers; I hoped it would turn into revival. Neither really happened, but I am very pleased we did it. It was a great gesture on Sandy's part.

Even until the final hour prior to my departure from Westminster Chapel, I held out hope that I would see revival come. I had hoped that I could include a chapter on revival at Westminster in this book, but it did not happen—at least not while I was there. I have also reconciled the fact that I may go to be with the Lord via death and not witness firsthand the

Second Coming of Christ (a grudging concession!). I believe revival will come, but perhaps not when I am around.

In May 1985, the registered Baptist churches invited Louise and me to visit the Soviet Union. Wherever we went we sensed a devotion to Christ quite unlike anything we had ever seen. Perhaps it was the result of a greater dependence upon God. The Rev. Michael Zidkoff, pastor of the Moscow Baptist Church, compared the churches in the East and West with the reference to Martha and Mary. "'Martha, Martha,' the Lord answered, 'you are worried and upset about many things, but only one thing is needed. Mary has chosen what is better, and it will not be taken away from her'" (Luke 10:41–42). Those in the West, he suggested, are like Martha. Those in the East are like Mary. Mary sat at the feet of Jesus while Martha was preparing the meal, then Martha became irked that Mary wasn't helping her. Martha was also amazed that Jesus didn't make Mary help. I suspect Michael Zidkoff was right in his assessment of us. We are too busy doing things that seem relevant, but which only distract us from the presence of Christ. It seemed to me there was a genuine touch of revival in the churches we visited.

While we were in Estonia, our translator Sergei Nikolaev asked me a question: "What do you want most in all the world, RT?"

I immediately replied: "Revival in Westminster Chapel."

He continued, "Why?"

That question took me by surprise. I remember how I struggled to answer and how I felt a need to justify my answer. He pressed me: "Why do you really want revival in Westminster Chapel? What are your motives?"

I struggled all the more to answer, saying that surely revival would be a wonderful thing in any church, so why shouldn't I want it in my own church? But his probing me made me see, perhaps for the first time, that the desire for revival is not necessarily a spiritual desire. It could arise from sheer selfish ambition. Perhaps this was my real motive. I certainly fear this may have partly been the case. If so, it may also help to explain why God did not seem pleased to bring revival to us during my time at the Chapel.

But Lyndon Bowring and Steve Chalke nearly laughed me to scorn—and caused me to roar with laughter as well—when I put this hypothesis as to why the Chapel hasn't been filled. Steve said, "RT, God likes you too much to do that to you."

Lyndon added, "Am I to believe that God said, 'I will bless Colin Dye, Richard Bewes, and Sandy Millar, but not you, RT,' because this success would go to your head? I don't believe that for one minute."

Steve is convinced that we are in an entirely different world from what it used to be. He believes that a team ministry is the answer.

Whatever the real reason, my lack of success when it comes to a filled church is a fact that I have to accept. I also believe God *would* have filled the Chapel had it meant greater glory to Him. This may not make sense to you, but it is what I believe with all my heart. If Job can say, "Though he slay me, yet will I hope in him" (Job 13:15), so I can say that I will honor Him regardless of His will to give or withhold great blessing. He can do either with perfect ease and be equally just. In a word: He could do either for His glory.

CONCLUSION

If I Could Turn the Clock Back

And we know that all things work together
for good to them that love God, to them who are the
called according to his purpose.
—ROMANS 8:28, KJV

IN THIS FINAL chapter, I sum up seven lessons I believe I have learned during my twenty-five years at Westminster Chapel. Five of these refer to mistakes I have made, some of which we began to rectify, and two of them show where I believe we did get it right, even from the beginning.

Paul said to Timothy, "For God did not give us a spirit of timidity, but a spirit of power, of love and of self-discipline" (2 Tim. 1:7). That word could have well applied to me when I came to the Chapel in 1977. Whether it made a difference in the young and fearful Timothy we don't know. But I am sure that the mistakes I made have largely sprung from a spirit of fear. How true are those words: "Do not fret—it only leads to evil" (Ps. 37:8).

When I refer to lessons I have learned and mistakes I have made, I do not mean for one moment to imply that I have learned the lessons so well that I would not make these mistakes again. For though I see so much of my folly and how I could improve, I still am on a journey. Perfection is not attainable in this life—a lesson Elijah apparently needed to learn since he seems to have been embarrassed by his short-comings: "I am no better than my ancestors" (1 Kings 19:4). But God wasn't finished with Elijah yet, and I pray the same is true with me.

LESSON 1

If I could start my ministry at the Chapel all over again, I would not take myself so seriously.

The trouble with taking yourself too seriously is that you never know you are doing it at the time. It is like being asleep; you don't know you were asleep until you wake up!

It has taken a number of years for me to realize what perhaps many around me noticed but didn't have the courage or needed wisdom to tell me. I realized what I was doing and tried to be different in my final weeks at the Chapel.

In the early days, it was important for me to be addressed as "Dr. Kendall." I blush to think how much I was that way. It was only symptomatic of a deeper problem I had. I was always fearful of not getting enough respect—whether from friends, visitors, or members, or from what was written about me. A negative comment would send me into a nervous or agitated state. It showed what a small man I was and how insecure I felt.

During a ten-day visit to the Holy Land in 1993, Bob Ferguson and I stopped by the Garden Tomb. I introduced myself to the people in charge, hoping that they would recognize my name, which they did. They even invited me to preach there on the following Sunday. But Bob Ferguson began to joke with them and imply they could surely do better than asking me for that Sunday! I was sadly unable to laugh at myself. It was a wake-up call to me that I must loosen up.

I was always afraid, not only that I would never be

treated with the dignity that was given to men like G. Campbell Morgan and Martyn Lloyd-Jones, but that the people would soon find out what a tragic mistake they made in calling me. I therefore was perpetually uptight and needing to prove myself. "The greatest freedom is having nothing to prove," says my friend Pete Cantrell. But sadly, I was largely governed by a spirit of fear.

The problem was that I did not trust God's wisdom in putting me there. Or, if He did indeed put me there, it must have been because the people of Westminster Chapel had already got out of God's will in the first place and I was the sign of God's judgment on them! Given my sense of unworthiness of who I was and where I came from, it seemed incredible that God put me in a place where the people deserved so much better.

LESSON 2

If I could turn the clock back and begin all over again, I would spend more time with my wife and family.

I put the Chapel first, thinking this was putting God first. I put sermon preparation first, thinking this was a priority God ordained since I was where I was. Wrong. I now believe that I would have preached just as well—probably better—had I spent adequate time with my precious family.

I am haunted by the words of Dr. Barrie White, my supervisor at Oxford, who cautioned me at the very first meeting I had with him: "Spend time with your children. You won't get those years back." But I rationalized that if I spent more hours in the Bodleian Library, getting my thesis finished, the sooner we would get back to America where I would *then* have time for them.

Next thing I knew we had decided to stay in London, but it was only for one year. Then one more year, and then five more years. We never made it back to America while our son and daughter were still children. They are now grown up, and I can't get those years back.

About ten years ago, the Billy Graham organization asked to make a video of me that they wanted to show to thousands of pastors via satellite. They asked me questions such as how did I prepare sermons; how did I see the church generally in Britain; what were my views about the Holy Spirit; and other questions. Then the director said, "We have one minute left; how shall we use up these sixty seconds? Oh, I know—tell us about your family and your role as a father." I replied that this was the one area of my life that would not interest them because I feel like a failure as a father, placing sermon preparation first—thinking that I was putting God first. I now believe I would have preached just as well had I put the family first, but I cannot get those years back.

They were filming the whole time I said that, and that is the part of the sixty-minute video they ended up using! They explained later that this might encourage pastors and church leaders who felt the same way.

Oh, how I wish I could have a second chance to spend more time with our children—to read with them, to play with them, to tell stories to them, to be less harsh in discipline, and to cry with them when they were hurting.

I write these lines to emphasize this matter again with the hope of saving some younger person's family or perhaps that of a church leader. If you read these lines, here is my recommendation:

1. Listen to them when they talk with you; they will never turn to you at a convenient time.

2. Do not dismiss their feelings of being hurt over the way their friends or teachers treat them.

3. Make mealtimes at the table last longer and family oriented again. Shut the TV off, and encourage them to talk.

4. Don't leave them when they are afraid to go to sleep or need you to read them a bedtime story.

5. Set a time to be with them, and keep your appointment as you would for the most important person on earth, for *your children are even more important yet.*

I am still counting on Romans 8:28 and the promise of Joel to restore the years that the locusts have eaten (Joel 2:25). God graciously began to do this at the dawn of the new millennia. Don't forget: the fact that something works together for good doesn't mean it was right at the time.

LESSON 3

I believe I just might have the courage to be myself if I were beginning my ministry at the Chapel today.

This has been one of the hardest things of all for me to learn. As I said earlier, I used to feel this need to prove myself and make people see that I was up to the job. The funny thing is that now I realize that the members of the Chapel never questioned that I was the right man for the job. The doubt was largely in *my* mind alone. But the anxiety was so great, owing to my feelings of inferiority, that I was terrified at being just myself.

Not to be oneself is to commit a sin. For one thing, it is a vote of no confidence in our Creator, who made us as we are, and in our Redeemer, who forgives us of all our shortcomings. It is also to question God's providence and sovereignty. I felt justified in my self-pity, as if God should be obliged to help me through. Instead He took years and years in enabling me to see some of these things for myself.

In March 1985, when I was addressing Assemblies of God young people at Westminster Central Hall, Margaret Brown, a lady from my friend Stuart Bell's church in Lincoln, came to me with a prophetic word she felt the Lord had given her for me. She believed the Lord revealed to her that I had not reached my potential or seen the reason why God brought us to Britain. I have never fully understood that "word" for me, but I do know that it had the effect of making me see that the time was long overdue to be myself. From then on I began more and more to be myself and risk the consequences.

The reason we are afraid to be ourselves is the fear of rejection. In order to avoid rejection, we entertain the idea that we must live up to another's expectation; we wear the mask to keep people from seeing who we really are. In my case, I can't say I was trying to imitate anybody, but I know that I was very stilted and confined to a picture I had in mind of how I was supposed to be. It all now seems so silly and ridiculous, and yet, I do wish in some ways I could start all over again and have the courage to be myself from day one. I am not implying that revival would have come or that I could have avoided controversy and difficulties. I am just a bit upset with myself for taking so long to realize it.

LESSON 4

If I could start all over again at the Chapel, I would have given the worship part of the service the profile it deserves.

My own thinking has changed. For one thing, in Britain, "worship" should refer to our adoration and praise of God, but it is often the word hastily used to depict singing—much as Americans hastily refer to "revival" to depict renewal. Whether true worship actually occurs in a "time of worship" is another matter.

In any case I would have given much more attention to the part of the service set aside to sing praise to God. When I first arrived at the Chapel in February 1977, the thought of singing a modern chorus was out of the question. We sang only hymns or psalms—nothing more. It wasn't until Paul Cain preached and talked about the "hydrological cycle"— the rising vapor forming rain clouds—and how our worship ascends to God to bring down His blessing that we took praising God in singing very seriously. We simply worked our way through the singing to get to the preaching.

We learned to give the "worship" part of the service the time it deserves. The preaching remains central, but we believe God loves our sincere adoration. I am so ashamed I took so long to see this. The psalms alone make this all too clear for us to minimize this matter. Singing the "new" was in fact what the psalmist did continually in his time (Ps. 96:1). Why are we so stuck into the inspiration of a former era?

LESSON 5

Consecutive expository preaching through a book in the Bible is one pattern I would not change.

One person once asked, "Is Dr. Lloyd-Jones made for the Chapel or the Chapel made for Dr. Lloyd-Jones?" On this question I too fit. The kind of preaching I did during those twenty-five years is all I know how to do, and I suspect there aren't many churches on either side of the Atlantic for whom this style is very desirable or acceptable.

To put it another way, I don't think I would have survived long in any church in the United States had I used the preaching style I used at Westminster Chapel. One famous Southern Baptist preacher—and one very able indeed—actually said to me that he would empty his own church if he carried on as I do. This sobered me and made me wonder if I am the minister of the only church in the world that would have me! I only know that Dr. Lloyd-Jones's style, which the people of the Chapel got used to and loved, set the pace for me. Had I not fit into the same pattern, they probably would not have called me.

People ask, "Why isn't there more expository preaching around?" It is a good question. On the other hand, if this way of doing preaching and ministry were so wonderful, why didn't God crown it with more success during those twenty-five years at the Chapel? On this question I have no answer.

I only know that I do not have a single regret that we worked through a good number of books in the Bible. If I had stayed another five or ten years, then I would have kept up the same exact style.

LESSON 6

If I were to begin my ministry today, I would teach the exact same theology.

I made a good number of changes over the years, but none of these were theological. There is one exegetical change: my view of Hebrews 6:4–6. As I stated earlier, I used to think this referred to the "illuminated but not regenerated": that is, those who made a profession of faith but were not really saved. In my early days, I followed the Puritan John Owen very carefully. But once I saw for myself that Hebrews 6:4–6 refers to true Christians who have become stone deaf to the Holy Spirit and never hear God speak any more (which is why they cannot be renewed again to repentance), I never looked back. It was not the result of a theological change. On the contrary, it brought my interpretation of Hebrews 6 in line with my basic theology.

I have been a "four-and-a-half-point" Calvinist since I left Oxford in the autumn of 1976, as I stated in chapter one. I have been open to the Holy Spirit since my baptism in the Holy Spirit on October 31, 1955. The combination of my theological views concerning the Word and the Spirit have been my hermeneutic in understanding the Bible. I love what I believe and preach. Theology, surely, can't get better than this. I only wish God had poured out His Spirit on my teaching and preaching in greater measure. Vindication would have suited me! I also suspect that God would have done so had He been able to trust me with such a seal of His approval.

LESSON 7

Finally, were I to start all over again, knowing what I now know, I would practice what I preach more than I have regarding the sovereignty of God.

I should have taken on board Dr. Carl F. H. Henry's own words to me, as though he was referring to himself, to remember that "only God can turn the water into wine." I fear that I tried too hard to make things happen. Lyndon Bowring says to me that although I preach like a Calvinist, I often behave like an Arminian! That loving rebuke hits me between the eyes.

If I could turn the clock back, I would try to practice what I preach about the sovereignty of God. I am without excuse in this area. It is a fault that I feared would haunt me right up to the last day.

I do not claim, then, to discover God's glory, and I certainly do not claim to have arrived at seeing that glory. I can, however, claim to have pursued it. Sometimes poorly, sometimes with such a meager faith that I do not deserve to be in the ministry. But, as for pursuing His glory, yes, we sincerely tried to do so.

February 16, 2004, I presented Palestinian leader Yasser Arafat with a copy of my book *Total Forgiveness.*

Epilogue

Since my retirement on February 1, 2002, God has given me what I should call a threefold ministry. First, I have teamed up with Jack Taylor and Charles Carrin in conducting "Word, Spirit, Power" conferences all over the United States. We have averaged about ten a year. This ministry has taken us into all denominations, especially Southern Baptist and charismatic churches. We seek to bridge the gap between solid evangelicals and those who are open to the immediate and direct witness of the Holy Spirit.

Second, my writing ministry continues. God has graciously given me favor with Stephen Strang of Charisma House as well as my old publishers in the United Kingdom, who continue to invite me to write for them. I have averaged flying to Britain to preach at least four times a year. Nothing is more heartwarming than being an American loved by Brits—even after I have retired in the United States.

Third, I have been given an opportunity to speak with the top political and religious leaders in the Middle East. This has come through Canon Andrew White of Coventry Cathedral, who is also the Archbishop of Canterbury's envoy to the Middle East. Andrew has opened the door for me to meet with Israeli and Palestinian leaders. I have spent a surprising amount of time with Yasser Arafat, witnessing to him and urging him to confess that Jesus Christ is the Son of God who died on the cross for his sins. Please pray for me that I will have wisdom and protection as I make trips to the Middle East, which will include visits to Iraq.

I did more bonefishing when I was minister of Westminster Chapel on summer holidays than I have done since retiring—even though we live right on Largo Sound in Key Largo, Florida! I have never been so busy in all my life. I thank God for His goodness to me. Please pray that I will consistently pursue His glory in all I say and do. May God bless you.

—R. T. KENDALL

Books Written
by R. T. Kendall

R. T. KENDALL HAS written the following books, which are arranged in order of publication.

- *Jonah* (Hodder & Stoughton, 1978 and 1985; Paternoster, 1995; U.S. edition, Zondervan, 1980). Sermons preached at Westminster Chapel on Jonah. Dedicated to Louise and Robert Tillman II and Melissa Louise.

- *Calvin and English Calvinism to 1648* (Oxford University Press, 1981; Paternoster, 1997). The differences between Calvin and the Calvinists, based on my Oxford PhD thesis. Dedicated to my father.

- *Who by Faith* (Hodder & Stoughton, 1981). Republished as *Believing God* (Paternoster, 1995; U.S. edition, Morning Star, 1997). Studies on faith from Hebrews 11. Dedicated to Harlan and Olive Milby.

- *Tithing* (Hodder & Stoughton, 1982; U.S. edition, Zondervan, 1983). Republished as *The Gift of Giving* (Hodder & Stoughton, 1998). A call to all Christians to discover what it means to tithe. Dedicated to every church leader. Foreword by Floyd McClung.

- *Once Saved, Always Saved* (Hodder & Stoughton, 1983; Paternoster, 1997; U.S. edition, Moody Press, 1985). A defense of our eternal security in Christ. Dedicated to Bruce and Sharon Porter.

- *Stand Up and Be Counted* (Hodder & Stoughton, 1984; U.S. edition, Zondervan, 1985). A case for calling people to confess Christ publicly. Dedicated to every evangelist. Foreword by Dr. Billy Graham.

- *Does Jesus Care?* (Hodder & Stoughton, 1986; Paternoster, 1997). An exposition of John 11. Dedicated to Marilyn (RT's sister).

- *God Meant It for Good* (Kingsway, 1986; Paternoster, 1998; U.S. editions, Tyndale House, 1987 and Morning Star, 1993). The life of Joseph. Dedicated to Josif Tson. Foreword by Paul Cain.

- *The Word of the Lord* (Marshall Pickering, 1988). Lectures in honor of G. Campbell Morgan, introduced by R. T. Kendall.

- *He Saves* (Hodder & Stoughton, 1988; OM/Paternoster, 2000). An exposition of Romans 1:16–17. Dedicated to Harry and June Kilbride.

- *Is God for the Homosexual?* (Marshall Pickering, 1988). A look at why God loves gay people but not homosexual practice. Dedicated to John.

- *Worshipping God* (Hodder & Stoughton, 1989 and 1999; U.S. edition published as *Before the Throne*, Broadman Press, 1995). How Christians can rediscover the full dimensions of worship. Dedicated to Meint and Linda, Brad, Brent and Bryce Huesman. Foreword by Darlene Zschech.

- *The God of the Bible* (Kingsway, 1990). Four years of Spring Harvest Bible readings from Romans, John, Acts, and Daniel. Dedicated to Lyndon Bowring.

- *Grace and Glory* (OM Publishing/Keswick convention, 1991). Keswick sermons on the life of Jacob. Foreword by Philip Hacking.

- *Meekness and Majesty* (Christian Focus Publications, 1992). An exposition of Philippians 2:5–11. Dedicated to Randy and Nancy Wall.

- *When God Says "Well Done!"* (Christian Focus Publications, 1993). An exposition of 1 Corinthians 3:6–15, looking at rewards in heaven. Dedicated to Richard and Dottie Oates.

- *Are You Stone Deaf to the Spirit?* (Christian Focus Publications, 1994). An exposition of Hebrews 5:11–6:12. Dedicated to Michael and Jenny Eaton.

- *Are You Ready for God?* (Scripture Union, 1995; U.S. edition published as *When God Shows Up, Staying Ready for the Unexpected*, Renew Books, 1998). An encouragement to Christians to expect the unexpected. Dedicated to Tony Hammon and the members of Island Community Church, Islamorada, Florida. U.S. edition dedicated to Harry and Kimberley Spear and John and Michelle Sutter. Foreword to U.S. edition by Jack Hayford.

- *Higher Ground* (Christian Focus Publications, 1995). Insights from the Psalms of Ascent (Psalms 120–134). Dedicated to Robert and Beth Amess.

- *The Word and the Spirit*, coauthored with Paul Cain (Kingsway and Struik Christian Books, South Africa, 1996; U.S. edition, Charisma House, 1998). Talks from the first Word and Spirit Conference at Wembley in October 1992. Dedicated to every Christian leader committed to the remarriage of the Word and the Spirit. Foreword by Colin Dye.

- *Understanding Theology 1* (Christian Focus Publications, 1996). Printed notes from the School of Theology. Dedicated to the deacons of Westminster Chapel.

- *Just Love* (Christian Focus Publications, 1997). An exposition of 1 Corinthians 13. Dedicated to Abbie Kendall.

- *All's Well That Ends Well* (Paternoster, 1998). The life of Jacob. Dedicated to Jenny and Charlie Ross. Foreword by Robert Amess.

- *The Anointing* (Hodder & Stoughton, 1998; U.S. edition, Thomas Nelson, 1999; Charisma House 2003). A fresh look at the anointing of the Holy Spirit, focusing on Yesterday's Man (Saul), Today's Man (Samuel), and Tomorrow's Man (David). Dedicated to T. R. Kendall. Foreword by Rob Parsons. Foreword to U.S. edition (Thomas Nelson) by Jim Bakker. Forewords to U.S. edition (Charisma House) by Michael Yousseff and Rob Parsons.

- *A Vision of Jesus* (Christian Focus Publications, 1999). Studies in Revelation 1. Dedicated to Desmond and Mary Burrows.

- *The Thorn in the Flesh* (Hodder & Stoughton, 1999; U.S. edition to be published by Charisma House in 2005). An exposition of 2 Corinthians 12:7–10. Dedicated to Rob and Di Parsons. Foreword by Lyndon Bowring.

- *Great Christian Prayers*, compiled and edited with Louise Kendall (Hodder & Stoughton, 2000). A selection of prayers for every day of the year, drawn from two thousand years of Christian prayers. Lovingly dedicated to Louise's mother, Mrs. Orville Hess. Foreword by the Rt. Rev. Richard Baughen.

- *Just Grace* (SPCK, 2000). The Ten Commandments. Dedicated to Ernie and Margaret Paddon. Foreword by Terry Virgo.

- *The Sensitivity of the Spirit* (Hodder & Stoughton, 2000; U.S. edition, Charisma House, 2002). An explanation of why and how the Holy Spirit is so sensitive and easily grieved. Dedicated to Bob and Diane Ferguson. Foreword by Alex Buchanan.

- *Understanding Theology 2* (Christian Focus Publications, 2000). Printed notes from the School of Theology. Dedicated to those who have enrolled in the School of Theology at Westminster Chapel 1992–2000.

- *A Man After God's Own Heart* (Christian Focus Publications, 2001). The life of David, from 1 & 2 Samuel. Dedicated to R. V. and Joy Reese.

- *Total Forgiveness* (Hodder and Stoughton, 2001; U.S. edition, Charisma House, 2002). How to achieve God's greatest challenge: forgiveness. Dedicated to Melissa Kendall. Foreword by Washington Okumu. In the U.S. edition, forewords by Dr. D. James Kennedy and Professor Washington Okumu.

- *Understanding Theology 3* (Christian Focus Publications, 2001). Printed notes from the School of Theology. Dedicated to Richard and Debbie Overfield.

- *Justification by Works* (Paternoster, 2001). James 1 and 2. Foreword by Clive Calver. Dedicated to Lee and Sally Wallis, Linda and Neal Otten, Lois and Bruce Malpass.

- *The Way of Wisdom* (Paternoster, 2001). Volume two of the above, looking at James 3, 4, and 5. Dedicated to Bill and Rachel Reynolds.

- *In Pursuit of His Glory* (Hodder & Stoughton, 2002; U.S. edition, Charisma House, 2004). Autobiography of Dr. Kendall's twenty-five year tenure at Westminster Chapel. Dedicated to every Chapel member, 1977–2002. Foreword by Ernie Paddon and Bill Reynolds. In the U.S. edition, forewords by Jack Hayford, Ernie Paddon, and Bill Reynolds.

- *Thanking God* (Hodder & Stoughton, 2003; U.S. edition to be published by Charisma House in 2005). Dedicated to Alan and Julia Bell.

- *Pure Joy* (Hodder & Stoughton, 2004; U.S. edition to be published by Charisma House in 2005). Dedicated to Dr. David and Lil Onstaad.

- *Between the Times* (Christian Focus, 2004). Exposition of the Book of Malachi. Dedicated to Dr. Anita Davies and Dr. Naomal Soysa.

- *The Parables of Jesus* (Sovereign World, 2004; U.S. edition, Baker Book House, 2004). Dedicated to Arthur Blessitt, Pete Cantrell, O. S. Hawkins, and Graham Ferguson Lacey.

- *Your God Is Too Nice* (Hodder & Stoughton, 2005).

- *Controlling the Tongue* (Charisma House, 2006).

- *The Next Move of God on the Earth* (Hodder & Stoughton, 2006).

- Sermons on 1, 2, and 3 John are to be published within the next two years.

- Sermons on Philippians are to be published within the next two years.

Sermons Series Preached
by R. T. Kendall

RT HAS PREACHED the following sermon series at Westminster Chapel. The list has been arranged in chronological order.

- Jonah—23 sermons preached on Sunday mornings between February 6 and October 2, 1977.

- Galatians—136 sermons preached on Friday evenings between February 11, 1977, and May 15, 1981.

- Revelation 1—33 sermons preached on Sunday evenings between October 9, 1977, and July 9, 1978.

- Hebrews 10:19–12:6: What Is Faith?—37 sermons preached on Sunday mornings between October 9, 1977, and October 1, 1978.

- 1 Samuel 1–28—34 sermons preached on Sunday evenings between October 8, 1978, and July 8, 1979.

- Jude—37 sermons preached on Sunday mornings between October 8, 1978, and September 30, 1979.

- Acts 1:1–7:3—35 sermons preached on Sunday evenings between October 7, 1979, and June 15, 1980.

- James—82 sermons preached on Sunday mornings between October 7, 1979, and November 22, 1981.

- Questions regarding heaven and the Book of Revelation—45 sermons preached on Sunday evenings between June 22, 1980, and July 12, 1981.

- Hebrews—312 Bible studies preached on Friday evenings between May 22, 1981, and January 24, 1992.

- 2 Samuel 11:1–12:14 and Psalm 51: David and Bathsheba—4 sermons preached on Sunday evenings between October 18 and November 8, 1981.

- 1 John—106 sermons preached on Sunday mornings between January 10, 1982, and December 9, 1984.

- 2 John—1 sermon preached on Sunday morning, January 6, 1985.

- 3 John—1 sermon preached on Sunday morning, January 13, 1985.

- The Sufferings of Jesus—6 sermons preached on Sunday evenings between February 28 and April 4, 1982.

- Genesis 37–50: Joseph—49 sermons preached on Sunday evenings between June 6, 1982, and October 9, 1983.

- Acts 7—31 sermons preached on Sunday evenings between October 16, 1983, and October 28, 1984.

- Jesus—13 sermons preached on Sunday evenings between January 6 and March 31, 1985.

- Philippians—140 sermons preached on Sunday mornings between January 20, 1985, and March 5, 1989.

- John 11: Does Jesus Care?—10 sermons preached on Sunday evenings between October 6 and December 8, 1985.

- Isaiah 52:7–53:12—11 sermons preached on Sunday evenings between January 5 and March 23, 1986.

- Romans 1—44 sermons preached on Sunday evenings between April 13, 1986, and September 27, 1987.

- 1 Samuel 16:1–1 Kings 1:31: David—64 sermons preached on Sunday evenings between October 4, 1987, and June 11, 1989.

- 1 Corinthians—187 sermons preached on Sunday mornings between March 12, 1989, and March 20, 1994.

- Selected psalms, mostly Davidic—7 sermons preached on Sunday evenings between June 25 and September 24, 1989.

- John 1:1–7:24—127 sermons preached on Sunday evenings between October 15, 1989, and March 21, 1993.

- Joel—7 sermons preached on Friday evenings between May 1, 1992, and June 26, 1992.

- School of Theology—begun on Friday evenings on October 2, 1992 and concluded on December 14, 2001.

- Revelation 6:9–7:17: Heaven—12 sermons preached on Sunday evenings between May 9 and July 25, 1993.

- Psalms 120–132: The Songs of the Ascents—13 sermons preached on Sunday evenings between September 19 and December 12, 1993.

- Genesis 25:19–47:31: Jacob—56 sermons preached on Sunday evenings between January 2, 1994, and May 21, 1995.

- 2 Corinthians—141 sermons (including 13 sermons on 2 Corinthians 12:7: The Thorn in the Flesh) preached on Sunday mornings between April 10, 1994, and April 19, 1998.

- Acts 8:1–28:31—89 sermons preached on Sunday evenings between May 28, 1995, and July 27, 1997.

- Esther—13 sermons preached on Sunday evenings between September 14 and December 7, 1997.

- Exodus 20:1–17: The Ten Commandments—12 sermons preached on Sunday evenings between January 4 and March 29, 1998.

- Matthew 5–7: The Sermon on the Mount—89 sermons preached on Sunday mornings between May 3, 1998, and July 30, 2000.

- Joshua—59 sermons preached on Sunday evenings between May 3, 1998, and October 17, 1999.

- Malachi—33 sermons preached on Sunday evenings between October 24, 1999, and July 23, 2000.

- The Parables of Jesus—40 sermons preached on Sunday mornings from September 17, 2000, to January 13, 2002.

- The Life and Times of Elijah—39 sermons preached on Sunday evenings from September 17, 2000, to December 2, 2001.

NOTE: These sermons may be ordered from Dr. Kendall's Web site at www.rtkendallministries.com.

Index of Names

Dr. R. T. Kendall
Ministries

Most of the 3,500 sermons Dr. Kendall preached at Westminster Chapel are available on audio, including School of Theology lectures (a three-volume set titled "Understanding Theology"). His most popular series:

> *Thorn in the Flesh*
> *God Meant It for Good* (the life of Joseph)
> *Gifts of the Spirit* (1 Corinthians 13;
>   Philippians 2:5–11)
> *A Man After God's Own Heart* (life of David)
> *All's Well That Ends Well* (life of Jacob)

For a complete listing of Dr. Kendall's materials, visit his Web site at:

www.rtkendallministries.com

or write to Dr. Kendall at:
R. T. Kendall Ministries
P. O. Box 226
Key Largo, FL 33037

Dr. Kendall is available for a limited number of speaking engagements and for "Word, Spirit, Power" Conferences with Jack Taylor and Charles Carrin. For the latest information on the conferences and to see if a conference will be in your area soon, please visit the Web site: www.rtkendallministries.com.

Take the next steps in your faith walk today.

We pray that God has encouraged and strengthened you with this autobiography. Dr. R. T. Kendall also has several other soul-refreshing messages that you won't want to miss!

Fresh Anointing for You Today

R. T. Kendall helps you identify your current role in the kingdom. Learn how to wait for God's perfect timing, promotion, and fresh anointing in each season of your life.
$13.99 / 1-59185-172-6 (Paperback)

Forgive and Forget?

When everything in you wants to hold a grudge, point a finger, and remember the pain, God wants you to lay it all aside.

"This is a book that should be read around the world."
—D. James Kennedy, PhD, Senior Minister, Coral Ridge Presbyterian Church
$13.99 / 0-88419-889-8 (Paperback)
* *Total Forgiveness* study guide available July 2004

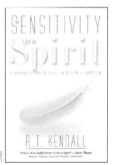

Make Sense Spiritually.

Learn the difference between being sensitive to the Holy Spirit and being aware of the sensitivity of the Holy Spirit. Find the road back from anywhere, which starts with repentance, and eventually you'll find peace.
$13.99 / 0-88419-844-8 (Paperback)

Strang Communications, the publisher of both Charisma House and *Charisma* magazine, wants to give you a FREE SUBSCRIPTION to our award-winning magazine.

Since its inception in 1975 *Charisma* magazine has helped thousands of Christians stay connected with what God is doing worldwide.

Within its pages you will discover in-depth reports and the latest news from a Christian perspective, biblical health tips, global events in the body of Christ, personality profiles, and so much more. Join the family of *Charisma* readers who enjoy feeding their spirit each month with miracle-filled testimonies and inspiring articles that bring clarity, provoke prayer, and demand answers.

To claim your **3 free issues** of *Charisma* send us your name and address to: Charisma 3 Free Issue Offer, 600 Rinehart Road, Lake Mary, FL 32746. Or you may call 1-800-829-3346 and ask for Offer # 93FREE. This offer is only valid in the USA.

---

www.charismamag.com

3581